TO

SEE

THE KINGDOM

TO

SEE

THE KINGDOM

The Theological Vision
of H. Richard Niebuhr

James W. Fowler

ABINGDON PRESS
Nashville   New York

Library of Congress Cataloging in Publication Data

FOWLER, JAMES W   1940-
   To see the kingdom; the theological vision of
H. Richard Niebuhr.
   Bibliography: p.
   1. Niebuhr, Helmut Richard, 1894-1962. I. Title.
BX4827.N47F68   230' .092' 4 [B]   74-688
               ISBN 0-687-42300-7

The author and publishers wish to thank the following for permission to reprint material:

The Christian Century Foundation for material from the following articles by H. Richard Niebuhr appearing in *The Christian Century*: "Back to Benedict?" "Can German and American Christians Understand Each Other?" "The Grace of Doing Nothing," "A Communication: The Only Way into the Kingdom of God," "War as the Judgment of God," "Is God in the War?" "War as Crucifixion"; and for "The Inconsistency of the Majority" from *The World Tomorrow*. Copyright by The Christian Century Foundation in 1925, 1930, 1932, 1932, 1942, 1942, 1943, 1934, respectively, and reprinted by permission.

Church History magazine for material from "The Idea of Covenant and American Democracy," appearing in *Church History* in 1954.

Harper & Row, Publishers, Inc. for material from *The Kingdom of God in America* by H. Richard Niebuhr, copyright, 1937 by Harper & Row, Publishers, Inc.; from *Radical Monotheism and Western Culture* by H. Richard Niebuhr (Harper & Row, 1960); from "Value Theory and Theology" by H. Richard Niebuhr, in *The Nature of Religious Experience: Essays in Honor of Douglas Clyde Macintosh*, edited by Julius Seelye Bixler et al. (Harper & Row, 1937). By permission of the publishers.

The University of Chicago Press for material from "Man the Sinner" by H. Richard Niebuhr, appearing in *Journal of Religion* in 1935.

The World Council of Churches for material from *Moral Relativism and the Christian Ethic*, published for the International Missionary Council in 1929.

MANUFACTURED BY THE PARTHENON PRESS AT
NASHVILLE, TENNESSEE, UNITED STATES OF AMERICA

To My Parents
LUCILE HAWORTH FOWLER
and
JAMES W. FOWLER, JR.
Who See the Kingdom

Preface

Across the thirty years of his teaching career at Yale Divinity School, H. Richard Niebuhr contributed to the preparation of more persons who today are influential as professors, heads of departments of religion, deans, and pastors than any other American theologian of the twentieth century. He wrote seven books, six of which remain in print. Each of these books has shown a remarkably durable ability to interest, intrigue, and inform contemporary students. Through his books he has gained a lasting place in the formative literature of sociology of religion and of American church history, as well as in Christian theology and ethics which were his chosen fields. Beyond this academic legacy Niebuhr's teachings and writings have been broadly influential in the life of the churches in the United States. In addition to the articles, lectures, and sermons which he contributed to the ecumenical movement Niebuhr's leadership in the study and rethinking of theological education in North America and his book *The Purpose of the Church and Its Ministry* gave his theology of the church and ministry extensive impact on theological students and practicing pastors.

Niebuhr came onto the American theological scene in a time of great turmoil: vast tides of immigration into the cities, World War I and its aftermath, an American labor movement finding its feet and being goaded by committed Communist and I.W.W. organizers, lynchings and race riots, a country no longer predominantly rural or predominantly Protestant. Add to these elements of change in American society the shock waves of a theological revolution in Europe, and you begin to grasp the ferment into which Niebuhr emerged. How could the gospel provide guidance and vision for a church caught up in these currents of change? Could the church recover a faithfulness to the steepness of the gospel's ethical ideals? And if it did, could it then impact upon the structures and institutions of society in such a way as to bring about a more just and righteous national life? These were the questions with which Niebuhr began.

This book, the first to study in depth the development of H. Richard Niebuhr's thought, begins with Niebuhr's wrestle with these questions. What came out of his struggle was a new direction in theology and ethics. Uniquely and indigenously American, it nonetheless draws knowledgeably on the principal theological alternatives of the Continent and of England. Convincedly and committedly Protestant, it exhibits a breadth and historical depth that make it truly Catholic. Firmly and consistently oriented to the church's confession of faith, it makes penetrating contributions to our understanding of culture and society.

This study seeks to present Niebuhr and his thought from the "inside." Drawing upon unpublished manuscripts, from the 1930s, forties, and fifties, not previously available, it gives careful attention to the period when Niebuhr's thought was developing into the form familiar to his readers and students across the last twenty-five years of his career. It demonstrates the unity, complexity, and dynamics of his mature theological-ethical teachings. By its reliance on notes taken by students in his course on Christian ethics at Yale, it endeavors to suggest something of the shape he might have given his projected magnum opus on Christian ethics had he lived to write it. The chapter reporting on the unpublished study on faith (from the 1950s) will show the reader a side of Niebuhr's thought which, though visible in suggestive ways in others of his writings, comes through in this substantial manuscript as remarkably bold and novel.

In contrast to the great systematic edifices left by his contemporaries Barth, Brunner, and Tillich, Niebuhr's theological writings constitute a more modest legacy. While the former built "cathedrals," Niebuhr, we might say, bequeathed us tents—movable dwellings to carry on pilgrimage, whose use requires the investment and development of our own constructive abilities. The steady annual production of doctoral dissertations on H. Richard Niebuhr, and the increasing number of college and theological school seminars on his thought, suggest that his influence is growing rather than waning. I hope that this book will serve well as a companion piece and guide to the reading (and rereading) of his work, and that students of Niebuhr, new and old, will find in it a focused, accurate, and passionate expression of his vision.

In the writing of this book I have incurred debts of gratitude which I want thankfully to acknowledge.

To my teacher, friend, and colleague Professor Richard R. Niebuhr I owe the inestimable privilege of access to the unpublished manuscripts left by his father.

To Dean Krister Stendahl and the faculty of Harvard Divinity School I am indebted for two separate semesters of leave from my teaching duties, during which I wrote this study.

For interviews regarding H. Richard Niebuhr I must thank his wife, Mrs. Florence M. Niebuhr, and Professors Raymond Morris, Robert Michaelson, George Riggan, and Nicholas Piediscalzi. Mr. Jon Diefenthaler, whose University of Iowa dissertation on Niebuhr promises to provide a great deal of biographical background on him, shared with me considerable valuable information from his thorough research.

Helpful criticism of this writing when parts of it constituted my Harvard doctoral dissertation came from Professors Arthur Dyck, Richard R. Niebuhr, Harvey Cox, and Gordon Kaufman. Professor Kaufman also read parts of the revised and expanded manuscript. My friend Professor Thomas P. Riggio, of the University of Connecticut, gave it an insightful reading from the standpoint of his perspective as a scholar of American literature. The Reverend Andrew Grannell, a careful student of Niebuhr's thought, also gave detailed and helpful criticism.

Mrs. Grace Friend Mullen typed the manuscript of the book. Her interest in and loyalty to the project have been a source of great help and encouragement.

My wife, Lurline, shared all the agonies and ecstasies of this enterprise. Books cost families a great deal. Lurline consistently managed to turn the cost to advantage by insisting that our fore-shortened family time should be commensurately improved in quality. As she begins a new direction in her own professional life, perhaps I shall have the opportunity to repay some of the generous investment of time and care she made to enable this writing.

JWF

Arlington, Massachusetts
June, 1973

Contents

Introduction

Helmut Richard Niebuhr was born on September 3, 1894, in Wright City, Missouri, the youngest of four surviving children. His father, Gustav Niebuhr, had become a distinguished pastor in the German Evangelical Synod of North America after emigrating alone to the United States from Germany as a boy of seventeen. Reinhold, the next youngest son and two years Richard's senior, told of his father's reading from the Bible in Hebrew and Greek each morning,[1] and of his introducing his growing children to the thought of Adolf von Harnack.[2] Their mother, Lydia Hosto Niebuhr, was the daughter of the senior pastor under whom Gustav

[1] Reported in Ronald H. Stone, *Reinhold Niebuhr: Prophet to Politicians* (Nashville: Abingdon Press, 1972), p. 18.
[2] Reinhold Niebuhr, "An Intellectual Autobiography," in Kegley and Bretall, eds., *The Theology of Reinhold Niebuhr* (New York: The Macmillan Co., 1956), p. 3.

had first served in San Francisco. A woman of great character and ability, after her husband's death she was to play a significant role in Reinhold Niebuhr's fruitful ministry in Detroit.[3] In the bilingual Niebuhr home, music, art, literature, and learned piety blended to create an atmosphere rich with mutual love and respect for excellence.

Richard followed his brother to Elmhurst, his denomination's college, which in those days (1908–12) was not accredited as a senior college. Then from 1912 to 1915, as had his father and brother, he studied at Eden Theological Seminary in preparation for ordination in the Evangelical Synod. During Niebuhr's time at Eden his father died (1913), and his mother moved back to Lincoln, Illinois, where the father had previously been pastor. It was in that church in Lincoln that Richard met Florence Marie Mittendorff, who would later become his wife. It was also in Lincoln, a town of 14,000 people, that he worked for a year as a reporter for a daily newspaper in 1915–16, helping with family expenses and, it seems, determining what would be his next step vocationally.

In 1916, at the age of twenty-two, he accepted ordination and a call to the ministry of the Walnut Park Evangelical Church in St. Louis. Mr. Jon Diefenthaler, of the University of Iowa, has interviewed members of that church who remember Niebuhr's time of ministry there. They recall him as serious and able, a highly committed and energetic, if scholarly, pastor. Sometime during his two years at Walnut Park an event occurred which the church members noted as having had a deeply saddening effect on Niebuhr. While camping in winter with a group of young people from the church, two boys, brothers, broke through thin ice and were drowned. Niebuhr, it was reported, made desperate but futile efforts to save them. The memory of that tragedy and his sense of responsibility for it may have contributed to his lifelong sensitivity to the presence and power of inexplicable evil in life, and to the suffering of innocents.

[3] See Stone, *Reinhold Niebuhr*, p. 19.

INTRODUCTION

From 1916 to 1918 Niebuhr earned a master's degree in history at Washington University in St. Louis.

In 1919, he was invited by his great professor of New Testament at Eden, Dr. Samuel D. Press, to return there as a teacher of theology and ethics. Niebuhr accepted, and for three years served on that faculty. In June of 1920 he married Florence Marie Mittendorff, who recalls that in these first Eden years he put in long hours preparing lectures and courses in order to stay ahead of his students. In the summer of 1921 he studied at the University of Chicago. It was probably at this time that he encountered the teaching of George Herbert Mead, the great Chicago philosopher and social psychologist, whose thought exerted a permanent, fruitful influence on his own thinking.

Niebuhr had known for some time that he wanted further formal study and that he wanted to pursue it at Yale Divinity School. In the fall of 1922 he and Mrs. Niebuhr moved to Clinton, Connecticut, where he served a congregational church as pastor while he studied at Yale. Because Eden did not then confer the B.D. degree he earned both a B.D. and a Ph.D. by the time he left Yale in 1924. During these years he worked with Professors Frank Porter and D. C. Macintosh, among others, and under the latter wrote his doctoral dissertation "Ernst Troeltsch's Philosophy of Religion." It is a tribute to Niebuhr's breadth as a scholar that as he was completing his study of Troeltsch he was invited by Yale to join the faculty as an assistant to Porter and to take over some of his courses in New Testament theology.

Instead, he accepted an invitation to become president of Elmhurst College. In 1924, at the age of thirty, Dr. Niebuhr assumed that office and for three years labored on behalf of his college. During those years Elmhurst received full accreditation. It also experienced growth in financial support and faculty improvement and made significant strides toward becoming a first-rate liberal arts college.

By 1927, however, the strain of administration and the pull of scholarship and writing led Niebuhr to accept an invitation to return to the faculty of Eden Theological Seminary. He and his wife and their two children, Cynthia and Richard Reinhold, spent four happy and, for him, productive years back at Eden, during which he completed *The Social Sources of Denominationalism*, his first published book and a model of research in the fields of the historical and sociological study of religion.

Upon completion of that work Niebuhr turned serious attention to the task of constructing a more adequate theological basis for Christian ethics and the reform of the church. In the spring and summer of 1930 an eight-month sabbatical from Eden made possible a trip to Germany. Prior to going, Niebuhr read widely in recent German theological writings, bringing German theology into critical, dialectical relation with the liberalism of Troeltsch and the theology of the late American Social Gospel. On his trip he met and talked with many theologians and professors, among whom Mrs. Niebuhr remembers Professor Karl Heim, then of Tübingen, as having made a strong impression on him. It is not clear whether he met Paul Tillich on this trip; but he must have read several of Tillich's books, for he translated one of them into English shortly after his return.[4] While in Germany an opportunity came to travel to Russia with a group led by Sherwood Eddy. Niebuhr spent August of 1930 in Russia, an experience which seems to have led him to an understanding of Marxism as a practical faith and a philosophy of history.

As the Niebuhrs were returning to the United States, at Ellis Island, in New York harbor, a letter was brought on board their ship inviting him to accept the post of associate professor of Christian ethics at Yale Divinity School. Niebuhr was deeply honored by the invitation, his third to Yale (he had refused one offered around 1927); but he was not eager to leave Eden, where they had deep friendships and church associations. Eventually he decided to accept the invitation, however, and after completing the year at Eden moved east in the summer of 1931.

Niebuhr gave the Alumni Lecture at Yale that fall. It gave a

---

[4] *Die Religiöse Lage der Gegenwart* (1926), which Niebuhr translated as *The Religious Situation* (New York: Henry Holt & Co., 1932).

review of his study of the German and American theological situations and shows the beginning emergence of his own decisive theological synthesis. During the next six years his theological response to an era of national emergency and crisis took shape in a series of incisive articles and books. In 1935, with Wilhelm Pauck and Francis P. Miller, he published a sharp critique of the American churches' ethical impotence and entanglement in social evils, entitled *The Church Against the World*. This was followed in 1937 by his study of the central theological thrust in the three hundred years of American Protestantism, *The Kingdom of God in America*.

In 1938 Niebuhr became a full professor at Yale. Later that year he and Mrs. Niebuhr purchased a large wooded lot and built the gracious clapboard home where she still lives in nearby Hamden, Connecticut. During this time he was at work on what many readers judge to be his finest book, *The Meaning of Revelation* (1941).

The war years were difficult ones for Niebuhr. As we shall see in chapter 4, he carried out some of his most sober and agonizing theological work in the midst of this unprecedented world crisis. Exhaustion and the struggle to shape a theological and ethical response to the horrors of the war drove Niebuhr into virtually paralyzing depression in the summer and fall of 1944. Hospitalized for a time in that period, he characteristically made this an occasion to reflect on the hospital as an institution, and the care of physicians and nurses as instruments in the healing and redemptive work of God.

After the war Niebuhr made important contributions to rethinking the role of the church in the postwar era. In 1949 he delivered the lectures which, two years later, were published as *Christ and Culture*. This book, a perennial classic, shows the blending of Niebuhr's broad historical grasp of Christian thought with his penchant for creating vivid typological constructs by which to organize and compare the many patterns of normative relation between the Christian message and its environing cultures.

During the years from 1952 to 1957 Niebuhr worked intermittently on a large manuscript on faith. Considering faith in both phenomenological and normative terms, these materials were given as lectures at several institutions in the fifties. They also incorporated some elements of an unpublished manuscript of the mid-forties called "Knowledge of Faith." Under the title "Faith on Earth" Niebuhr had planned to publish these materials on faith with those which later appeared as *Radical Monotheism and Western Culture* (1960). The potential publisher failed to grasp the significance and novelty of these chapters. The part of the manuscript dealing with faith as a phenomenon was rejected for publication, while the chapters on "radical monotheism" were accepted. ("Faith on Earth" will receive extensive treatment in chapter 5.)

From 1954 to 1956 Niebuhr, assisted by Daniel Day Williams and James Gustafson, headed up an American Association of Theological Schools study of theological education in the United States and Canada. Their work included both an extensive survey of existing educational practices and an effort to develop normative guidelines for the future of education for ministry. The results of their study appeared in a jointly authored volume, *The Advancement of Theological Education*. Niebuhr and Williams edited another book, entitled *The Ministry in Historical Perspective*. And Niebuhr, speaking partly for his colleagues, wrote a broadly influential statement on the mission of the church and ministry, drawing out its implications for theological education. This work he called *The Purpose of the Church and Its Ministry* (1956).

In 1960 Niebuhr went abroad again, giving lectures at the University of Glasgow, at Cambridge University, and at the University of Bonn in West Germany. These, supplemented by his Earl Lectures at the Pacific School of Religion in 1962, were published posthumously as *The Responsible Self* in 1963.

When H. Richard Niebuhr died on July 5, 1962, he was within a year of retirement. At the time of his death he had just begun to draw together notes from several years of his lecture course on ethics. It seems likely that he had planned to begin work that summer on his *Ethics*, a comprehensive presentation of the ripe fruit of his forty-year career as teacher and writer in theological ethics. Sadly, he had not committed an outline to paper. Professor James Gustafson's introduction to *The Responsible Self* gives a most helpful overview of Niebuhr's approach to ethics, and suggests the form his magnum opus might have taken. In chapter 4 I report extensively on the structure and content of Niebuhr's class lectures and show some of their interrelations with his written work.

Niebuhr was an impressively systematic thinker. It is unlikely, however, that his *Ethics* would have resembled any usual approach taken in systematic theology or ethics. For his systematic exposition was addressed more to the description and analysis of moral *action* than to moral *concepts;* more to the *dynamics* of faith in evolution and revolution than to the *doctrines* expressed in belief. Whether the topic is revelation, responsibility as an ethical norm, or faith, Niebuhr characteristically began with description. And his descriptions are dynamic. They are studies of processes, events, encounters, relations, changings, transformations. They aim to give the reader or hearer access to the *experience* of revelation, the *awareness* of responsibility, the *imperativeness* of trust and loyalty in faith.

Though rarely autobiographical in any explicit way, Niebuhr's theological work clearly had its roots in his own struggle of faith and in his identification with the struggles of contemporaries and forebears in the communion of saints. He was fascinated and absorbed by autobiography. He read widely in philosophy and history. He was attentive to the work of sociologists and psychologists and took seriously the implications of their investigations for illumining the dynamics of faith and religious experience. But most of all, one senses that Niebuhr was consistently involved in his own highly personal "experiments with truth." Though he would have been uncomfortable with the comparison, some words he once spoke about Luther also apply to him:

He found freshly minted parables. He brought forth new symbols because he wrestled with, he encountered, he experienced, he heard, he searched out himself before God and God before himself. What he communicated was not the word of God in scriptures but the word he had heard God speaking to him, Martin Luther, in scriptures. It was not the word that anyone could hear but which came to the ears of an agonized listener, of one who was fighting for his life, who was crying for help and heard the distant answer of the helper.[5]

While he avoided the ostentation of direct self-revelation, Niebuhr's theology is clearly the work of one who "meant it," and who kept submitting his understandings and expressions of faith to the tests and validations of experience.

[5] Cole Lectures, Vanderbilt University, 1960. Lecture 2, "Towards New Symbols," tape transcript pp. 28-29 (unpublished).

Chapter I
Theological Preludes
and Prophetic Inquiry

1. YOUNG IN EDEN

H. Richard Niebuhr's teaching career began in 1919 at Eden
Theological Seminary. Since graduating from Eden in 1915, he had
had two years as pastor of a St. Louis church, earned a master of
arts in history from Washington University, and worked for a year
as a reporter for a daily newspaper. What was he working on and
thinking about in these years prior to his study at Yale? Is the older
man and mature scholar visible in the early writings from the
first years of his teaching career?

During these first Eden years Niebuhr published three articles,
all appearing in the *Magazin für Evangelische Theologie und
Kirche,* a publication of the German Evangelical Synod of North

America.[1] Looking back at these articles from the vantage point of his later development, it is possible to see in them methods of inquiry, problems, and emphases that later become consistently characteristic of Niebuhr's work.

THE PHILOSOPHERS' GOD

"An Aspect of the Idea of God in Recent Thought" is the first and, in many ways, the most interesting of Niebuhr's three early articles.[2] His own position is not explicitly stated in this compact description and appraisal of contemporary philosophers' reflections on God and the human condition. What is important for us is the assumptions Niebuhr brings to the inquiry, the questions he asks, and the kinds of analyses he carries out. Already there are signs of awareness that ideas are conditioned by the environment and needs of the thinker: "Our definitions of God's nature are conditioned by our need of Him. . . . Our interpretations of the world-order change with external variations in our environment and . . . we apprehend those characteristics of the nature of God best which most adequately answer to the particular needs of our life." [3] In a manner characteristic of his more mature work, Niebuhr sees the analysis of modern man's religious needs and the efforts to meet them by philosophers as "not without significance for Christian theology." [4] He observes that science and naturalism, based on a mechanistic theory of determinism, had heightened two crucial needs for God in modern man: "one [need] arising out of the scientific explanations of the cosmos and the evolutionary theory of life and the other rooting in the problem of evil." [5] Of the three types of philosophical reaction to those needs the "stoic" answer of Bertrand Russell (that though man cannot understand or make

[1] Until later in the twenties (when it was retitled *Theological Magazine*) this periodical was published in German. Some of the articles did appear in English, however, as did all of Niebuhr's.

[2] *Magazin für Evangelische Theologie und Kirche* (hereafter cited as *METK*), 48 (January, 1920), 39 ff.

[3] "An Aspect of the Idea of God in Recent Thought, p. 39.

[4] *Ibid.*

[5] *Ibid.*

sense of his existence he can do his duty) simply evades the question. The second type of reaction, Hegelian idealism with its scientific agnosticism, Niebuhr also holds to be an evasion. The third type of reaction, which Niebuhr sees as "rapidly becoming the dominant tendency in America at least," is Jamesian pragmatism and the neorealistic school of Elof John Boodin.[6] These latter approaches, he points out, accept the world of science, but they see in it teleological development rather than mechanism.[7] The important feature of the pragmatist and neorealist positions for Niebuhr, however, is their significance for religion as doctrines of *pluralism.* For James, Niebuhr writes, "God is a part and not the whole." He is the God of spiritual life or of tendencies making for righteousness, but he does not have to be "the responsible author of evil," as he must be "according to Hegelian conceptions."[8]

The intriguing thing that emerges from a careful reading of this somewhat opaque article is the recognition that over against the naturalists and determinists on the one hand, and the idealistic monists on the other, Niebuhr finds himself philosophically more in agreement with the pragmatist, neorealist, and evolutionist (Bergson) doctrines of a *finite* God, who continues in creative activity "on the side of life thru the evolution of species and the formation of human personalities."[9] If this interpretation is right, it suggests the likelihood of a tension in Niebuhr's thought between this philosophical position he finds attractive and a biblical understanding of *one* God, infinite in power and goodness. This article raises the suspicion that without acknowledging it Niebuhr, at age twenty-six, finds himself wrestling between what he

[6] *Ibid.,* p. 40. Elof John Boodin (1869–1950). Born in Sweden, he came to U.S. in 1887. He took his Ph.D. with Royce at Harvard in 1899. By 1920 he had published three major books. *Time and Reality* (1905), *Truth and Reality* (1911), and *A Realistic Universe* (1916). He combined a concept of time as "dynamic non-being" with a pragmatic, realist epistemology, blending them, in the latter book, as a basis for a realist metaphysics that incorporated scientific procedures and results.

[7] Note Niebuhr's sensitivity to the importance of the "root-metaphors" of the positions he is examining. (See Stephen C. Pepper, *World Hypotheses,* Berkeley: University of California Press, 1942.)

[8] "An Aspect of the Idea of God," pp. 41, 44.

[9] *Ibid.,* p. 42.

11

will later call "monotheism" and various forms of dualism or meta-physical pluralism, the latter being attractive to him because they acknowledged the reality of evil and suffering in life without indict-ing either the power or the goodness of God. On the basis of this article this suspicion can be neither confirmed nor removed. But the article definitely plants in our minds the intuition that for Niebuhr at this point, as certainly was the case at later points in his career, the reality of evil, suffering, and tragedy presented espe-cially deep-going challenges to the faith out of which his theology grew. Of this much we can be sure: that massive affirmation of the oneness, the supreme power, and the goodness of God that would later become the foundation of Niebuhr's theology is not yet incontestably present. But we should mark this openness to process conceptions of God and nature as an early influence that will show up clearly in the development of Niebuhr's mature position.

IN THE WAKE OF THE SOCIAL GOSPEL

The two other Eden articles do not afford us any view of Niebuhr working on the problems raised in the first paper. Instead we see him engaging the social challenges of the urban frontier from a Rauschenbuschian Social Gospel stance. In "The Alliance Between Labor and Religion" [10] Niebuhr makes three main points: (1) historically there have been many connections between the Chris-tian movement and the labor movement; (2) the contemporary labor movement is religious in character, by reason both of its origins in the Christian impulse and of its present religious quali-ties;[11] and (3) despite the historical relationship and the common goals of labor and the churches these movements are tragically divided. The church has objected to labor's use of violence, not

---

[10] *METK*, 49 (May, 1921), pp. 197-203.

[11] Niebuhr describes the labor movement's religious qualities as "its in-spiring hope for a better world and its faith in the ideal, . . . its bitter discon-tent with the sins of the present order, its insistence on the worth of personality, its sense for realities, and its underlying conviction of the solidarity of men." "The Alliance Between Labor and Religion," pp. 198-99.

so much on the basis of the ethics of Jesus, but because of its interest in its own salvation, mistakenly conceived in economic, materialistic terms. "Not until the church is ready to fight the same battle that labor is fighting, but by the better method of aggressive suffering, will it be in a position to declare against labor's method in the fight." [12] The church, Niebuhr concludes, faces a decision "weightier in import even than that which was forced on Luther." [13] Will it dare to stand alone, "to lead the way to the goal by way of the cross," or will it continue, in rejecting labor's method of warfare, to make common cause with labor's enemies? [14]

The final article in this early trilogy appeared just before Niebuhr left for Yale in 1922. "Christianity and the Social Problem" [15] presents Niebuhr's normative interpretation of the Social Gospel and shows us, before his Yale work on Troeltsch, his way of conceptualizing society, societal problems, and the tasks of the church in relation to them.

> The social gospel is no new gospel. It is the *Sermon on the Mount* and the *message* about the *Kingdom of God*. It is the parable of the Good Samaritan and of Dives and Lazarus. It is the prophecy of the Old Testament and the good news of the New Covenant. It is Paul's description of the universal church and John's vision of the end. [16]

From that sweeping beginning Niebuhr moves to assert that the New Testament simultaneously affirms "the absolute value of human personality" and its comparative value over institutions, while subsuming all individual*ism* under the imperative to seek first the kingdom of God. "The value of human lives can be realized, according to the Gospel, only in losing of the individual life within the Kingdom of God." [17] Niebuhr will later call this kind of paradoxical relation between the absolute value of the individual and the requisite for its realization of "losing itself" in the kingdom a *polarity*—a polarity in thought and in reality. In this article he

[12] *Ibid.*, p. 202.
[13] *Ibid.*, p. 207.
[14] *Ibid.*, p. 203.
[15] METK, 50 (July, 1922), pp. 278-91.
[16] "Christianity and the Social Problem," p. 278.
[17] *Ibid.*, p. 279.

hinges his analysis of specific social evils on these two polar principles:

These evils we may consider under two heads: insofar as they violate the principles of the kingdom of God, they show themselves in rampant individualism; insofar as they are denials of the supreme value of the individual, they appear as the suppression of personality.[18]

In pointing to evils that result from denial of the principle of the kingdom—and from substitution for it of the principle of highest loyalty to the self's cause—Niebuhr names the high divorce rate, exploitation of wage workers by industry, and, in more comprehensive terms, "a general breakdown in morals." [19] He devotes several pages to an examination of the background causes of this moral breakdown, tracing it to (1) a "one-sided development of the principle of individual liberty" growing out of the Reformation and French Revolution responses to the historical abuses of political, economic, and religious authority;[20] (2) the emergence of machine production which placed excessive power in the hands of the individual owners of machines, separated individual workers from the earlier family productive units, and gave birth to class consciousness, which is "an individualistic principle, though it be the consciousness of a group";[21] and (3) the confusion of morals and standards of conduct introduced by the admission into the United States of large numbers of immigrants.[22] In his summation of

---

[18] *Ibid.*, p. 281. As Niebuhr reiterates the principle of the kingdom he uses concepts and terminology indicating that Josiah Royce, as well as the New Testament, has been his teacher: "The end of life is social. This is not an esoteric truth. It is a fundamental law of life. Individualism leads always and everywhere to destruction. Consecration of self to the cause of the social group leads to self-realization, tho complete self-realization be impossible until the social group includes the whole of man's social environment, God and mankind." The Roycean themes are the *cause* of the social group, and of the universal community.

[19] *Ibid.*, p. 282.

[20] *Ibid.*

[21] *Ibid.*, p. 283.

[22] On this Niebuhr writes: "Whenever varying civilizations mingle we can look for a mutual breakdown of the morals which guided the conduct of each group so long as it was separate. Like-mindedness, which is especially important for social peace and solidarity, is especially absent in American society as a whole." *Ibid.*

the situation, which stresses the structural dimensions of the evil in society, Niebuhr wrote:

The conditions of our times are such that human selfishness is given an especial opportunity to assert itself. The fault does not lie only within human nature,—it lies within the social structure to which this human nature must make its adaptation.[23]

In the light of this analysis Niebuhr outlines the mission of the church in service of the kingdom principle. First, as never before the church must preach the higher righteousness of the Sermon on the Mount. Second, while the church must not evade the responsibility of urging the state to pass and enforce legislation protecting the rights of women and children in industry and in divorce law, "it has before it the task of creating a new set of morals directly in the hearts of the people," for "no law can ever be enforced until the conscience of the people is behind it." [24] Finally, the church has the "task of restoring to our social life the value of an ideal held in common," the creation of a national homogeneity "in which the higher righteousness shall come to group expression." [25]

In the rest of the article Niebuhr deals with the results of denying the other polar principle in his summation of the Social Gospel, the absolute value of the individual. Here he speaks of economic exploitation of individuals and institutions, pointing especially to "the *institution of modern industry*." [26] He shows an awareness of the deprivation of economic freedom suffered by farmers and agricultural workers through the amalgamation of small farms into large conglomerates; and of industrial workers through the rigid structuring of work opportunities in accordance with the low wages and rationalized procedures of machine production. "Economic

---

[23] In the text this entire passage is italicized. One might conclude that this is indicative of a breakthrough, a new insight for Niebuhr. I hardly think this is the case. More likely he is stressing the point that he most wants to press on his fellow churchmen who, as his statement pointing out the individualistic character of Lutheran ethics (*ibid.*, p. 279) would suggest, likely tended toward an ethics of individual conversion and responsibility.

[24] *Ibid.*, p. 284.

[25] *Ibid.*, p. 285.

[26] *Ibid.*, p. 287.

freedom," he wrote, "is at least as important as political freedom." [27] It is interesting to note that while Niebuhr catalogs some
of the then more radical demands of labor, such as recognition of
the right to organize and granting to workers a share in the control
of industry, his admonition to the church in reference to them is
relatively weak: "The church of Christ cannot but have sympathy
with the demands for reduction of the labor day and for the steady
increase of wages to the point where the service of the worker
rather than the service of material things, of capital, is fully recognized." [28]

Though he recognizes that "the social gospel as applied to industry will be revolutionary finally in its outworkings," Niebuhr's
concluding counsel on the proper posture of the church is mild and
melioristic. He urges that the application of the Social Gospel
must be *sympathetic;* "the employer and the employee of today
are results largely of their environment." The preaching of the
church must be *definite,* addressing specific problems. The preaching of the Social Gospel must be *Christian.* "May it preach the
law of sacrifice to employer and employee but sacrifice not for the
sake of present peace." [29]

TO YALE

Niebuhr's early trilogy of articles offers us the only available
evidence from which to construct a "portrait of the author as a
young man." Though far from conclusive, an examination of the
intellectual baggage young Niebuhr carried to New Haven in 1922,
based on these articles, would seem to reveal at least the following:
(1) an interpretation of the biblical basis of faith understood primarily in line with an amalgam of nineteenth-century European
Protestant liberalism and the liberalism of the American Social
Gospel; (2) some breadth and depth of acquaintance with the
writings of contemporary philosophers, particularly Bertrand Rus-

[27] *Ibid.,* p. 288.
[28] *Ibid.,* p. 290.
[29] *Ibid.,* pp. 290-91.

16

sell, William James, Henri Bergson, and Josiah Royce; (3) the likelihood of a tension between biblical monotheism and some version of dualistic or pluralistic metaphysics in which responsibility for evil does not have to be ascribed to God; (4) an awareness of the problems of ideological and ethical relativism, though (at least in these articles) not named or focused on as such; (5) an implicitly organic theory of society in which church and society are not clearly differentiated, unity as homogeneity is conceived as a societal ideal, and harmony rather than conflict is "normal" (this way of thinking results in an almost paralyzing awareness of the tension between the goals of social peace, cohesion, and order and those of economic and social justice); and (6) a tendency to reflect on social ethics and the task of the church at a somewhat abstract level, thereby circumventing the necessity of developing the imperatives of the gospel in other than mainly general terms.[30]

2. THE FORMATIVE ENCOUNTER WITH TROELTSCH

THE CHOICE OF TROELTSCH

When H. Richard Niebuhr arrived at Yale Divinity School in 1922 he was, as doctoral candidates go, a mature man and a very mature student. It is highly probable that D. C. Macintosh, professor of theology at Yale from 1909 and devoted lifelong proponent of a critical-empirical epistemology of religious knowledge, guided Niebuhr toward the writings of Ernst Troeltsch. In 1919 Macintosh had written a penetrating analysis of Troeltsch's theory of religious knowledge, in which several of the emphases of Niebuhr's dis-

[30] These observations are intended as descriptive rather than evaluative. For a context against which the characteristics here described may be evaluated see Donald B. Meyer, *The Protestant Search for Political Realism, 1919–1941* (Berkeley: University of California Press, 1961), especially chaps. 1-5. In relation to Meyer's characterization of the dominant ethos of Social Gospel churches and churchmen in the early twenties, those features of Niebuhr's mode of thinking that from later vantage may seem worthy of criticism appear as highly typical of the era.

sertation were foreshadowed.[31] The task Niebuhr assumed in writing about Troeltsch was a formidable one. Only a miniscule amount of the large corpus of Troeltsch's writings had been translated into English. Virtually all the important secondary sources on Troeltsch were in German. Troeltsch's German afforded little difficulty for Niebuhr, however, because his family had been bilingual. The greater difficulties in interpreting Troeltsch resulted from the continually evolving character of his position and from the intense, dialectical character of his style of thought.

Troeltsch has to be viewed in the context of a very dynamic and multileveled intellectual situation. He self-consciously made very fine distinctions between the positions of various neo-Kantian epistemologists, of neo-Hegelian evolutionists, of the historicists (the members of the history-of-religions school), as well as of the various contemporary schools of psychology of religion. This meant that any adequate interpreter of Troeltsch's development had to work his way patiently into the complex crosscurrents of thought that stimulated and challenged Troeltsch.

But the adequate interpreter of Troeltsch had to be more than merely intellectually sophisticated and capable of sustained, discriminating attention to a wide variety of largely abstract positions. He also had to have what Max Weber somewhere calls "religious musicality" with his subject—the empathetic sensitivity to the deep tide of religious passion that drove, sustained, and came to expression in Troeltsch's often abstruse work. Troeltsch found, in Niebuhr, an interpreter adequate on each of these counts.

Niebuhr's dissertation, "Ernst Troeltsch's Philosophy of Religion," is important for us primarily as a formative event in Niebuhr's life and thought. Choosing the topic of a doctoral dissertation is what Niebuhr would have called a "moral" act: it is an act of

---

[31] See D. C. Macintosh, "Troeltsch's Theory of Religious Knowledge," *American Journal of Theology*, 22 (1919), pp. 274 ff. Particularly Macintosh called attention to the duality of the Kantian-rational and Jamesian-empirical thrusts in Troeltsch's modification of Ritschlian value-judgment theory and his insistence "that a value judgment is the foundation and strength of all human knowledge" (p. 283). Both these points find important development in Niebuhr's dissertation.

self-definition, as are all acts of significant commitment and self-investment. Like most other major acts of self-definition (marriage, entering a profession, joining a church, adopting an ideological stance or world view), the choice of a dissertation subject grows out of a complex constellation of factors, some of which are conscious for the chooser, some of which are not. The temptation to try a phenomenological analysis of the moral act of choosing a topic must be resisted, though as a task it would have intrigued Niebuhr. What this discussion aims to do, rather, is to help clarify what it means to view Niebuhr's dissertation as a formative event in his life and thought. In a very broad sense we are asking: What did Niebuhr "learn" in the course of living intensively with the writings and ideas of Troeltsch? What did he "decide" in his dialogue with this thinker? In what self-defining interests and long-range work commitments did the choice of Troeltsch result?

THE ANALYSIS OF TROELTSCH

The influence that his work on Troeltsch had on Niebuhr's mind and life cannot be understood from reading the dissertation alone. Missing from it is any systematic critique of Troeltsch's position. It contains no effort at a constructive statement that would have revealed Niebuhr's ideas about a fruitful direction beyond Troeltsch. Nor does the text reveal any conspicuous sudden breakthroughs to new insights for the author. In order, then, to assess the dissertation as a formative event for Niebuhr, we must view it in the context of his later work. What themes, what modes of thought, what problematics, discussed in the dissertation, reappear as pivotal elements in Niebuhr's subsequent development? How did Niebuhr alter and develop key Troeltschian ideas or approaches in his mature teaching and writing? What options did Niebuhr decisively reject as a result of working on Troeltsch?

Niebuhr devotes the first third of his dissertation to an account of Troeltsch's intellectual development, finding four clearly distinguishable periods in it and tracing the decisive influences on each of them. He does a masterly job of presenting the major themes in their interrelatedness. Troeltsch's intellectual growth appears as

19

an organism, evolving with continuities and persistencies as well as new departures.

The backbone of the dissertation is Niebuhr's definition of the major tension in Troeltsch's philosophy of religion as arising out of two different main ideas that Troeltsch combines without bringing them into complete accord.[32] The first of these is a Kantian-rationalist approach that posits a necessarily valid truth content in religious experience on the basis of an *a priori* correspondence between human reason and the nature of divine reality. Though the psychology of religion discovers much that is spurious in religious experience, the philosopher of religion, Troeltsch believed, guided by the *a priori* of religious reason, will know how to discern the real, the necessarily valid truth content in the manifold of religious experience. Undergirding this approach is a metaphysics with a modified monadology that sees "a connection between the rational principle in human consciousness and a rational world ground which comes to expression in the principles of human reason." [33] The *a priori* element never presents itself as pure form alone, but is always implicated in concrete religious content. It is the universally valid element present in every genuine religious experience. This first approach tended to dominate in Troeltsch's work during what Niebuhr identified as his neo-Kantian phase—roughly 1903 to 1913. The metaphysical tendency here is toward a monism.

Alongside this rationalist approach, and tending to supplant it after 1913, is an empiricist and realist approach that evolved out of Troeltsch's exposure to Max Weber and sociological method, out of his research for *The Social Teaching of the Christian Churches*, and out of the influence of Jamesian psychology of religion and Bergsonian vitalism. Here the concern is not with the rationally necessary, formal truth in religious experience, but with the uniqueness, the singularity, of every historical individual [34] and the

[32] "Ernst Troeltsch's Philosophy of Religion," p. 116.
[33] See *ibid.*, p. 68. See also pp. 26-27, 115-16, 167-68, 196.
[34] "Individual" here does not refer to individual *persons* but rather is a category referring to events, to constellations of values or ideas, or to cultural entities, in their unique particularity.

interplay of rational with nonrational or antirational factors in human history. Whereas in the rationalist approach the focus is epistemological and the goal abstract truth, in the empiricist approach the focus is historical-cultural and the task is to interpret the essence of concrete historical social-cultural entities—the value synthesis that gives a culture or a historical idea its character and integrity.[35] The normativity and "truth" to be found by this approach are not universal or eternal; they are historically conditional and limited. This is a relative apriorism, but "though the relativity of values needs to be conceded their validity need not be surrendered." [36] Nor does such "relative apriorism . . . mean subjectivism." [37] This second kind of apriorism in Troeltsch is linked to the first through a similar kind of metaphysical conviction of a correlation between human thought and divine nature as we saw in the first: "Thought must have some secret alliance with reality, be connected somehow with it by means of a common ground of both." [38] But here the rational character of this relation is much less certain and is deeply qualified by an awareness of nonrational factors. Just as irrational and nonconscious elements enter into the value synthesis constituting the *essence*, the normative value center, of a historical culture, so an element of risk and choice enters into the discerning and identifying of this value center by the interpreter. If the metaphysical tendency of the rationalist approach is toward a monism, the tendency of the realistic empiricist approach is toward a pluralism.

To sum up this central tension and what Niebuhr sees at stake in it, we will do well to look at one of Niebuhr's formulations:

This realism [of Troeltsch's second phase] with its acceptance of the non-rational totality of life and of pluralism but with its demand for

[35] "The essential character of an historical complex is the value which it possesses and which is immanent within it. The primary question is not as to the value of an historical individuality from the viewpoint of the observer, but as to the actual value-relations which, in human history, have served to individualize complex reality into wholes possessing value or meaning." *Ibid.*, pp. 241-42.
[36] *Ibid.*, p. 252.
[37] *Ibid.*, p. 255.
[38] *Ibid.*, pp. 256-57.

the forcing in of the rational into the non-rational and its tendency toward monism, is an incomplete synthesis of the rationalist and anti-rationalistic elements in Troeltsch's thought. In it we have once more the compromise between antitheses which is so characteristic of actual life. . . . Here Spinoza and William James represent the antipodes. It is impossible to work the two elements together. . . . In religion the contradiction comes to light again as between the idea of the plural, living and free character of the world in God and the creative activity of God on the one hand, and the unity of the world, the rule of the Supersensual on the other hand. Practically the two sides are held together in theism, but theoretically they can never be harmonized." [39]

CONTINUITIES BETWEEN NIEBUHR AND TROELTSCH

With the sketch of the pivotal contention of Niebuhr's dissertation in hand we can return to the main question of this section: In what ways does this work on Troeltsch seem to have been a formative event in Niebuhr's life and thought? Our effort to answer this can be organized under three categories: (1) elements of Troeltsch's style, modes of thought, and methods of inquiry that also become characteristic of Niebuhr's way of working; (2) patterns or structures of thought present in Troeltsch for which there are parallel central patterns or structures in Niebuhr's later works, but in which Niebuhr has made significant modifications; and (3) aspects of Troeltschian thought which Niebuhr rejected, with significant consequences for his later work.[40]

Under the first category, Troeltschian characteristics of thought that became Niebuhrian characteristics, the most massive and comprehensive entry will have to be what Niebuhr calls "Troeltsch's realism." This aspect of Troeltsch's work is like a twentieth-century revised version of the Kantian statement of reason's awareness

---

[39] *Ibid.*, p. 216. This last sentence is of surpassing interest. Note its relation to the seminal issue in "An Aspect of the Idea of God in Recent Thought," above. Niebuhr is summarizing Troeltsch. An important question for this study is whether Niebuhr's later theistic synthesis under the idea of the sovereignty of God really meets and overcomes this difficulty; and if so, how.

[40] Of course, in pointing to similarities and drawing parallels between Niebuhr's later mode of thinking and his interpretation of Troeltsch's thought, neither the influence of other intervening figures and experiences nor Niebuhr's own maturing pre-Troeltschian intellectual style may be overlooked. The work on Troeltsch is a very significant formative event for Niebuhr, but certainly not *the* formative event.

of its own limits. Niebuhr summarizes the main principles of this realism:

(1) All concepts of the natural sciences are working hypotheses; (2) . . . all concepts of the historical sciences are transformations, systematizations and concentrations of a much richer reality of facts; (3) . . . all isolations of the subject and especially of the conscious subject are only artificial abstractions from a continuous racial consciousness (*Gattungsbewusstsein*) and from a subconscious life which flows into some sort of unity with the physical; (4) . . . all our culture and religious ideals are emanations out of a complicated movement of life which no kind of research can completely illuminate; (5) . . . the whole realm of rationally clear facts and norms in nature and history is embraced by a much broader realm, a wide, dark mass of the purely actual and living; and (6) . . . the relation between the rational and the non-rational or "irrational" cannot be rationally determined.[41]

Because Niebuhr was always more impressed by the historicist side of neo-Kantianism than by its rationalist side, his congruence with Troeltsch's realism did not have to involve the syndrome of reason attacking reason in the interest of the "irrational" as Troeltsch's statement does.[42] Nor, because Niebuhr had a more developed social psychology at his disposal, did he have to deal with the danger of rationalist individualism in terms of ideas like "racial consciousness" and "subconscious life." Shorn of these features, however, the spirit of this statement of Troeltsch's realism is a spirit that pervades Niebuhr's stance in relation to the claims of positivists—whether they be positivists of some empirical method in science or philosophy, or positivists of revelation in theology. It characterizes his response to excessively confident intellectual systems of any kind. In regard to his own work this spirit of realism was a significant element in his humility, his willingness to attend with care to any responsible theological or philosophical vision, his continual willingness to be taught.

[41] "Troeltsch's Philosophy of Religion," pp. 214-16.
[42] I think it may also be true to say that Niebuhr recognized, in a way Troeltsch perhaps never did, how much confidence in itself reason shows when it states its limits, and that in delimiting the "irrational" the philosopher is also subsuming it under reason, though in a manner different from the old reason it supplants.

The importance of Troeltsch's realism for Niebuhr cannot be fully appreciated, however, until it is seen that this realism is a mood or temper that comprehends several of the really central emphases in Troeltsch's thought, all of which carry over into Niebuhr's work in decisive ways. Perhaps the most important of these—certainly the one for which Troeltsch is best known—is his teaching about *relativism*. By this I mean Troeltsch's consciousness that every idea or belief is decisively conditioned by value patterns, by forms of social relations, and by the time consciousness characteristic of its thinkers or believers.[43] What is important for us is that nowhere in the dissertation or later does Niebuhr express anything but implicit agreement with and appreciation of this standpoint. Most significant is the fact that Niebuhr does not regard as a retreat Troeltsch's movement away from efforts to ground religious truth on the rationally necessary basis of the religious *a priori*. He sees and accepts Troeltsch's forthright development of the consequences of the relativist standpoint, not as a blow to be absorbed, but as an aid to truth and a clarification of the meaning of faith. It is a mistake, Niebuhr argued at the end of his dissertation, to label Troeltsch a relativist. "There are," he wrote, "three elements in [Troeltsch's] discussion of the truth or value of religion. . . . The one is the idea of the relativity of all historical values, and so of religion, the other is the apriori and imperative obligation which such values impose upon us, the third is the presentiment, the intuition, the direct inner experience of the Divine Life." [44] Though in his last, incomplete book (*Der Historismus und Seine*

---

[43] It is clear that Troeltsch's early exposure to a comparative religious perspective by Legarde, his rejection of the Ritschlian effort to ground the superiority of Christianity on exclusive miracle apologetic, and his similar refusal to adopt a Hegelian-speculative viewpoint in which Christianity is held to be the culminating realization and expression of the world spirit, are all aspects of this consciousness. His appropriation of the historicists' appreciation for the particularity and uniqueness of historical complexes was a factor in it, as was the empiricist influence of James. Probably most decisive was the extended research and writing for *The Social Teaching of the Christian Churches*, during which time Troeltsch became acquainted with Max Weber and through his stimulus absorbed understandings deriving from Marx and many others about the interrelationships of ideologies and social structures.

[44] "Troeltsch's Philosophy of Religion," pp. 262-63.

Probleme) Troeltsch emphasized the first of these elements, Niebuhr writes, relativism represents the negative side of his thought. "And in view of his insistent emphasis upon the *apriori* character of religion, upon its independence and causal inexplicability and, finally, in view of the constant trend toward a metaphysical interpretation of apriorism in his 'Historism,' it is impossible to escape the conclusion that the emphasis, for Troeltsch, was really placed on the second and third elements." [45]

At the beginning of *Christ and Culture* Niebuhr gives an indication of how the Troeltschian teaching on relativism influenced him. Here we see that this relativism, the negative side of Troeltsch's thought, becomes an aspect or correlate of the positive side of Niebuhr's theology:

Troeltsch has taught me to respect the multiformity and individuality of men and movements in Christian history, to be loath to force this rich variety into prefashioned conceptual molds, and yet to seek *logos* in *mythos*, reason in history, essence in existence. He has helped me to accept and to profit by the acceptance of the relativity not only of historical objects but, more, of the historical subject, the observer and interpreter. If I think of my essay as an effort to correct Troeltsch's analysis of the encounters of church and world it is mostly because I try to understand this historical relativism in the light of theological and theo-centric relativism." [46]

It seems fair to say that in Troeltsch the ideas of realism and relativism have their specific character as part of a vision anchored primarily in a faith in reason. Troeltsch, I think, remains an idealist. Finally his God is *nous* and the primal fact about man is the mystical, intuitional, rational link between his mind and the divine mind. Though it carries us ahead of ourselves, it is important to see that in Niebuhr's mature thought realism and relativism take their character in the context of quite a different vision, one that sees the primal fact about persons as being our relation, in absolute dependence, to a God who is One, who is comprehensive of all power, and who is loyal in love to dependent being. As the visional contexts are changed the ideas undergo transformation. Realism in

[45] *Ibid.*, p. 263.
[46] *Christ and Culture* (New York: Harper & Brothers, 1951), p. xii.

Troeltsch means humility before the penumbra of mystery that sets the bounds on human reason; relativism means that no conception of the absolute or of reality is adequate. Realism in Niebuhr means discerning, valuing, and responding in life in light of a trust that the mystery has integrity, is personal, and exercises its power redemptively, inviting human collaboration; relativism means "that it is an aberration of faith as well as of reason to absolutize the finite but that all this relative history of finite men and movements is under the governance of the absolute God." [47] Though it caricatures both men somewhat, we can say that for Troeltsch *realism* and *relativism* are aspects of the stance of a rational intellectual inquirer, while for Niebuhr they are dimensions in the existential posture of a "faithing" man or community.

Having suggested how these two aspects of Troeltsch's thought are carried over into Niebuhr's, and how the change of visional contexts alters their meanings, we can briefly allude to several other continuities between Troeltsch and Niebuhr. The first of these continuities is in some ways a matter of intellectual style, though in both men the characteristics to be described have deep convictional rootage in their central outlooks. I refer here to the *catholicity* of both men's thought, investigations, and development of positions. On principle neither man could be an exclusivist—either as a Christian, claiming a singular supremacy for his way over that of non-Christians, or as a theologian, declaring the absolute independence of his method of inquiry from the findings and claims of other disciplines. On principle both men devoted considerable attention to the investigations of philosophers, sociologists, psychologists, and others. Both men followed Schleiermacher in examining religion as part of human culture, and man's religiousness as an intrinsic part of his self-definition and orientation in the world. Both men showed an openness to the visions of others—a teachability and willingness to revise hard-carved concepts and formulations in the light of changed circumstances or new insights. In both men there was a sense of the value of a very catholic tradition and a commitment, fulfilled through continuing immer-

[47] *Ibid.*

sion in it, to be faithful to the variegated richness of the church's memory. As Troeltsch moved from an apologetic stance, trying to ground Christianity in rational certainty, to a confessional stance, Niebuhr consistently and continually viewed defensiveness and aggressive apologetic in theology as one of the prime manifestations of distrust and of crippling faith.[48] In all this it is of course impossible and unnecessary to say that these qualities in Niebuhr are due solely to the influence of Troeltsch upon him. Certainly that is not the case. It does seem fair to say, however, that in his dialogue with the writing of Troeltsch these tendencies in Niebuhr found confirmation and consolidation.

Just as all the elements of style just enumerated are directly related to the realism, with its correlative relativism, in the ways of thinking of both these men, so is one other very important common characteristic of their thinking. In another summary of the central tension in Troeltsch's philosophy of religion Niebuhr writes:

> Troeltsch's philosophy reveals itself as an attempt to combine social, traditional religion with personal, more or less mystical religion, to carry the assurance of mysticism and Kantian rationalism into the realm of mediate and non-rational, empirical religion, but to do justice to the social necessity of cult and the historical character of religious thought. Troeltsch deals with *antinomies*, or at least with *polar contrasts*, in religion. Conservatism and liberalism, rationalism and antirationalism, logos and myth, individual and community—these are the factors he seeks to combine.[49]

In Troeltsch, Niebuhr found a thinker of such multidimensional scope and such honesty that he could not and would not force into a smooth, unifying synthesis all the interpretations of the real that, from different perspectives, commended themselves to him. For Troeltsch, to express the unity in the sensible plurality of experience was beyond the descriptive capacity of any rational theory.[50] So in trying to achieve clarity about aspects of this

---

[48] See especially *The Meaning of Revelation* (New York: The Macmillan Co., 1941), esp. pp. viii-ix.

[49] "Troeltsch's Philosophy of Religion" p. 116 (Italics added by present writer).

[50] *Ibid.*, pp. 214-15.

experience Troeltsch necessarily spoke in such a way as to reflect the conceptual as well as experiential tensions which the person as thinker, and the thinker as person, encounters. This drove Troeltsch into dealing with what Niebuhr called *antinomies* or *polar contrasts* in religion and in history. Perhaps an illustration from Niebuhr's text can make this a little more concrete. Niebuhr asks the question at one point: Is the essential element in religion, for Troeltsch, belief in revealed God or gods, or is it the religious cult? He presents statements from Troeltsch which from one viewpoint affirm the primacy of the cult. Then he places alongside them other statements which, from quite another perspective, assert just as emphatically the primacy of the ideational element, of belief in God. Niebuhr came to see that the positions taken by Troeltsch were both right and were not contradictory:

Both definitions of the essence of religion have their place in Troeltsch's psychology and philosophy of religion, the one is the essence of personal religion, the other of social religion, the one also is the essence of latent religion, the other of positive, historical religion, and the two are united in the dialectic of individual and community, and of reason and non-rational fact.[51]

Though Niebuhr uses the Kantian term "antinomies" again to refer to this characteristic of Troeltsch's thinking,[52] the term "polar" is the one that Niebuhr most consistently applies to this kind of thinking in his later writings. Though I have been able to find only one place in which Niebuhr reflects somewhat systematically on the character of polar thinking and the necessity for it,[53] the method of polarity, or what I choose to call a "logic of polarity," is

[51] *Ibid.*, pp. 139-40.
[52] *Ibid.*, p. 163.
[53] Cole Lectures 1, "The Position of Theology Today," pp. 3-21, where Niebuhr characterizes the dominant contemporary theological tendencies in terms of their dispositions in relation "to some of the great polarities that characterize our human existence. For theology like all movements in human thought does seem to move inevitably between these universal poles such as those of past and future, subject and object, contemplative and practical reasoning" (p. 3). In this lecture he distinguished (not altogether without ambiguity) between *dualities* in our experience, and *polarities*. A genuine polarity is a polarity in "that one element in this dyad is not definable without reference to the other" (p. 9).

a permeative characteristic of his thought throughout his career and constitutes a major factor in the subtlety, richness, and balance of his writings. Can we provide a definition of a "logic of polarity" that will bring the meaning of the phrase and the method of thinking it describes into better focus? A logic of polarity, we might say, is a mode of thinking and writing that tries to attend to the wholeness, the unity, of a complex phenomenon, by juxtaposing the detailed but partial views of it acquired from the several possible points of vantage (each of which may tend to make totalistic claims for its perspective), and by combining those perspectives, making such reconciliations of their contradictions as can legitimately be made, but without any specious removal of the tensions between them.

I have defined a logic of polarity in ideal terms—as an ideal that even the best human minds can only approximate when dealing with anything but the most limited aspects of reality. In studying and writing on Troeltsch, Niebuhr lived in intimate interaction with a mind capable in extraordinary measure of that kind of thinking. It may be that a mind as able as Niebuhr's intuitively develops the capacity for exercising something like a logic of polarity. I cannot help but believe, however, that Niebuhr's self-conscious development of such a manner of thinking and investigation was due in significant measure to the example of Troeltsch and to the standard he represented.[54]

In turning now to the second category of Troeltschian influences on Niebuhr we can move more swiftly. Here we have in view patterns or structures of thought present in Troeltsch for which there are parallel central patterns or structures in Niebuhr's later work, but on which Niebuhr has made significant modifications.

In many ways the natural offspring of the application of a logic of polarity to the conceptualization and analysis of complex realities is the development of typologies. We have already referred to

[54] One rather playful indication that Niebuhr self-consciously approached theological problems with this kind of logic comes in the preface to *Meaning of Revelation*: "It may appear that I have tried to seize both horns of every dilemma with which the problems of Christian faith in history confronted me. But I trust that I have not fallen into paradox" (p. viii).

Troeltsch's highly developed capacity for differentiating between similar intellectual positions. One of his more memorable contributions to the sociology of religion and to Christian ethics is his adaptation, in *The Social Teaching of the Christian Churches*, of Weber's church-sect typology into the tripartite typology of church-sect-mysticism. That schema correlated the doctrinal positions of historical Christian religious organizations with such variables as group morphology, the economic attitudes and the social class of adherents, and their stance toward social and cultural institutions and process. Though Niebuhr makes little mention of this typology or of typological method in the dissertation,[55] the fruitfulness of his application and development of the typological approach is one of the most impressive features of his later work.[56]

Perhaps the most decisive theme and pattern of thought that Niebuhr seems to have "learned" with or from Troeltsch is that having to do with value and valuation. Among the papers on Niebuhr's desk at the time of his death in 1962 was a handwritten manuscript entitled "Valuation"—apparently part of a projected book on Christian ethics. It begins, "Man's fundamental moral act seems to be that of valuing." [57] Even a slight familiarity with Niebuhr's works shows that the theme of value-valuation is consistently near the center of his thought from the time of the dissertation on Troeltsch to the time of his death. Some of his most lucid

[55] See "Troeltsch's Philosophy of Religion," pp. 147-61, for the most sustained discussions of the sociological dimension of Troeltsch's work. The church-sect-mysticism typology is mentioned on pp. 156-57.

[56] Troeltsch is specifically cited as influencing the typological approaches taken in *The Social Sources of Denominationalism* (Meridian Books; Cleveland: World Publishing Co. [1929], 1967) (see especially pp. 17-21, 29), and *Christ and Culture* (pp. xi-xii). Niebuhr also acknowledges indebtedness to C. G. Jung's *Psychological Types* (1921) and Etienne Gilson's *Reason and Revelation in the Middle Ages* (1938) in his development of the typology of *Christ and Culture* (p. xii). In an unpublished paper which presents the argument and typology of *Christ and Culture* in briefer forms Niebuhr makes his most complete statement of the rationale and limitations of typological method. There again he mentions Jung along with Weber, Troeltsch, and William James as exemplars of the method. ("Types of Christian Ethics," unpublished typescript, dated by Niebuhr 1942, 9 pp. See especially pp. 1-2.)

[57] Unpublished manuscript, "Pt. II Responsibility to Divine Action," p. 1.

articles and essays deal with the valuing dimension of faith, of knowledge, of ethical action.[58] Here again it would be erroneous to overemphasize Troeltsch's importance in accounting for the primary role valuation plays in Niebuhr's work. Macintosh was surely an influence of great significance in this regard, as was Josiah Royce. Nonetheless, there is such a marked parallel between the way Troeltsch seems to have understood and dealt with the problem, and the structure of Niebuhr's later thinking on valuation, that the conclusion is almost inescapable that Niebuhr began to think this way through working with Troeltsch. In summary form, here are the Troeltschian teachings about valuation as Niebuhr interprets them: (1) Fundamentally the problem of *knowing* is a problem of *valuing*. "When we recognize that the postulating or establishing of anything as real presupposes the recognition of the value of truth, and when we see furthermore that the work of natural science is carried on only for the sake of its value for life, we understand that values, and the norms derivable from them, are the last foundation of knowledge. . . . The necessity of relating all reality to an ultimate value is grounded in the very essence of reason. . . . The ultimate value is . . . the *apriori* of all knowledge and the center of the epistemological subject, which can organize its knowledge only upon this basis." [59] (2) Formal ethics, the Kantian ethics of the categorical imperative, is unsatisfactory as an expression of the Christian ethic, and is of little practical use because it does not take into account the diverse, real, absolute, and obligating values that exist in culture and compete for men's loyalties: religion, the state, economic life, art, science, etc.[60] (3) Reconciliation of these cultural goals can only be attained by a "compromise," a synthesis of cultural values: "We cannot avoid the task of welding the cul-

[58] See especially "Value Theory and Theology," from *The Nature of Religious Experience* (New York: Harper & Brothers, 1937), pp. 93-116; *Meaning of Revelation;* "The Nature and Existence of God," *Motive* (December, 1943); "The Center of Value," from R. N. Anshen, ed., *Moral Principles of Action* (New York: Harper & Brothers, 1952); *Radical Monotheism and Western Culture* (New York: Harper & Brothers, 1960).

[59] "Troeltsch's Philosophy of Religion," pp. 185-86.

[60] *Ibid.*, pp. 31-32, 100.

tural values, which are values for us, into a 'homogeneous whole for the present and the future within a large area of culture.' This synthesis of culture, a system of concrete goods harmonized with each other, is the standard of evaluation." [61] In each such synthesis there is a central value by reference to which the synthesis is formed, and "the definition of this central value is the essential point." [62] For Troeltsch such a cultural value synthesis arises in history "unconsciously" (that is to say, not as a result of conscious, collective decision and construction) and can only be identified after its formation in an act of discernment and choice by an observer.[63]

Structurally this synthesis-of-values model is precisely parallel to that which Niebuhr employs in "The Center of Value," "The Nature and Existence of God," and *Radical Monotheism and Western Culture*. As a description of man's collective and personal self-unification through valuation he does not alter it. The decisive difference, when you change this valuation schema from a Troeltschian to a Niebuhrian context, comes at the point of the normativity and locus of the central or ultimate value. For Niebuhr the center of value is a given: it is God's cause, the fulfillment of the Creation, of all being, to which God is loyal. That center of value is not merely an emergent from cultural processes, through approximations of it do emerge there. The decisive vision of this divine cause comes in the self's realization that as part of being *he is being valued* and *is valued being*. Then it is that personal and cultural valuing begin to be transformed toward a synthesis centering in God's cause.[64]

In passing we may suggest some of the other ideas Niebuhr encountered in working on Troeltsch which found a significant place in his later work. These include Bergson's idea of *time* as *duration* developed in Troeltsch's *Historismus*[65] and usefully employed in

[61] *Ibid.*, p. 252.
[62] *Ibid.*, p. 253.
[63] *Ibid.*
[64] See especially "Value Theory and Theology," in *Nature of Religious Experience*, pp. 114-16. These points receive extensive treatment in chaps. 4 and 5 below.
[65] "Troeltsch's Philosophy of Religion," pp. 242-43.

Niebuhr's *Meaning of Revelation* (chap. 2). Also we might mention the neo-Kantian distinction between the methods of the *Naturwissenschaften* and the *Geisteswissenchaften* as formulated by Rickert and employed by Troeltsch,[66] and as utilized in modified form as the distinction between "inner" and "outer" history by Niebuhr in *The Meaning of Revelation* (chap. 2).

Now I want to turn briefly to some aspects of Troeltsch's position that Niebuhr must have consciously chosen to avoid in his later work, probably because he saw in Troeltsch's work their unfortunate consequences for theology.

Niebuhr, it seems, was never tempted to emulate the rationalist-epistemological side of neo-Kantian philosophy. Nor does he ever seem to have given much thought to grounding his theology in an explicit metaphysical outlook. Perhaps he was turned away from metaphysics by Troeltsch's unsatisfactory attempt to develop the idea of the rational religious *a priori*. Certainly his awareness of the impossibility of a metaphysical resolution of the tension between monist and pluralistic outlooks made this direction seem untenable. Nonetheless, the religious function of the *a priori* does find its equivalent in Niebuhr in two ways. Parallel to Troeltsch's stress on the priority of the religious *a priori* in ordering the other *a prioris* and in welding a cultural synthesis,[67] Niebuhr, in personal and relational terms, speaks of the sovereignty of God and of the absolute priority and centrality of his cause. Parallel to Troeltsch's modified monadology, in which the *a priori* is that element in human consciousness that correlates with divine nature, making necessarily valid religious knowledge possible, Niebuhr affirms in more confessional and relational terms like those of St. Augustine, "Thou madest us for thyself, and our heart is restless until it repose in thee." [68]

[66] *Ibid.*, pp. 69-70.

[67] See *ibid.* p. 187: "In Troeltsch's case the religious apriori is a *primus inter pares*, which provides for the unity of the other norms of consciousness and relates them to transcendental reality while it also expressed itself in an independent way as the awareness of God."

[68] Augustine, *Confessions* (New York: Collier Macmillan, 1961), bk. 1, p. 11. For Niebuhr's statement see "Value Theory and Theology" in *Nature of Religious Experience*, p. 113.

Hard on the heels of his dissertation Niebuhr rejected psychology of religion as the necessary handmaiden of theology.[69] That rejection is only one expression of a larger lesson that he learned through his work on Troeltsch. Niebuhr saw clearly that there is no way one can move from a stance committed to objective, purely rational or empirical inquiry into the phenomenon of religion to a stance committed to faith in the God of Jesus Christ. To begin with a philosophy or a psychology or a sociology that serves other values than the value which is the object of theology is already to have put obstacles in the way of focusing on the object of theology—the relationship between God and man. Theology, for Niebuhr, must learn from these other, valid methods of reflection on human experience, but their employment by the theologian must be theologically controlled. Theological *knowing* is a matter of *valuing*— a matter grounded in the experience of being valued and thereby coming to value the Valuer. Until there is a consciousness of the real value situation in the relation of God and being, the object of theological knowing does not—cannot—come into view.

3. SOCIAL SOURCES AND A THEOLOGICAL MORATORIUM

It is always good to be through with a dissertation. Not many Ph.D. candidates, however, have college presidencies waiting for them upon completion of their degrees. In 1924, Dr. H. Richard Niebuhr assumed the duties of president of Elmhurst College. Many years later in alluding to this period, he said jokingly, "I went on to make a failure of a college presidency, but I eventually got back into theology." [70] "Eventually" was 1927, when he returned to the faculty of Eden Theological Seminary. He taught at Eden until he accepted the offer of an associate professorship at Yale Divinity School in 1931. During the Elmhurst years Niebuhr

[69] See "Theology and Psychology: A Sterile Union," *Christian Century*, 44 (January 13, 1927), pp. 47-48 and below, pp. 46-47.
[70] Cole Lectures, 4, p. 1.

published four articles[71] and began work on what was to become *The Social Sources of Denominationalism*. Between 1927 and the end of 1929, while at Eden, he published three articles[72] and completed *Social Sources*, which appeared in October of 1929.

In my judgment the five-year period from 1924 to 1929 was extremely important for Niebuhr's development as a theologian. An attentive reading of his publications for that period reveals two principle directions of growth. One of these developed through the systematic application of a critical Troeltschian analysis to the relation between the churches and societal factors in the United States. Combining value analysis and detailed historical research, Niebuhr's pioneering work on denominationalism as an American phenomenon, and on the corresponding ethical impotence of American Protestantism, offers a fine example of what Kenneth Underwood has recently called "prophetic inquiry." [73] The other of these two major directions of development consists in a steadily growing confidence in the *reality* of the subject matter of theology and ethics. At the heart of this development is a growing conviction of the validity and reliability of Christian revelation as a basis for a Christian ethic that has binding *content* as well as imperative *form*.

THE CONSTRUCTIVE CRITIQUE OF TROELTSCH

In presenting the continuities and parallels between Troeltsch and Niebuhr in the previous section, I may have made it appear that

[71] "Back to Benedict?" *Christian Century*, 42 (July 2, 1925), pp. 860-66); "What Holds Churches Together?" *Christian Century*, 43 (March 18, 1926), pp. 346-48; "Theology and Psychology: A Sterile Union," *Christian Century*, 44 (January 13, 1927), pp. 47-48; and "Jesus Christ Intercessor," *International Journal of Religious Education*, 3 (January, 1927), pp. 6-8.

[72] "Christianity and the Industrial Classes," *Theological Magazine* (formerly *Magazin für Theologie und Kirche*), 57 (January, 1929), pp. 12-18; "Churches That Might Unite," *Christian Century*, 46 (February 21, 1929), pp. 259-61; *Moral Relativism and the Christian Ethic*, published as a pamphlet by the International Missionary Council as one of the primary papers for a Conference on Theological Education held at Drew Theological Seminary, November 30–December 1, 1929, 11 pp.

[73] See Kenneth Underwood, *The Church, the University and Social Policy* (Middletown, Conn.: Wesleyan University Press, 1969), vol. 1, pp. 211 ff.

Niebuhr appropriated key Troeltschian themes and made them his own with very little difficulty. Such a view of the relationship of their ways of thinking can be misleading. If my interpretation of Troeltsch's impact on Niebuhr revealed structural similarities and shared approaches between them, the writings of this 1925–29 period show us Niebuhr in the process of establishing a theological basis and stance *over against* certain aspects of the critical position of Troeltsch. Let me try to make this explicit. As we have seen, Niebuhr, broadly speaking, embraced Troeltsch's realism, his description of relativism, and his ethical and historical approach through value theory. He had come to share with Troeltsch (perhaps unselfconsciously during this early period) a tendency to think in polar terms and to employ typological method. But there were some aspects of Troeltsch's thinking that must have seemed to Niebuhr to threaten the very spinal cord of any genuinely Christian faith or theology. Of these aspects we may mention two.

The first is the pervasive *rationalism* of Troeltsch's stance. There are some good reasons for agreeing with Karl Barth when he implies that Troeltsch was really always more a philosopher of religion than a theologian.[74] Rationally defining the limits of reason, Troeltsch trusted (had faith in) the intuitional, mystical, rational link between the spirit of man and that of the Absolute to create, discern, and live in obedience to obligatory and unifying value imperatives. For Troeltsch the norms for theological or philosophical ethics arise in culture and must be discerned there. This meant that Troeltsch's doctrine of God culminated in a static, largely formal concept, the substantive ethical content of which is only accessible through human consciousness and the value productions of human cultural processes. His doctrine of man, even in the

[74] Barth seems to have seen as symbolic of the theological poverty of late liberalism Troeltsch's move from teaching systematic theology at Heidelberg to join the philosophy department at Berlin in 1914–15: "The actual end of the 19th century as the 'good old days' came for theology as for everything else with the fateful year of 1914. Accidentally or not, a significant event took place during that very year. Ernst Troeltsch, the well-known professor of systematic theology and the leader of the then most modern school, gave up his chair in theology for one in philosophy." Barth, *The Humanity of God* (Richmond: John Knox Press, 1960), p. 14.

chastened, more existential approach of his later years, still affirmed an optimism about human ability to recognize valid religious truth, and through its hidden correspondence to the Ultimate, to participate in the generation of true religious insight. For Troeltsch, reason, finally, is the arbiter of the nature of God and the normativity of the basis of ethics. Confronted with the culture-bound character of the American Protestant ethos, Niebuhr could hardly hope to establish a cutting, critical, *Christian* ethic on such an indeterminate basis.

The second aspect of Troeltsch's position which Niebuhr found unusable and theologically limiting is largely a resultant of the first. It has to do with the difficulty of speaking, from a Troeltschian perspective, of the normativity of certain specific historical events as being in some sense revelational of the Absolute. Here there seem to be two problems: (1) Given the thorough conditionedness of all perceptions and ideas, as the theory of relativism describes it, how can particular historical events be legitimately singled out as supremely clear manifestations of the Absolute? and (2) even if it were legitimate to make such a claim for a particular configuration of events, how is it possible to achieve reliable clarity about what *really* was the case, for example, in the story of Jesus, on the basis of the kind of sources available to us? Troeltsch ends with a kind of revelational agnosticism that makes authenticating the claims of allegedly revelatory events a matter, finally, of gauging their ethical-valuational impact on the history of culture and its results. Such a standpoint might be compelling for the phenomenologist of cultural values, whose task it is to discuss the normative intentionality of a culture;[75] but for a theologian concerned with the recovery of an ethical integrity by the Christian church, it has decisive limitations.

This construction of Niebuhr's dilemma over against Troeltsch at the time of completing his dissertation is largely inferred from three considerations: (1) the criticisms Niebuhr does offer in the

[75] This kind of approach with both its strengths and weaknesses is represented among contemporary religious ethicists by Gibson Winter in his *Elements for a Social Ethic* (New York: The Macmillan Co., 1966). See esp. chap. 6.

37

course of the dissertation; (2) his silence in the dissertation as regards any correcting alternative to Troeltsch; and (3) the tone and pattern of development in these 1925–29 writings. As I see it, Niebuhr encountered in Troeltsch the epitomes of the same liberalism that Karl Barth had a little earlier rejected and denounced so powerfully.[76] In these years we see the same pressures at work on Niebuhr that pushed Barth to a consciously antithetical stance toward liberalism. But, for Niebuhr, to have categorically rejected liberalism would have been to jettison convictions and modes of thinking that had become central to his own personal and professional integrity. His task, therefore, had to be to keep, refine, and develop that critical-empirical side of Troeltsch, with its twin basis of historical and sociological analysis, but to integrate it with a genuinely Christian confession of the gospel that neither blunted the steepness of the ethical teachings of Jesus nor entered too cheaply upon compromises with the culture. Thus, while Barth was building a massive antithesis to liberalism, with, of course, its own positive thrust and integrity, Niebuhr (not yet as self-consciously as Barth, I think) was at work on a genuine synthesis of the polarities in his situation, which largely parallel the liberal-neo-orthodox antinomies.[77] For Niebuhr these issues did not arise primarily

---

[76] Karl Barth's *Römerbrief* in the decisive second edition had appeared in 1921. Though Niebuhr's writings never explicitly mention this book or its shock wave during this period, his copy, now belonging to Prof. Hans Frei of Yale, is covered with marks and notations suggesting many readings.

[77] This, I believe, is the real meaning of this often quoted and often misunderstood passage from the preface to *Meaning of Revelation:* "Students of theology will recognize that Ernst Troeltsch and Karl Barth have also been my teachers, though only through their writings. These two leaders in twentieth century religious thought are frequently set in diametrical opposition to each other. I have tried to combine their main interests, for it appears to me that the critical thought of the former and the constructive work of the latter belong together" (p. x). Barthian interpreters of Niebuhr have seized upon this passage as a basis for attributing a more decisive positive influence upon Niebuhr by Barth than a careful study of Niebuhr's writings will sustain. I believe the positional and conceptual influence of Tillich from 1929 to 1932 was much more important constructively for Niebuhr than that of Barth. I would not want to deny or play down, however, the importance for Niebuhr of the Barthian *confessional passion,* his insistent proclamation of the *righteousness of God,* and his call for a return to "the strange new world within the Bible." (See Barth, *The Word of God and the Word of Man,* chaps. 1 and 2.)

in the context of recovering the integrity of dogmatics and of the theological disciplines, though this was an issue for him. More decisive in his concern was the practical matter of finding a constructive ethical basis for reformation of the church to complement the powerful social critique which his Troeltschian studies enabled him to make. The decisive breakthrough to an integrating stance came later, and will be covered in the next two chapters, but important movements toward it occurred in 1925–29.

ASCETIC RENEWAL AND PROPHETIC INQUIRY

"Christianity has made a startling discovery in recent years. It has suddenly become aware of the steepness of the ideal of Jesus and of the intransigent character of his ethics. At the same time it has been painfully disillusioned of its dream of the automatic progress of the world toward the kingdom of God. The old antithesis, long conveniently forgotten, is again with us: the world, the flesh, and the devil over against a transcendent God, the state against the church, mammon against Christ." [78] With these sober words Niebuhr begins his first *Christian Century* article, published about a year after his leaving Yale. It is impossible to sort out the precipitating factors in this new pessimism, with its vivid sense of the dualities in existence. Niebuhr, using Benedict as a symbol of principled withdrawal from a chaotically opulent, degenerate culture, seems to be engaging in a soliloquy—an effort to come to terms, for himself and for the church, with the gap between the steep ethics of Jesus and the virtual identification of the Christian ethos with the nationalistic and capitalistic values in contemporary American society. Though the focus of the article's thesis is diffused by Niebuhr's mixture of description, prescription, and prediction, the point is clear enough: the previous extreme response of sensitive Christians to a time of extreme church-world compromise in *monasticism* may represent the path the church must take again. This calls for an undivided interest in "the spiritual world," a disciplined

---

[78] "Back to Benedict?" *Christian Century*, 42 (July 2, 1925), p. 860.

mysticism that may have to take philosophical dualism, the meta-physical bases for mysticism, seriously again.[79] It calls for recovery of the meaning and purpose of asceticism, the disciplining of life in obedience, poverty, and chastity.[80] Of obedience Niebuhr says: "It is not the obedience to superior force that is wanted but the hard and unyielding honesty of those who understand the command of their own categorical imperative in the pursuit of beauty, truth and goodness. The iron self-discipline of monasticism cannot be without defenders in these days of luxury and self-indulgence." [81] For the church to take seriously the monastic ideal once more would mean "that it would abandon the policy of boring from within. Separating itself from the world it might recover its integrity for a while until confronted with another Calvary it either suffered crucifixion or made its uneasy compromise with pharisee and sadducee." [82]

Niebuhr's research and writing along the lines that culminated in the publication of *The Social Source of Denominationalism* in 1929 were aimed at helping the church achieve the kind of clarity about itself that would make possible a principled separation from its compromising relations with the institutions, processes, and

[79] This passage is very interesting in light of our earlier reference to what seemed to be a struggle in 1920 between various pluralistic phiosophical doctrines and biblical monotheism: "All efforts to define the world monistically have only succeeded in reducing the spiritual to the level of the material; and all this-worldliness, despite its high claim of bringing the other world into the present sphere, has only succeeded in banishing the spiritual realm from human thought. Dualism is perhaps not so discredited a philosophical doctrine as the fashion in thought would have us believe; at all events a practical dualism is emerging out of the critical antithesis modern men experience between the ideal and the real" (*ibid.*, pp. 860-61). It seems characteristic of Niebuhr not to engage the question of monism versus dualism at the level of the intrinsic metaphysical satisfactoriness one or the other might possess; his choice would be made more on the practical grounds of their actual ethical effects.

[80] The details of this argument are too long to present in full here, but are too interesting not to mention. Niebuhr, writing for a very Protestant audience and prior to the 1928 presidential campaign of Al Smith, takes a highly critical stance toward many of the sacred cows and the smugness of Protestantism, and mounts some telling arguments for reconsideration of monastic ideals—without, however, explicitly recommending their adoption by Protestants.

[81] *Ibid.*, p. 861.

[82] *Ibid.*

values of the culture.[83] The preparation for the book began when Niebuhr was asked to teach a course on symbolics (probably in 1925–26). Of this course Niebuhr wrote:

The effort to distinguish churches primarily by reference to their doctrine and to approach the problem of church unity from a purely theological point of view appeared . . . to be a procedure so artificial and fruitless that [I] found [myself] compelled to turn from theology to history, sociology and ethics for a more satisfactory account of denominational differences and a more significant approach to the question of union.[84]

Prior to the publication of the book Niebuhr wrote two articles giving previews of its analysis. These came in 1926 and early 1929.[85] It is important to take note of Niebuhr's prime points in this line of his thought, and to attend to the theological and ethical bases on which he grounds his critique. We can do this primarily with reference to the book itself.

The Social Sources of Denominationalism (hereafter referred to as *Social Sources*) is a masterpiece of organization. Niebuhr takes a genuine problematic, "The Ethical Failure of the Divided Church," and analyzes it from virtually every relevant angle. He begins with the premise that the actual principles of the moral behavior of churches as groups and of most Christians give the lie to the gospel they proclaim. With compassion as well as prophetic criticism, Niebuhr renders the usual charges of hypocrisy largely irrelevant: man does not orient himself in the world or identify himself with groups primarily because of *ideas*;[86] nor are his ideas and values the resultants of dispassionate rational choice. The social form, the doctrinal positions, the disposition toward "the

---

[83] Niebuhr always insisted in his lecture course on Christian ethics that one of the principal critical tasks and goals of Christian ethics is to aid in the achievement of clarity about the actual moral principles implicit in our personal and institutional or social life.

[84] *Social Sources* p. vii.

[85] "What Holds Churches Together?" *Christian Century*, 43 (March 18, 1926), pp. 346-48; and "Churches That Might Unite," *Christian Century*, 46 (February 21, 1929), pp. 259-61.

[86] See especially "What Holds Churches Together?" p. 346, for a discussion of this "intellectualist fallacy," and *Social Sources*, pp. 11-17.

world" of religious groups and individuals, are directly related to intermingled factors such as the economic position of adherents, their class and educational status, their nationalistic and ethnic identifications, sectional histories and loyalties (especially in the United States), and their racial identity and status. Resisting mono-causal explanations and faithfully presenting the complexity and polarities in personal and social-organizational processes, Niebuhr weaves an intricate pattern of historical analysis and contemporary ethical criticism. The book is informed by a full appreciation of the multifaceted character of the evils it exposes, and is filled with a compassion that does not exclude the supposed beneficiaries of the social ills while it upholds the legitimate claims of the victims. In this sense the book is prophetic, often specifically and trenchantly so, but is at the same time pastoral.

When he comes to the last chapter, "Ways to Unity," Niebuhr's argument shows that his ethical thinking is still very close to that of Troeltsch. In ethical terms the dividedness and moral impotence of the churches, Niebuhr finds, are rooted in the diverse and conflict-ing pluralism of their valuing.[87] His solution for this condition draws on the Troeltschian theory of the necessity for a synthesis of cultural values under the unifying power of a supreme ideal:

In its [the church's] saner moments it becomes aware that it can save neither its self-esteem nor its existence nor yet the finer values its thinkers, prophets, artists and its toiling masses have wrought out, unless it is made captive to some compelling and integrating ideal which will restore to it a sense of the whole and will equip it with an ethics commensurate with the scope of its interests and of its world-embracing organization. The problem of the world is the problem of a synthesis of culture—of the building up of an organic whole in which the various

[87] In later writings Niebuhr designates such pluralistic patterns of valuing in personal and cultural life with the term "polytheism." This is, of course, an "ethicization" of a term from history of religions which, so far as I can tell, Niebuhr learned to use in this way from Troeltsch (see "Troeltsch's Philosophy of Religion," p. 107). For Niebuhr's later use of the term and the idea see "The Church Against the World" (1935) in Sydney Ahlstrom, ed., *Theology in America* (Indianapolis: Bobbs-Merrill, 1967), p. 605; "Man the Sinner," *Journal of Religion*, 15 (1935), p. 278; "Faith in Gods and in God" (1943) and "The Center of Value" (1952) both in *Radical Monotheism*. See also chap. 2 of *Radical Monotheism*.

interests and the separate nations and classes will be integrated into a harmonious interacting society, serving one common end in diverse manners.[88]

Niebuhr finishes that paragraph by saying that such a synthesis of culture depends on a common ethics and world view. Civilization must, he affirms, receive such a synthesis from its religion. This leads him to paint in vivid terms the dilemma of the Western world, which "lies in the fact that while it depends upon religion for the creation of a common mind and the birth of a common loyalty, the only religion available seems incapable of establishing, even within its own structure, the desired harmony." [89]

But Niebuhr cannot rest content with the impotent pessimism of that analysis. He reiterates that in their present ethical conditions the churches have no prospect of doing anything but sacralizing divisions and differences. To be sure, there are also social sources tending to church unity, such as national unification of previously distinct denominational groups.[90] But this may, he points out, "lead to an even greater subordination of Christian ethics to nationalistic ethics than now prevails.[91]

In his examination of alternatives to denominational Christianity Niebuhr turns to what is his first written assessment of the significance of European "crisis theology." He speaks explicitly of "crisis theology of Germany" but does not mention any particular figures. Clearly Barth's position is at the center of his attention, however.

There is another type of Christianity which is quite as ineffective though perhaps not as destructive in its contacts with civilization as is denominational Christianity. The other-worldly faith which regards the message of the gospel as applying to the individual's relation to a transcendental sphere alone and condemns every aspect of the present world, including culture, religious striving and every attempt at amelioration of social evils as the expression of a depraved and lost will, has been resurrected today by the crisis theology of Germany.[92]

[88] *Social Sources*, p. 266.
[89] *Ibid.*, p. 268.
[90] *Ibid.*, pp. 270-72; see also "Churches That Might Unite," p. 260.
[91] *Social Sources*, p. 272.
[92] *Ibid.*, p. 275.

Niebuhr acknowledges the value of crisis theology's recovery of the Reformation doctrine of sin and the absolute dependence of man on God's grace as a needed corrective to "a frequently provincial social gospel." But then he asserts that the theology of crisis "appears simply irrelevant so far as the social task of Christianity is concerned." [93] Affirming crisis theology's insistence that the final significance of the kingdom of God transcends all the relative versions of the ideal for which men work, Niebuhr asks, "Yet is there no relationship between these [relative] ideals and the cosmic fact? Is there no continuity between the divine mercy and those angels of man's better nature which struggle with the demons of the jungle in his individual and corporate life?" [94] The upshot of Niebuhr's criticism is clear:

The church cannot escape responsibility for the present order of civilization by referring men to some transcendental sphere where all their efforts are revealed as equally marked with guilt and imperfection. . . . To anticipate the attainment of His righteous rule by reliance on eschatological miracle and meanwhile to condemn all efforts to work out human salvation by the best endeavor of which men are capable, is to reduce religion to an ethical anodyne.[95]

If neither denominational Christianity nor the Continental neo-Reformation theological movement has the ethical potency to shape a new synthesis of cultural values, to what hope and what strategy should Christians turn? Niebuhr's answer is a reassertion that the Christian gospel *does* contain the required ideal; that its purpose is to reveal to men, in the life of Christ, "their potential childhood to the Father and their possible brotherhood with each

[93] *Ibid.*, p. 276.
[94] *Ibid.*, pp. 276-77.
[95] *Ibid.*, pp. 277-78. These passages are quoted at length in order to convey the unusually sharp language Niebuhr uses in refuting the ethical implications of crisis theology as they appeared to him. His critique is right, but perhaps he protests overmuch. The passion of his critique suggests that perhaps the Barthian emphasis may have made Niebuhr more uncomfortable with his warmed-over Troeltschianism than he can yet admit. The major Barthian influence on Niebuhr, in all likelihood, came not as a powerful vision to which he responded with embrace, but as a barbed exposure of the ethical indeterminateness of the Troeltschian value theory. Barth may have helped *goad* Niebuhr into his mature position; Niebuhr was, however, never a Barthian.

other." [96] This is, he contends, a revelation of the character of ultimate reality, in accordance with which men will fix on the *summum bonum* of "the eternal harmony of love, in which each individual can realize the full potentiality of an eternal life in self-sacrificing devotion to the Beloved Community of the father and all the brethren." [97] This ideal, he affirms, is the secret goal of every profound religion and answers the deepest desires of the oppressed people of the world, who are rightly cynical about denominational Christianity. There is a great latent fund of energy and passion awaiting release and guidance by such an ideal.[98] For the proclamation of this gospel a church is needed that transcends all parochial loyalties and provincial visions, that obeys the command to love the enemy, and abjures economic distinctions in a "communism of love." [99] Such a church will not be a new sect, moving through the typical pattern of evolution from sect to church. Rather, drawing (perhaps unconsciously) on Troeltsch's idea of *latency*, Niebuhr affirms that such a *church* has always existed within the *churches*.[100] It is a fellowship of reconciliation whose acts of healing, mercy, and aggressive love must permeate the divided consciousness and skewed values of culture with an ever-new potential of unity, peace, and harmonious love.

It is hard not to feel that Niebuhr is unsatisfied with this blend of Troeltschian analysis and Social Gospel rhetoric even as he writes it.[101] The concluding section is an example, very rare in Niebuhr,

---

[96] *Ibid.*, p. 278.

[97] *Ibid.*, p. 279.

[98] *Ibid.*, pp. 279-80.

[99] *Ibid.*, pp. 280-81. This is Niebuhr's first allusion to the comparison between the Communist movement and radical Christianity. In the first half of the 1930s that comparison is made often and is part of Niebuhr's model for a revolutionary Christianity.

[100] *Ibid.*, pp. 281-83. Niebuhr cites manifestations of this latent, essential church in the Jerusalem and Antiochian early Christian communities, in the Franciscan movement, and in The Society of Friends.

[101] In the preface to *The Kingdom of God in America* (Torchbooks; New York: Harper & Brothers [1937], 1959) he makes this dissatisfaction explicit: "The only answer I was able to give to the problem of Christian disunity was in the form of a new appeal to good will to overcome stubborn social divisions and to incarnate the ideal of Jesus. This appeal seemed, upon critical reflection, to be wholly inadequate" (p. x).

of that kind of preaching that substitutes emotion and eloquence for the substance of assurance. But if the position just described seems shaky, I think it is not only due to Niebuhr's sense of its deficiency. I believe it is also because something new in the way of a faith stance and theological basis is forming in Niebuhr, by comparison with which the tired hope and impotent imperatives of the *Social Sources* conclusion had to be recognized for what they were.

PORTENTS AND PRELUDES

Interspersed with the articles that grew out of the *Social Sources* research were several others in which a development of another kind seems to be taking place. This is what I spoke of above as a growing confidence in the *reality* of the subject matter of theology and ethics, and in the reliability of the revelation of God in Christ as a basis for an ethic that has binding content as well as imperative form. Niebuhr's scholarly energies during 1924–27 were undoubtedly diffused owing to his administrative responsibilities. It seems clear that when he went to Eden in 1927 he devoted his principal writing time to *Social Sources*. The articles we have in view here, then, were occasional pieces, most probably written (with one exception) [102] at the solicitation of others. If I am right in discerning the embryo of a new stance in these articles, which are on several themes, it seems to have been necessary for Niebuhr to complete *Social Sources* before the emerging new stance could take the center of his attention. But such a shift in center does seem to begin to become explicit in the last of the articles, "Moral Relativism and the Christian Ethic," which may be seen as the hinge to the explicit development of the foundations of Niebuhr's mature position.

In the main these articles serve as momentary manifestations of a largely subterranean development in Niebuhr toward a new faith stance and theological position. In the first, "Theology and Psychology: A Sterile Union," Niebuhr writes a declaration of theology's independence from control by or excessive dependence upon

[102] "Theology and Psychology: A Sterile Union," *Christian Century*, 44 (January 13, 1927), pp. 47-48.

other disciplines, especially psychology. Neither German epistemology nor American pragmatism, he asserts, succeeds in discovering the categorical element in religious experience. Theology took a "blind alley" in fixing upon the subjective religious consciousness of religious man as its beginning point—a mistake as consequential, Niebuhr suggests, "as that into which the early physicists might have led the natural sciences had they begun their work by observing man's consciousness of physical objects." [103] Clearly the Barthian critique of Schleiermacher had made its impact upon him. But he also shows the influence of Macintosh when he calls for a theology that will be "truly an empirical science and not an empiricist philosophy in which object and subject are dissolved in psychological experience." [104] Though Schleiermacher gets the blame here for initiating the subjectivist tendency, it is hard to avoid the feeling that this article is part of Niebuhr's unwritten critique of Troeltsch.[105] In our perspective the importance of this article lies in its insistence that theology attend to the real *object* of religious consciousness and that it be "no longer the obsequious servitor of psychology." [106]

So recognition of the reality of the object of theology and of the correlative independence of theology are aspects of this emerging posture. It seems we can also perceive in this period a new willingness to speak of the *personal* character of God, and of a Jesus Christ who intercedes for men with God and actively reconciles them to him, as well as being the prophetic teacher and exemplar of faith. These themes emerge in late 1926 when Niebuhr wrote what was originally probably an address or a sermon entitled "Jesus Christ Intercessor." [107] Here Niebuhr speaks of the high-priestly role of Jesus as presented in the New Testament and as present in

[103] Ibid.
[104] *Ibid.*
[105] It is not much of an exaggeration to say that for Troeltsch theology in effect became an adjunct or a subtype of philosophy of religion, and was dependent upon epistemology and psychology of religion to bring the norm of its subject matter into proper view. See Troeltsch, "Das Wesen der Religion und der Religionswissenschaft," *Gesammelte Schriften,* vol. 2, pp. 452-99.
[106] Theology and Psychology," p. 48.
[107] *International Journal of Religious Education,* 3 (January, 1927), pp. 6-8.

contemporary life and experience. He speaks of Jesus' faith as trust in a loving Father and of his loyalty to men, for whom he makes intercession. In one of the few instances in his published writings where he speaks about prayer,[108] Niebuhr answers the charge of "psychologism" that prayer is only meditation and autosuggestion: "Prayer is meditation and reflection and suggestion *and also* communion with God. In that communion the heart of man may be changed; may not the heart of God be also affected? In such a social community as the Kingdom of God, as it exists at any time, the relationship of all members may and must be changed through the activity of one." [109] Although this may be an overinterpretation, I take this passage as a *muted* indication of two beliefs that will later emerge with centrality in Niebuhr's thought: (1) that the kingdom of God is a presently existent social community, and (2) that the Divine Other in this community is *personal* and is personally related to humanity.

The notable feature of a third of these articles, "Christianity and the Industrial Classes," [110] is its expression of confidence that there is no *inherent* incompatibility between Christianity and the necessities of modern industrial production. Niebuhr asserts this in refutation of the contentions of Bertrand Russell and Karl Heim to the effect that urbanization and industrialization necessarily spell extinction for an agrarian-rooted Christianity. Niebuhr cites Weber and Troeltsch in support of the thesis that Christianity had its rise and spread among city folk, and that its utopias were conceived in urban symbols. The separation from Christianity of working people is due, he argues, more to the ethical failures of the church than to any fundamental contradiction between Christianity and industrialism. In many ways the confidence and hopeful outlook of this article contrast with the doleful recital of social ills

---

[108] There is a series of sermons on prayer dating from the 1930s in Niebuhr's papers. I have not worked through these with care owing to the need to draw a limit to this research.

[109] "Jesus Christ Intercessor," pp. 7-8.

[110] *Theological Magazine*, 57 (January, 1929), pp. 12 ff. This piece also was probably written as an address.

and churchly impotence that Niebuhr had written seven years before.[111]

The real milestone article of this group is one Niebuhr prepared as a preliminary paper for a Conference on Theological Education, held at Drew Theological Seminary between November 30 and December 1, 1929—*Moral Relativism and the Christian Ethic.* As best I can calculate, this paper was written after the completion of *Social Sources,* which apparently went to the publisher in October of 1929. In Niebuhr's talk about God and about revelation in *Social Sources,* the Troeltschian formality and statisticity are never really overcome. God is still basically the Absolute of philosophical idealism, even when Niebuhr uses the Fatherhood terminology of the Social Gospel. Though it is hard to pin this down explicitly, it seems that in *Social Sources,* as in Troeltsch, the biblical sources and norms of revelation, because of a mistrust of historical revelation, are still somehow subordinated to external rational norms. The shift I think I detect in *Moral Relativism and the Christian Ethic* is equally hard to pinpoint; but it seems that in this paper Niebuhr has come to the point where the balance between idealist-rational norms and biblical revelation, so long weighted on the side of the former, now perceptibly shifts, and a new degree of confidence in the independent validity of Christian revelation comes to expression. It is not a dramatic change in a quantitative sense, but it represents a kind of quiet culmination of a growing confidence in matters native to historical faith and Christian theology that the critical rationalism of Troeltsch had, for a time at least, made it difficult for Niebuhr to rely on theologically.

Niebuhr begins by pointing out the relativity of the doctrine of relativity.[112] "Relativity really is not so much a theory as a report of experience." [113] There really can be no privileged nonrelativized domains in history. Even the teachings of Jesus, it must be said, are relative to his religious background and to the currents of religious

---

[111] "Christianity and the Social Problem" (see above, pp. 13-16).

[112] A point that Michael Novak makes tellingly in his *Experience of Nothingness* (New York: Harper & Row, 1970), pp. 52 ff.

[113] *Moral Relativism,* p. 4.

and political life around him.[114] Christians can neither "dogmati-
cally . . . assert the absolute superiority of their religious and ethical
heritage, claiming that Christianity is revelation while all other
religions are merely human aspirations," [115] nor can they rely on a
Christian rationalism which claims to identify with certainty the
rational absolute within the traditional teachings and beliefs of the
church.[116] Neither position escapes the suspicion of relativism.
Christian ethics must accept the truth of relativism and resist the
temptation of absolutizing, as "valid for all times and all places,
such insights into principle as come to it under the pressure of new
conditions." [117]

But now comes the point at which Niebuhr tilts the balance
toward dominant reliance on norms shaped by historical revelation. We must "undertake the task of criticizing all our current
interpretations of the Christian ethic in order that the purely cultural and Western influences may be distinguished from the original Christian content." [118] This can be done because

> the Christian ethic, which has always been proclaimed as the absolute
> ethic of the will of God, not relative to Jew or Greek, is under no
> compulsion to give up the claims which it has made to unswerving
> loyalty and universal validity because it must be formulated in relative
> terminology, and applied to changing conditions. . . . The absolute
> within the relative comes to appearance at two points—in the absolute
> obligation of an individual or a society to follow its highest insights,
> *and in the element of revelation of ultimate reality.*[119]

It is not necessary to claim that the Christian ethic is universally
valid in order for it to be absolute and obligatory for Christians.
Niebuhr affirms that "the obligation of the Christian to follow the
Christian ethics [arises] from the fact that he is a Christian, whether
as the result of religious experience or as a result of his commitment to Christianity by an act of faith." [120] In a very real sense

[114] *Ibid.*, pp. 5-6.
[115] *Ibid.*, p. 6.
[116] *Ibid.*, p. 7.
[117] *Ibid.*, pp. 7-8.
[118] *Ibid.*, p. 7.
[119] *Ibid.*, p. 9. (Italics added.)
[120] *Ibid.*

Christ is the fate of the man born into a Christian society.[121] If, however, the obligation to obey the Christian ethic in this fated sense is a *formal* obligation for the Christian, Christianity also "has the right to claim that its experience of the will of God is not only obligatory in form but also in content; that its claim to absoluteness does not rest only upon the character of human experience but also on the character of reality; that goodness does not depend upon human judgment but on the pattern of existence, or the will of God." [122]

Here Niebuhr sounds the note of a revelational realism that has a different timbre from anything we have heard yet. The Christian experience of the will of God will necessarily be partial, and all explications of it will be relative; "but incomplete experience of the absolutely good is not experience of the incompletely good, nor is relatively true definition of moral reality a definition of a relatively moral reality." [123]

It is not, I think, until this point in his career that the experience of relativism, which Niebuhr knew firsthand and found developed theoretically in Troeltsch, really ceases to be a threat and a block to the possibility of grounding a radical Christian ethic on faith in the disclosure of the *real* in Jesus the Christ. To the development and implications of such a position we now turn.

---

[121] *Ibid.*, pp. 9-10. In this Niebuhr follows Troeltsch. He repeats this point in the prologue to the posthumously published lectures in *The Responsible Self* (New York: Harper & Row, 1963), p. 43.

[122] *Moral Relativism*, p. 10.

[123] *Ibid.*, p. 11.

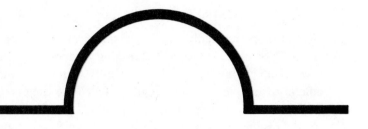

Chapter II
The Conviction
of the Sovereignty of God

1. THE COMING OF THE CENTRAL CONVICTION

From one perspective (though this is by no means the only possible one) the period in Niebuhr's life from 1924 to 1929 represents a kind of theological moratorium. This is not to be confused with an intellectual or professional moratorium, for it is indisputably clear that the research and reflection that culminated in *Social Sources* are of the highest order in terms of originality and creative power. But Niebuhr's preoccupation with that major work, in addition to the administrative responsibilities he carried in these years, allowed or made inevitable his postponement of any sustained theological wrestling of a kind that would enable him to absorb the critical position of Troeltsch and move on in a clearly new direction.

By the beginning of 1930, however, Niebuhr's context of reflection had changed markedly. New perceptions of his vocation and of the demands of the times were breaking in upon him. Preparations were being made for a sabbatical trip to Germany, which was to come in the spring and summer of 1930. The reading and study involved in these preparations gave Niebuhr a profound appreciation of the disillusionment and pessimism of social, economic, and political life in post–World War I Germany. Reading the works of the young crisis theologians and of the young Tillich, Niebuhr must have been vividly impressed by the relevance of and necessity for new theological responses to this crisis in national and cultural existence. Nor was all the disillusionment on the European side of the Atlantic. In this country the economic boom of the late twenties had turned to bust. In face of the new insecurity and fears which overtook the nation, the hopeful rhetoric and utilitarian theology of the late Social Gospel had turned tinny, rapidly losing all experiential resonance.

Niebuhr's writings of the early thirties have a contemporaneity and timeliness for present-day American readers. Niebuhr's description of the theological and existential situation of that time fits our own with equal accuracy: he called it "a time that confronts mysteries because it has lost dogmas." [1] There is some comfort in seeing the seriousness of our own time of fissured meaning relativized by Niebuhr's account of the experience of nothingness forty years ago. But if we find ready empathy with the perplexity and anomie reflected in Niebuhr's analysis of religion and culture in the early thirties, it is by no means certain that many in our time can really grasp or be grasped by the central positive affirmation that began to emerge in Niebuhr's writings of that period. For in those troubled years there happened in and to Niebuhr a mature conversion of faith. He came to—or there came to him—a new depth of conviction that the One called God is *real* being, power, and action; that God is *the prime reality*. It was a personal comprehension and embracing of the fact that God *is*, and that *God* is, and of the

---

[1] "Theology in a Time of Disillusionment" (unpublished handwritten lecture; annotated, in Niebuhr's hand, as "Alumni Lecture Yale 1931," 22 pp.), p. 15.

implications of that fact for man's life as valuer, initiator, and responder. Not, I think, since Jonathan Edwards has any American theologian been so authentically and so profoundly captured by the conviction that the fundamental fact about man and about creation is their relationship of radical dependence on—and, in man's case, of responsibility to—a sovereign God.[2]

In an autobiographical reflection on the course of his thought over three decades, written in 1960, Niebuhr talked about the coming of this ground conviction:

The fundamental certainty given to me then (sad to say, not in such a way that my unconscious as well as conscious mind has been wholly permeated by it) was that of God's sovereignty. . . . I came to understand that unless being itself, the constitution of things, the One beyond all the many, the ground of my being and of all being, the ground of its "that-ness" and its "so-ness," was trustworthy—could be counted on by what proceeded from it—I had no God at all. . . . Since I came to that conviction or since it came to me, I have worked considerably at the problem of the nature and meaning of "value" and at efforts to understand the basic relation of the self to that on which it is absolutely dependent. But the old theological phrase, "the sovereignty of God," indicates what for me is fundamental.[3]

In that same reflection Niebuhr spoke of the years from 1930 to 1935 as "the time in which I began to think the way I do now." [4] This was "the decisive period in the formation of personal convictions and in the establishment of theological formulations of these convictions." [5]

---

[2] I have belabored the point of this paragraph to this degree because of the strangeness and radicality of this conviction to most of us nowadays. I am continually amazed by the essential simplicity of the idea, on the one hand, and, on the other, by the *massive revolution in consciousness* it brings as it comes to dominate one's outlook.

[3] In Harold E. Fey, ed., *How My Mind Has Changed* (Meridian Books; Cleveland: World Publishing Co., 1961), pp. 71-72.

[4] *Ibid.*, p. 74.

[5] *Ibid.*, p. 71. Note the distinction Niebuhr makes between "personal convictions" and "theological formulations of these convictions." He is a theologian who is clear about and unembarrassed by the rootage of theological expressions and style in what he, in another passage, calls "the highly personal, not to say private, experiences" that most immediately affect the basic formulations of our faith (*ibid.*, p. 70). The distinction between convictions and formulations— or at least the differentiation of the levels of consciousness and immediacy they

In this chapter and the next, we shall examine Niebuhr's development in this central conviction as it is formulated and expressed in the writings from summer 1930 through the publication of *The Kingdom of God in America* in April of 1937.[6] We do not know, and probably cannot know, the private joys and sorrows, fears and hopes, the bouts with meaninglessness and the void, as well as the breakthroughs and "peak experiences," that lie behind Niebuhr's development in this faith stance. We do, however, have his efforts to work toward clarity about the *content* of these experiences and to express the *character of the Ultimate One* whom he met in them. To read Niebuhr as *Niebuhr* would have read him, we should try to let these formulations point us to the *reality* to which he attended in the experiences out of which they grew. Criticism is beside the point until the object, by reference to which any relevant criticism of the formulations would be made, has come into common view.

Before we undertake this kind of approach to the writings of 1930–37, one brief additional point needs to be made. Though Niebuhr characterizes the new faith stance which came to him in this period as "the conviction of the sovereignty of God," the particular phrase "sovereignty of God" does not figure prominently in his theological expressions of this faith, either in the period under consideration or in subsequent years.[7] The *substance*, the *content*,

---

imply—is present in writings throughout Niebuhr's career. Though, to my knowledge, he never troubles to give a formal definition of a "fundamental conviction," in his usage I think it means something like the following: a self's more or less stable disposition to trust in and rely upon a reality, as apprehended in a comprehensive, personalized, interpretative construct, that gives coherence and integrity to the self's valuing and to its responses to action upon it. (Such a "construct," it should be made clear, has conscious, preconscious, and unconscious dimensions.)

[6] Niebuhr's dates of 1930–35 are basically right, I suppose, for this seminal period. To me, however, the real culmination and confirmation in this mature stance comes with Niebuhr's radical reinterpretation, by means of it, of the integrity in American religious, cultural, and political development in *Kingdom of God.*

[7] The phrase does not appear until Niebuhr wrote his parts of *The Church Against the World*, a volume co-authored by Niebuhr, Wilhelm Pauck, and Francis P. Miller in 1935. The phrase makes its most frequent appearances in *Kingdom of God*, particularly in chap. 2 which has the title "The Sovereignty of God."

the *reality*, to which the phrase as symbol gives expression, is what "happened" to and for Niebuhr in these years. The authentically personal character of this experience is underscored, in my judgment, by the variety of largely unsystematized metaphors and images Niebuhr employed in trying to grasp and express the heart of the matter.

The central emergent in Niebuhr's writings from 1930 to 1937 is the certainty of the reality and the priority in being, value, and power, of God. This shorthand formula sums up what was for Niebuhr really an emergent out of a process of engagement with several major types of problem areas. It happens that these particular problem areas, like the emergent central theme, subsequently become more or less permanent points of theological engagement for him. For this reason, in tracing the theme of the sovereignty of God in the 1930–37 writings, we see it developing in relation to most of the other pivotal themes of Niebuhr's later writings and teaching. Therefore it is imperative for us to see the various meanings and implications of the central theme in the context of the problematics in which Niebuhr worked them out.

2. CONCEIVING A NEW SYNTHESIS

The context of the major writings of 1930–31 is Niebuhr's effort to conceive a new theological synthesis that would adequately emphasize the priority and independence of God in relation to all other dependent being, but which at the same time could give expression to the decisive involvement of God *in* time and *in* human experience. Niebuhr found that contemporary German theology, in the main, emphasized the pole of God's independence and radical transcendence, whereas American religious empiricism placed the weight too uncritically on God in his immanence.

TOWARD A THIRD WAY

In a 1930 article in the *Christian Century* written during his trip to Germany, Niebuhr stresses the importance of serious conversa-

tions between German and American theologians. Characteristically his concern is expressed at the point of theology's ethical adequacy. Scoring the "pure activism" of an American Social Gospel
that had largely lost its theistic anchor, Niebuhr urged the need
for Americans to encounter the theocentrism of German theology.
German Christianity, on the other hand, "which possesses a theology and philosophy but no commensurate ethics," will benefit from
exposure to the genuine efforts to reform social institutions and
renew cultural values that the Social Gospel, at its best, inspired
and sustained.[8] Turning the vectors of these polar tendencies
toward each other, Niebuhr found himself standing in the tension
where they met. "What is required [in theology], we discover is a
third piece, one which will unite the two and in doing so change
and reveal the meaning of the partial picture which appeared on
either unintegrated block." [9] His statement of what the "third
piece" might look like reveals the influence of two figures who are
to be very important in the development of his new third way:

> The way . . . appears to be only in a *realism* which will apprehend in
> all their stubborn actuality the *facts* of *history* and the *fact* of *God*,
> which will neither substitute a romantic idea of natural man for the
> petty and ignoble creature whom our novelists have so often seen and
> described better than our theologians and which will not replace the
> God with whom the soul struggles, *God* the *enemy* and *God* the
> *ultimate reality*, with some man-made deity, some projection of the
> wish or the social whole.[10]

The appeal to realism reflects Niebuhr's reading of Paul Tillich's

---

[8] "Can German and American Christians Understand Each Other?" *Christian Century*, 47 (July 23, 1930), p. 915.

[9] *Ibid.*

[10] *Ibid.* (Italics added by present author.) The reference to "realism" in
this quote and on succeeding pages should recall Niebuhr's acquaintance with
and acceptance of Troeltsch's critical realism. However, Niebuhr is writing in
these years under the immediate impact of the "Belief-ful Realism" of Paul
Tillich (on whom Troeltsch was also a major influence), and in critical reaction to the American empiricism of Macintosh and Wieman, also known as
"Religious Realism." Tillich's realism expressed an existential stance of faith
that viewed the destruction and chaos of post–World War I Europe as a manifestation of divine self-revelation and judgment. American "Religious Realism,"
on the other hand, was a more optimistic epistemological effort to derive
reliable knowledge of God from less traumatic kinds of religious experience.

writings of the twenties, especially *Die Religiöse Lage der Gegenwart* (1926).[11] In Tillich, Niebuhr found a theologian whose indebtedness to Troeltsch and nineteenth-century liberalism showed in his effort to take seriously the human value constructions and patterns of meaning in history and culture. But Tillich moved beyond Troeltsch and liberalism in the realist direction by contending that history and culture are also the arenas in which the unconditional breaks into the present in determinative self-manifestation and revelation of intent.[12]

The other figure whose influence shows in Niebuhr's characterization of the realism of the new synthesis is Alfred North Whitehead. In his little book of lectures, *Religion in the Making* (1926), Whitehead penned a sentence that epitomized with powerful precision the consciousness Niebuhr had been developing of the religious significance of contemporary disillusionment. In this one sentence Niebuhr found a formula that so resonated with his experiences and observations that it was to become the backbone of his phenomenology of faith,[13] and the most quoted nonbiblical formulation in his corpus of writings. The sentence is Whitehead's characterization of the three stages in religion's evolution: "It [religion] is the transition from God the void to God the enemy, and from God the enemy to God the companion." [14] In a lecture given at Yale in the fall of 1931, Niebuhr devotes a section to

[11] A theological interpretation and critique of contemporary Western "technocratic" and "anthropocratic" culture, sensitive to the religious content and significance of art, literature, music, and politics. Niebuhr translated this volume as *The Religious Situation* (1932) and wrote an interpretative preface to it. I have not been able to determine whether Niebuhr met Tillich while in Germany. Mrs. Niebuhr thinks not.

[12] For Niebuhr's expositions of Tillich in this period see "Can German and American Christians Understand Each Other?" pp. 915-16; "Religious Realism and the Twentieth Century" in D. C. Macintosh, ed., *Religious Realism* (New York: The Macmillan Co., 1931), esp. pp. 421-23; "Theology in a Time of Disillusionment," pp. 14, 21; and "Translator's Preface" to Tillich, *The Religious Situation* (Meridian Books; Cleveland: World Publishing Co. [1932], 1956), pp. 9-24.

[13] See especially chap. 5 below.

[14] Alfred North Whitehead, *Religion in the Making* (Meridian Books; Cleveland: World Publishing Co. [1926], 1960), p. 16.

the discussion and critique of Barthian crisis theology. "It is the virtue of this Barthian theology," he writes, "that it has discovered the religious significance of the void. . . . This theology reminds us, as Whitehead also does, that religion is transition from God the void to God the enemy and from God the enemy to God the companion, but that access to the companion may be too cheaply purchased to be real where it is not gained by way of the void and the enemy." [15]

This Barthian extension by Niebuhr of Whitehead's formula serves as a pregnant summary of one of the key dimensions of Niebuhr's "conviction of the sovereignty of God." If Niebuhr may in any sense be accurately described as a Barthian, it is in respect to his own development of the Barthian insight that the experience of the absence of God—and of the "otherness" of God from the mundane objects of human trust—is negatively revelational of the character of true godliness. "This renewed appreciation for the transcendence of the object of religion is probably the most characteristic and valuable feature of the theology of a day of disillusionment. . . . The theology of crisis . . . has built upon this foundation." [16] But it is important for those who would too quickly make a Barthian out of Niebuhr to see two things. First, for Niebuhr this idea of transcendence "is primarily a negative concept, the statement of a void in life rather than of fulfillment." [17] Important as this negative revelation is in the process of overcoming idolatry and the false shelters of anthropocentric religion, it is no resting-place in itself. "If an anthropocentric mode of thought tried to define religion within the limits of humanity then this purely theocentric approach tends to present faith within the limits of deity After reducing all experience and reason in the religious realm to purely subjective processes the Barthian movement succeeds only in arriving at a Kantian agnosticism in which God re-

---

[15] "Theology in a Time of Disillusionment," p. 16. See also *Radical Monotheism*, pp. 123-24.

[16] "Theology in a Time of Disillusionment," p. 16.

[17] *Ibid.*

mains for ever unknown." [18] And second, if the negativity of the void is revelatory, it is so not merely because it destroys the false, but because it also draws us through itself into the real. "The failure of the relative points us to the absolute and if it makes the discovery of the absolute more difficult it also makes it much more urgent. The revelation of the transiency of the transient points us to the permanent and requires us to find the anchorage of life in a rock of ages that is not in the age." [19]

The point of the preceding paragraph is that, while the transcendence of God—the *independence*, the *strangeness*, the *otherness* of God—is an important dimension of what God's sovereignty means for Niebuhr, it is *only* a dimension. And the judgment on finite being and value implicit in the experience of transcendence is not a judgment unto extinction, but a judgment toward the end of transformation, restoration, and redemption of conserved finite being and value. And so Niebuhr speaks of the God the *void*, but not apart from the God the *enemy*; and he speaks of neither of these two apart from the God the *companion*. He is undoubtedly indebted to Barth's theology in some degree, for the insight that to speak of the companion without enduring the anguish of the void and of the enemy, is to speak of an idol. But the experience of God's transcendence has its significance for Niebuhr chiefly as a necessary propaedeutic to the reception of a more positive revelational content, rather than as a culminating experience of the reality of God.[20]

NIEBUHR'S DIALOGUE WITH TILLICH

In order to do justice to the more positive revelational content in Niebuhr's idea of the sovereignty of God, it is necessary to look closely at the influence of Tillich upon him in 1930–31. The decision

---

[18] "Religious Realism and the Twentieth Century," pp. 420-21.

[19] "Theology in a Time of Disillusionment," p. 17.

[20] For Niebuhr's on the whole critical assessments of crisis theology in these years see "Religious Realism and the Twentieth Century," pp. 420-21; "Theology in a Time of Disillusionment," pp. 16, 17-20; "Translator's Preface" to *Religious Situation*, p. 22. Barth and Brunner are the only theologians of crisis he mentions by name in 1930–31.

to translate Tillich's *Religiöse Lage der Gegenwart* indicates Niebuhr's estimate of Tillich's importance for English readers. In "Theology in a Time of Disillusionment," written in 1931 after his return from Germany, Niebuhr speaks of Tillich as the "most promising of the new generation of German theologians." [21]

It is not exaggeration to say that the relation between the thought of Tillich and the formative position of Niebuhr in these years deserves a substantial study in itself. Here I must restrict myself to a few observations. First of all, it is important to note that Niebuhr's interpretation and critique of the nineteenth-century tendencies in philosophy, art, literature, and theology derive more from Tillich (and from Niebuhr's and Tillich's common learning from Troeltsch) than from the very influential critique offered by Barth.[22] But more importantly, Niebuhr found in Tillich's "belief-ful realism" a Troeltsch-like critical idealism that largely overcame the Troeltschian difficulty in drawing on the normative content of particular events and structures in history and culture. It also seemed to overcome, in considerable measure, the static and formal quality of Troeltsch's kind of idealism. Tillich's method, Niebuhr wrote,

does go beyond neo-Kantian and phenomenological analysis in seeking to apprehend the content as well as the forms of mental functions and in trying to do justice to the individual and creative as well as to the formal elements to be found in them. The substitution of a dynamic for a static view of mind, of a partly mystic, partly pragmatic view of truth for a purely formal one, appear to make this philosophy strain hard at the limits imposed upon it by the Kantian tradition and to incline its theory of knowledge more and more toward a realism comparable to that of the Anglo-Saxon countries.[23]

Briefly, what Niebuhr found most attractive in Tillich's position in these years was his powerful combination of a primary faith

---

[21] "Theology in a Time of Disillusionment," p. 14.

[22] See "Religious Realism and the Twentieth Century," pp. 413-16, and esp. n. 1, p. 414: "This analysis of nineteenth century culture is indebted in many important points to Paul Tillich's *Religiöse Lage der Gegenwart*, Berlin, 1926, and to his *Religiöse Verwirklichung*, Berlin, 1930." The analysis of the rootage of contemporary disillusionment in "Theology in a Time of Disillusionment" is also indebted to Tillich in many respects.

[23] "Religious Realism and the Twentieth Century," p. 422.

postulate of the reality and primacy of "the unconditional" with a steadfast effort to interpret the meaning of present events and patterns of history as expressive of (and as relativized by) the unconditional. To get to the heart of these matters we can do no better than to quote Tillich's own explication of "the unconditional":

The term "unconditional" points to that element in every religious experience which makes it religious. In every symbol of the divine an unconditional claim is expressed, most powerfully in the command: "Thou shalt love the Lord thy God with *all* thy heart and with all thy soul and with all thy mind." No partial, restricted, conditioned love of God is admitted. The term "unconditioned" or the adjective made into the substantive, "the unconditional," is an abstraction from such sayings which abound in the Bible and in great religious literature. The unconditional is a quality not a being. It characterizes that which is our ultimate and, consequently, unconditioned concern, whether we call it "God" or "Being as such" or the "Good as such" or the "Truth as such," or whether we give it any other name. . . . Unconditional is a quality which we experience in encountering reality.[24]

Tillich's insistence that "the unconditional" is "no thing" or "no being" is one side of the paradox he tries to maintain in the position which is variously described by Niebuhr as "criticial Realism,"[25] "belief-ful realism,"[26] and "faith-realism."[27] In this thrust, the independence of the Divine, so much the concern of crisis theology, finds powerful expression. But alongside of, and in tension with, this transcendent side of the paradox is the other side, that of "historical realism." Here the focus is on the concrete, the historical, where "the power of reality" or "the really real" comes to expression:

The really real is not reached until the unconditioned ground of everything real, or the unconditioned power in every power of being is

[24] Paul Tillich, *The Protestant Era*, 2d ed. (abridged), trans. James Luther Adams (Chicago: University of Chicago Press, 1957). See n. 1, p. 32, in the essay entitled "Kairos" written in 1922 and read by Niebuhr, by this time. (It is my belief, however, that the footnote from which I quoted was written later—at the time these articles were gathered and translated into English in 1948).
[25] "Theology in a Time of Disillusionment," pp. 21-22.
[26] "Translator's Preface" to *Religious Situation*, pp. 13 ff.
[27] "Religious Realism and the Twentieth Century," pp. 421 ff.

reached. Historical realism remains on a comparatively unrealistic level if it does not grasp that depth of reality in which its divine foundation and meaning become visible.[28]

In Tillich critical idealism finds the kind of normative beginning in a faith stance that Troeltsch's position, insofar as it thought of itself as theology, clearly lacked. This centrality of faith made an impression on Niebuhr:

The Unconditioned is the goal and pre-supposition of all thought and all reality; yet, in the nature of the case, it transcends all reality and cannot be regarded as an object alongside of others. Hence a true realism, which apprehends things in their independence and individuality must see in them also this self-transcending element, this reference to their unconditioned basis. True realism, therefore, involves an element of faith or must, at all events, be associated with a faith that sees the individual not only as independent of the beholder but as a function of the Unconditioned.[29]

We made reference earlier to Niebuhr's identification with the emphasis in crisis theology that discerns the religious significance of the void. If the negative sense of the transcendence of God is underscored in the theology of crisis, in Tillich's theology there is an articulation of the positive side and content of the experience of God *over against* finite being and meaning. To the faith that attempts to discern the unconditional power in every power and the unconditional depth in every being, there can be no ignoring the actuality of evil and chaos in the experience of the world. Nor can disappointments and the failures of the world to meet our expectations be overlooked. If earlier we saw Niebuhr extend Whitehead's formula in a Barthian direction, we must also take note of a Tillichian extension of it which, despite the philosophical language, brings Niebuhr very close to a biblical and prophetic interpretation of the judgment and condemnation of God:

A theology of transcendence begins to function positively not only when it traces the relationship of our life to its last unconditioned source and meaning and so becomes a theology of faith; its function

---

[28] Tillich, "Realism and Faith," *Protestant Era*, p. 78. This essay appeared in *Die Religiöse Verwirklichung* (Berlin, 1930). Niebuhr quotes from it extensively in his preface to *Religious Situation*, pp. 13-16.
[29] "Religious Realism and the Twentieth Century," pp. 422-23.

in history and in our time is also the interpretation of another sort of religious experience, of the experience of condemnation. It is the *theoria* of God the enemy.[30]

There are, Niebuhr continues, a number of ways in which we can interpret our disappointments. "We may interpret them as mere disappointments, as failures of the world to meet our expectations, or we may regard them as our failure to meet expectations which the world has rightly had of us. We may regard them as deceits or we may experience them as judgments." [31] Writing in the midst of economic failure, international tensions, ideological disorder, and churchly despair, Niebuhr points out that the most typical response to disappointment is to curse the scheme of things, to protest the unfairness of our surroundings which betray our hopes and expectations. Others respond in stoic resignation, developing a withdrawing, sideline wisdom. There are, he adds, "less disciplined ways of dealing with the disillusionment but of these we need not speak." The point of a "theoria of God the enemy," however, is that

all of these ways are an evasion—an evasion of the necessary transition from the void of God to God the enemy. When we have faced the fact that meaninglessness is intolerable only because there is a prior meaning, and that relativity is insufficient only because there is an absolute, that our whole disappointment has been possible only because faith is more fundamental than disappointment—or when, at all events, we have come to regard our disappointment in the light of a possible eternal meaning, an ultimate, last fact, we cannot deal with failure any longer as an inconsequential thing in an inconsequential universe. Our pettiness and our meanness, our futility, face the enemy, the judgment. Our social system, its war, its poverty, all its brutal carelessness of life and finer values, no longer appears as a betrayal of our hopes but as our betrayal of God. It is not we, then, who have been betrayed, but we who have betrayed.[32]

Working through and appropriating Tillich's "belief-ful realism" was, in my judgment, an exceedingly important stage or step in the consolidation of Niebuhr's mature position. In Tillich, as we

[30] "Theology in a Time of Disillusionment," pp. 17-18.
[31] *Ibid.*, p. 18.
[32] *Ibid.*, pp. 18-19.

have seen, he found a powerful philosophical fusing of the critical realism, which he had found convincing (if theologically unproductive) in Troeltsch, with a forthright confession of faith in God as the nonobjectifiable divine depth, the unconditionally Real, behind and in all the real. By using Tillich's position as the standard, Niebuhr developed a telling criticism of the American religious realism of his teacher Macintosh and others.[33]

But Tillich's greatest importance for Niebuhr in this period seems to reside in the fact that, for a time, his position provided a very helpful and well-developed set of formulations over against which Niebuhr could bring his own new perceptions, his growing insights and commitments, into clarifying focus. Tillich's work undoubtedly contributed to the new consciousness developing in Niebuhr. But, for Niebuhr, the major function of Tillich's writings, I am suggesting, lay in providing one model for the kind of theological synthesis which faithfulness and the present shape of events seemed to call for. The result of a contribution like that which Tillich's work made to Niebuhr's development in 1930–31 is not discipleship and captivity in the catalytic system. Rather it is confirmation, a new personal and professional consolidation, and, at its depth, a deepening and nurturing of the primal vision or fundamental conviction that sustains the theologian as person and the person as theologian.

It must be said that Niebuhr nowhere attributes this kind of significance to his encounter with Tillich in 1930–31. Tillich's name is not even mentioned in the autobiographical account referred to in

[33] See "Religious Realism and the Twentieth Century," pp. 424-28. The main points of Niebuhr's critique are these: (1) American realism is insufficiently observant of the dualism in religious experience—the dualism between the event or relation or symbol in which the unconditional comes to expression, and the unconditional. It is too ready to identify the symbol or the occasion with the unconditional. (2) American realism is still too much bound to cultural confidence in technocratic capacity and inevitable progress. It is too utilitarian; religion and God are subordinated to the self-realization of man and the conservation of human values. (3) Being too confident about the availability of God in religious experience, it is prone to individualism; it neglects the importance of tradition, of historical revelation, and of the "Gestalt of Grace" (Tillich) which is a collective manifestation of the unconditional in social life and history. And (4) American realism runs the risk of spuriously absolutizing and universalizing its own religious experience.

the previous section. Yet as I have studied Niebuhr's work throughout the seminal phase of 1930–37, and particularly in the transi-
tional years of 1930–31, I have become more and more convinced
that Tillich's importance for him was as I tried to state it above.
Never again were Niebuhr's writings to rely as heavily and as
approvingly on the thought of another theologian as they did on
Tillich in 1930–31.

THE WAY FORWARD

It is clear that, despite Tillich's influence on him, Niebuhr did not
become a Tillichian. Though I would argue that structurally and
ideationally Niebuhr's position continued to congrue with that of
Tillich during the early 1930s, Niebuhr turned to non-Tillichian
metaphors for formulating the conviction of the sovereignty of
God—metaphors that were at once more biblical, more self-consciously relational, and more indigenously American than those of
Tillich. And, it is important to note, Niebuhr's formulations
worked hard to overcome what must have seemed to him to be
serious limitations in Tillich's position—the abstractness, the formal indefinability, and the finally mystic intuitive character of its
idea of God. Despite the beauty and power of its synthesis, I think
Niebuhr would have said of Tillich's theology in this period much
the same thing he said about the religious insufficiency of late
American liberalism. Because of its abstractness it has an "inability
to capture the religious imagination of the people and the same
failure to unite with the strong forces of human need and yearning
which alone make a theology capable of directing as well as expressing the religion of the human heart." [34]

Writing near the end of the two decisive years, 1930–31, Niebuhr
indicates what to him now seems the way forward. If the path he
describes moves away from the pattern of Tillich's thought in the
twenties, it also carries forward much of what accrued to Niebuhr in
and through that temporary convergence of their thinking in 1930–
31:

[34] "Theology in a Time of Disillusionment," p. 14.

The chief task which faces theology in an age of disillusionment does not lie primarily in the religious interpretation of disillusionment, though this has its important place, it lies rather in building upon the foundation of disillusionment—not by its denial—*the theory of an immanence which is present and which yet must be attained,* in making the transition from God the enemy to God the companion, or God the Savior. . . . We may anticipate the development or, rather, sketch the task which confronts us, by saying that the transition may most promisingly be sought in three spheres, all inter-dependent—[1] in continued wrestling with the problem of Jesus and the historical meaning of the revelation of God in history, [2] in continued realistic analysis of religious experience and the search for divine reality in actual religious life, and [3] in even more urgent effort to realize the eternal will of God, as we must see it from the relative point of view of the present moment, in some form of social and personal justice which will carry within it, as immanent, a revelation of the God who yet remains transcendent; which will be adequate to our own situation, but which will contain the absolute demand.[35]

3. A GOD WHO ACTS?

Part of the indeterminateness and abstraction of the conception of God in those works of Tillich that most influenced Niebuhr appears when you ask: Can Tillich's God be said to "act" in history? Is there any sense in which God, as portrayed in Tillich's writings, has the character of a personal agent? [36] The answer to both questions would seem to be "no." For Tillich, to be sure, the *Real* has character, in the sense of pattern and intentionality. But the attribution of action or willing to the Unconditional would seem to be a misleading way of speaking of its eternal being. It is a permanent structure, eternal and absolute. Its apparent dynamism, relative to finite consciousness, is an illusion to which that consciousness is subject, much as a child's consciousness is subject to the mistaken supposition that the moon moves on a parallel course and at the

[35] *Ibid.,* pp. 21-22. (Italics and numerals added by present writer.)
[36] My thinking on these questions has been aided by an article by Gordon Kaufman, "On the Meaning of 'Act of God,'" *Harvard Theological Review,* 61, no. 2 (April, 1968), pp. 175-201. See also chap. 6 of Kaufman, *God the Problem* (Cambridge, Mass.: Harvard University Press, 1972).

same speed as the automobile in which he is riding. For Tillich every "time," or, better, every "present," has significance not as a movement toward a new present, or as the fulfillment of a previous present, but insofar as it is the occasion for the manifestation or the partial concretization of the Unconditional. The Unconditional comes to expression when men in their finite freedom founder and break themselves and their structures of finite meaning on the eternal character of the Real. Man's freedom finds its true ground when, beyond the shambles of broken culture and fissured meaning, it discerns, embraces, and submits to the pattern of the Real. In that reconciliation, and the partial realization of the Unconditional that it involves, God is not affected. The eternality and absoluteness of God are constant, unchanging, complete.

Specialists on Tillich will have to judge the fairness and rightness of this interpretation of his portrayal of God in that early-middle phase of his career in view here. The question which it tries to answer, however, points to the most important context for coming to terms with the writings of Niebuhr from 1930 to 1937. Can the God of Niebuhr's growing faith-knowledge be said to *act* in any meaningful sense of the word? And if so, is the acting of such a God the acting of a *personal* agent? [37] To try to clarify an answer to these questions, we will consider in detail some of the key documents in the evolution of Niebuhr's fundamental conviction and its theological expression.

[37] We have not yet come to the point in Niebuhr's development where he begins to insist that the object of theological inquiry and reflection is the *relationship* between God and his creation, and not God as he might be in himself. But he already does his theological thinking in accordance with that insistence. So when we ask, Is God personal agent? Is God person? we do not ask about God's character in itself—a reality noncomprehensible for human consciousness—but rather about the character of God in relation to men and to dependent being. "Sovereignty of God" as a symbol says as much about man and other dependent being as it does about God. To say that God is *personal* in his sovereignty would be to speak of a quality of the relationship between God and man. To make such a claim, therefore, is different from saying either that man *experiences* God as personal, or that God's character, in itself, is personal. As a relational doctrine the thought of the person-hood of God has mutuality and reciprocity in it, as does the relational understanding of the doctrine of God's sovereignty.

"THE GRACE OF DOING NOTHING"

After fall, 1931, Niebuhr's explicit dialogue with Tillich drops out of his writings. Niebuhr returned to America ready, so it seems, to let the events and movements of a troubled national life be the occasions for practical ethical reflection and interpretation grounded in the conviction of God's sovereignty as he was coming to hold it and work out its implications. In late 1931 and early 1932 Japan invaded Manchuria in an act of international aggression that provided the first issue on which Niebuhr publicly brought to bear the ethical implications of a theology of the sovereignty of God. What, he asked, should be the stance of American Christians in relation to this situation? The *Christian Century* article he wrote on this question received a memorable, if subtly misleading, title from the editor: "The Grace of Doing Nothing." [38] We must look at it with some care.

Niebuhr begins by observing that the greatest moral problems for individuals or societies may arise when there is nothing clearly right and effective to be done. "It is when we stand aside from the conflict, before we know what our relations to it really are, when we seem to be condemned to doing nothing, that our moral problems become the greatest. How shall we do nothing?" [39] Yet, he points out, to be inactive is also to affect the course of history. Therefore it is important to reflect on some of the various alternative ways of being inactive. Three kinds of inactivity are alluded to and rejected: the inactivity of the pessimist who expects the disintegration of the world, and who contributes resignedly to it by his inactivity; the inactivity of the opportunist who, vis-a-vis Japan and China, remains watchfully inactive, awaiting his turn to exploit this situation or another like it; and the inactivity of frustration and moral indignation which Niebuhr identifies with a pacifism that is not truly nonresistant of evil, as he seems to believe a consistent pacifism

---

[38] *Christian Century*, 49 (March 23, 1932), pp. 378-80. On the typed carbon of the original manuscript, which is without title, Niebuhr noted in pencil that the title was supplied by the editor (as were the subtitles and divisions of the article into sections).

[39] "The Grace of Doing Nothing," p. 378.

would be. This pragmatic pacifism hurls violent invective and judgments on the aggressor and will eventually—in the absence of other restraints upon his aggression—either enter the fray with force, ignoring its scruples, or else give way to apoplexy.[40] "Righteous indignation, not allowed to issue in action, is a dangerous thing—as dangerous as any great emotion nurtured and repressed at the same time. It is the source of sudden explosions of the ground of long, bitter and ugly hatreds." [41]

In his consideration of modes of inactivity, Niebuhr turns to look at the stance of the most radical political faith of the day—a faith that informs a way of doing nothing that "offers more hope," and which, by analogy, provides a model for the inactivity of an authentic Christian faith. This is the Communist stance. "Theirs is the inactivity of those who see that there is indeed nothing constructive to be done in the present situation, but that, rightly understood, this situation is after all preliminary to a radical change which will eliminate the conditions of which the conflict is a product." [42] Theirs is an inactivity that holds no hope for good or justice in the present corrupt order, but believes steadfastly in the coming of a new future order. They wait, knowing that the misery of war often precipitates revolution. They see the present crisis as an opportunity "not for direct entrance into the conflict, nor for the watchful waiting of those who seek their self-interest, but for the slow laborious process of building up within the fighting groups those cells of communism which will be ready to inherit the new

---

[40] Niebuhr's critique of pragmatic and self-assertive pacifism as an aggression and as inconsistent with its nonviolent faith (which, for him, seems to entail a radical commitment to nonresistance) is more clearly presented in a 1934 article on a split in the Fellowship of Reconciliation. In this split Reinhold Niebuhr and a minority of the F.O.R. directorate left the organization because they felt it necessary to recognize the possible necessity of the responsible use of force in restraining international and domestic aggression or exploitative violence. HRN's article scored the majority (while expressing sympathy for their stand) for their subsumption of pacifism under rational utilitarian principles, turning it into a form of "non-violent aggression." See Niebuhr, "The Inconsistency of the Majority" World Tomorrow, (January 18, 1934), pp. 43-44. For detailed background on the controversy see Meyer, Protestant Search for Political Realism, 1919–1941, chap. 12, esp. pp. 213-16.
[41] "The Grace of Doing Nothing," p. 378.
[42] Ibid.

world and be able to build a classless international commonwealth on the ruins of capitalism and nationalism." Here, he adds, "is inactivity with a long vision, a steadfast hope, and a realistic program of non-interfering action." [43]

Niebuhr's trip to Russia in August of 1930 had made a deep impression on him. Doubtless it was this encounter with the Russian experiment which awakened his interest in parallels between the Communist philosophy of history and radical Christianity, though his commitment to the Socialist party in the U.S. antedated and helped prepare the way for this.[44] What is interesting to us is that as Niebuhr is working out the pattern of Christian life and involvement in history implied by radical faith in the sovereignty of God, the revolutionary strategy of contemporary communism provides his dominant model. This Communist model enables Niebuhr to see with new clarity and power the revolutionary character of Jesus' teaching and of his faith in the sovereign God. And time after time in these articles of the thirties Niebuhr draws this parallel and likens the strategy of the church to that of "a revolutionary community in a pre-revolutionary society." [45] After the mid-thirties the terminology taken over from Communist theory drops away, and the notion of revolution becomes transmuted into the idea of continuing *metanoia* and transformation in personal and group life.[46] But the understanding of how concrete forces and events in

[43] *Ibid.*, p. 379. Just after his return from Russia, in "The Irreligion of Communist and Capitalist," *Christian Century*, 47 (October 29, 1930), pp. 1306-7, Niebuhr had examined the anti-Christian secularism of communism and argued (1) that for Russia, which underwent no secularization under religious auspices such as the West did in the Reformation, communistic secularization was necessary to make industrialization possible; and (2) that modern capitalism is equally as "secular, this-worldly and irreligious" as communism. In 1932, in this different context, he is focusing on what might be called the radical "faith" of communism.

[44] It is also significant to note that during this period Reinhold Niebuhr actively worked in Third Party affairs and in 1932 "supported the Socialist party, and continued to do so during the decade." (Meyer, *Protestant Search for Political Realism, 1919–1941*, pp. 231 ff.)

[45] "The Church Against the World" ("Toward the Independence of the Church") (1935), in Ahlstrom, ed., *Theology in America*, p. 618.

[46] See *Meaning of Revelation*, p. iv: Christianity is "permanent revolution or *metanoia* which does not come to an end in this world, this life, or this time." See esp. chap. 4.

human history are to be interpreted as modes of God's action and as signs of the kingdom is an enduring theme. I find it hard to avoid concluding that the possibility of interpreting the action of God in present history in this concrete way came to Niebuhr in significant measure through the Communist example. To be sure, behind him and behind Marxism lies the Old Testament prophetic tradition. Niebuhr's work authentically recovers the perspective on God's sovereignty in history held by Amos, Isaiah, and Jesus. But that recovery was also substantially indebted to the nineteenth- and twentieth-century prophetic vision of a modern "secular" Jew.

Let us turn back now to "The Grace of Doing Nothing" and pick up Niebuhr's characterization of the inactivity of radical Christian faith:

There is yet another way of doing nothing. It appears to be highly impracticable because it rests on the well nigh obsolete faith that there is a God—a real God. Those who follow this way share with communism the belief that the fact that men can do nothing constructive is no indication of the fact that nothing constructive is being done. Like the communists they are assured that the actual processes of history will inevitably and really bring a different kind of world with lasting peace. They do not rely on human aspirations after ideals to accomplish this end, but on forces which often seem very impersonal —as impersonal as those which eliminated slavery in spite of abolitionists. The forces may be as impersonal and as actual as machine production, rapid transportation, the physical mixture of the races, etc., but as parts of the real world they are as much a part of the total divine process as are human thoughts and prayers.[47]

Like Hegel, Niebuhr affirms that "the history of the world is the judgment of the world," but he adds, "and also its redemption."[48] Because of the "actual structure of things" the seeds of national or individual self-interest, once planted, must inexorably bear their bitter fruit. "This God of things as they are is inevitable

[47] "The Grace of Doing Nothing," p. 379.
[48] I, following many spokesmen, attributed to Hegel the statement "Die Weltgeschichte ist das Weltgericht." (See Karl Löwith, *Meaning in History*, Chicago: University of Chicago Press, 1949, p. 58.) I was not able, however, to locate this in any of Hegel's writings. Prof. Gordon Kaufman, in a memo responding to my request for help in locating this statement, indicates that it comes from the poem "Resignation" by Schiller.

and quite merciless. His mercy lies beyond, not this side of judgment." [49] This inactive Christian faith believes, as does communism, that the results of the historical process will be good. But it
also recognizes that the good may, and probably will, require revolutionary change involving considerable destruction. "While [this
faith] does nothing it knows that something is being done, something which is divine both in its threat and in its promise." [50]

Niebuhr likens this faith stance, with its inactivity, to that of the
early Christians, "whose millenarian mythology it replaces with the
contemporary mythology of social forces." [51] Like early Christianity, and like communism today, it can make preparations for the
future and its developments:

It also can build cells of those within each nation who, divorcing
themselves from the program of nationalism and capitalism, unite in a
higher loyalty which transcends national and class lines of division and
prepares for the future. There is no such Christian international today
because radical Christianity has not arrived as yet at a program and a
philosophy of history, but such little cells are forming.[52]

And then in a rhetorical flourish Niebuhr shows us in political
metaphors the strategy that underlies his writing about the church
in the coming two years:

The first Christian international of Rome has had its day; the Second
Christian international of Stockholm is likely to go the way of the
Second Socialist International. There is need of and opportunity for a
Third Christian International.[53]

[49] "The Grace of Doing Nothing," p. 379.
[50] *Ibid.*
[51] *Ibid.* Niebuhr adds, parenthetically, "Mythology is after all not fiction but
a deep philosophy."
[52] *Ibid.*
[53] The reference to Stockholm is to the Universal Christian Conference on
Life and Work held in that city in 1925. At this, the first great international
conference of Christians following World War I, there was considerable
euphoria as participants experienced the power of common commitment to
transcend and heal the deep divisions that resulted from the war. (See W. A.
Brown, *Toward a United Church*, New York: Charles Scribner's Sons, 1946,
pp. 63 ff.) Niebuhr did not attend the conference, but his imagination was
clearly stirred. Note the continuity between the spirit of the Stockholm meeting
and the idea of a supranational church, transcending all parochial loyalties, to
which Niebuhr pointed in the conclusion of *Social Sources*, pp. 280-81.

Niebuhr concludes the article by delineating some important differences between the inactivity of radical Christians and that of Communists. The Christian knows that his inability to act constructively in the situation is due in large part to his own faults and failings—which are similar to those of the offender and are certain to make his intervention less than disinterested. He recognizes, if he is an American, that Japan is following the example of his own country and therefore can hardly be expected to accept American intervention as disinterested. The Christian inactivity, therefore, calls for rigorous self-analysis by Americans, and for renunciation of self-interest in any effort to intervene. This kind of inactivity, Niebuhr continues, "is not the inactivity of those who call evil good, it is the inaction of those who do not judge their neighbors because they cannot fool themselves into a sense of superior righteousness." [54] It is not based on a resigned patience, but a patience full of hope, based on faith. "It is not the inactivity of the non-combatant, for it knows that there are no non-combatants, that everyone is involved, that China is being crucified (though the term is very inaccurate), by our sins and those of the whole world." [55] Such inactivity, Niebuhr concludes, calls for works of mercy "though they are only palliatives to ease present pain while the process of healing depends on deeper, more actual and urgent forces." [56]

Then comes the line which shows Niebuhr's consciousness of how far out over the sea of faith he has sprung in this audacious article: "But if there is no God, or if God is up in heaven and not in time itself, it is a very foolish inactivity." [57]

[54] "The Grace of Doing Nothing," pp. 379-80.
[55] *Ibid.*, p. 380. The figure of crucifixion apparently had considerable precision for Niebuhr as applied to this kind of situation. A decade later, in a series of personally determinative articles on the agony of World War II, Niebuhr entitled a profound wrestle with the theological meaning of the suffering of millions of innocents in the war "War as Crucifixion" (*Christian Century*, 60, April 28, 1943).
[56] "The Grace of Doing Nothing," p. 380.
[57] *Ibid.*

TO SEE THE KINGDOM

At the solicitation of the editor of the *Christian Century*, Reinhold Niebuhr wrote a critical response to "The Grace of Doing Nothing" that is notable both for the urgency and precision of its argument and for its almost total failure to comprehend the depth and radicality of H. Richard Niebuhr's faith in the God who is sovereign in and through history. Reinhold Niebuhr reads his brother's article as a call to pacifism and ethical purity, centered in the radical application of an ethic of love. It is difficult to see how he could interpret the piece this way when it contains no specific argument for pacifism as a general, categorical stance, and when the word "love" does not appear in it at all. These difficulties notwithstanding, Reinhold affirms that the position he attributes to his brother is closer to that of the gospel than his own, and then proceeds to give a powerful and persuasive argument against the, to him, fatuous hope "that a kingdom of pure love will emerge out of the catastrophes of history." Since life is tragic and will be until the end of history, justice—or the "judicious use of the forces of nature in the service of the ideal"—is the only realistic and responsible goal for Christians and society to pursue, despite the imperativeness of the love ideal.[58]

Reinhold Niebuhr's critique reads as though it were dealing with a different article altogether. After reading the original article, it is hard to see how anyone could interpret it as being primarily an argument for pacifism as a categorical position. We can only conjecture that the Niebuhr brothers had an argument in progress involving nonresistance (HRN) versus responsible restraint, employing violence if necessary (RN). In his critique Reinhold must have been drawing on material to which we have no access. To meet H. Richard's argument simply as an appeal to the radical ethic of love, and as an injunction to avoid coercion until it can be pure and disinterested, as Reinhold did, is to remove it from the one context in which nonresistance is plausible—the context of radical

[58] Reinhold Niebuhr, "Must We Do Nothing?" *Christian Century*, 49 (March 30, 1932), pp. 415-17.

faith in a sovereign God. H. Richard Niebuhr wrote a final re-joinder, which appeared in the *Century* the following week, in which he makes that context unmistakably clear. This letter contains some of the clearest statements that we have of Niebuhr's understanding of the meaning of God's sovereignty and mode of action in history.

The difference between the brothers, Niebuhr writes, does not lie in the question of activity or inactivity, for "we are speaking after all of two kinds of activity." Rather, the question is

whether "the history of mankind is a perennial tragedy" which can derive meaning only from a goal which lies beyond history, as my brother maintains, or whether the "eschatological" faith, to which I seek to adhere, is justifiable. In that faith tragedy is only the prelude to fulfillment, and a prelude which is necessary because of human nature; the kingdom of God comes inevitably, though whether we shall see it or not, depends on our recognition of its presence and our acceptance of the only kind of life which will enable us to enter it, the life of repentance and forgiveness.[59]

For Reinhold Niebuhr, he writes, God is external to the historic process—"so much so that he charges me with faith in a miracle-working deity which interferes occasionally, sometimes brutally, sometimes redemptively in history." And then he tries to bring his own position to utmost clarity:

But God, I believe, is always in history, he is the structure of things, the source of all meaning, the "I am that I am," that which is that it is. He is the rock against which we beat in vain, that which bruises and overwhelms us when we seek to impose our wishes, contrary to his, upon him. That structure of the universe, that creative will, can no more be said to interfere brutally in history than the violated laws of my organism can be said to interfere brutally with my life if they make me pay the cost of my violation.[60]

There follows a line of argument which gives a number of illustrations of the way the divine structure makes it inevitable that self-assertion, contrary to God's will, must bring destructive conse-

[59] "A Communication: The Only Way into the Kingdom of God," *Christian Century*, 49 (April 6, 1932), p. 447.
[60] *Ibid.*

quences. Then Niebuhr makes the transition from God the enemy to God the companion:

> But this same structure in things which is our enemy is our redeemer; "it means intensely and means good"—not the good which we desire, but the good which we would desire if we were good and really wise. History is not a perennial tragedy but a road to fulfillment and that fulfillment requires the tragic outcome of every self-assertion, for it is a fulfillment which can only be designated as "love." It has created fellowship in atoms and organisms at bitter cost to electrons and cells; and it is creating something better than human self hood but at bitter cost to that self hood. This is not faith in progress for evil grows as well as good and every self-assertion must be eliminated somewhere and somehow—by innocence suffering for guilt is seems.[61]

Finally, as a human ideal the kingdom of God or society of love is impossible of attainment. "It is not an ideal toward which we can strive, but an 'emergent,' a potentiality in our situation which remains unrealized so long as we try to impose our pattern and our wishes upon the divine creative process." [62]

UNRESOLVED QUESTIONS

Two issues require comment here. The first is the question whether H. Richard Niebuhr's original article was in fact an argument for radical pacifism, as his brother seemed to think. In beginning his letter of response to Reinhold's critique Niebuhr wrote, "Since you [the editor] have given me leave to fire one more shot in the fraternal war between my brother and me *over the question of pacifism,* I shall attempt to place it as well as I can, not for the purpose of demolishing my opponent's position—which our thirty years' war has shown me to be impossible—but for the sake of pointing as accurately as I can to the exact locus of the issue between us." [63] The locus of the issue, it becomes clear, is the difference between the brothers' beliefs concerning the involvement of God in history and how much and what kind of reliance can be placed by responsible men on that involvement. It seems probable that both Reinhold

---

[61] *Ibid.*
[62] *Ibid.*
[63] *Ibid.* (Italics added by present author.)

and H. Richard Niebuhr had been inclined to a radical pacifism in this period. Reinhold, as the Fellowship of Reconciliation debate shows, had begun to move toward a political realism that saw the need for intervention—employing violence if necessary—to check and restrain aggression in the protection of life and rights of exploited peoples.[64] Nowhere have I found H. Richard Niebuhr arguing for pacifism as a categorical stance. As this article shows, his attention is given more to trying to express and explicate the meaning of his conviction that the *real* (which conditions history and which is inexorably working toward realization of its will in and through history) is God. Clearly the kind of position he advocates rules out a military intervention which is based on either a desire to protect or extend national interests, on the one hand, or that claims to act out of a presumed moral superiority on the other. Indisputably his prime concern is to press toward a kind of response to the Japan-China affair in the light of the "total divine process," that will break the cycle of national self-assertions and the self-righteous rhetoric of a hypocritical disinterestedness. But whether for him during these years violent restraint is categorically ruled out is not clarified. In the 1935 article "Man the Sinner," where Niebuhr provides guidelines for the exercise of restraint as they are informed by a Christian doctrine of man,[65] it becomes apparent that if he was previously a pacifist, by this time he no longer unqualifiedly holds that position.

The second issue that requires preliminary comment has to do with the question raised at the beginning of this section: whether and in what sense Niebuhr's God may be said to *act*; and whether his God is, in any sense, to be thought of as a personal agent. On the basis of a terminological analysis of Niebuhr's references to God, it can be said plainly that there is very little direct anthropomorphism in the conception of God we have seen emerge so far. No less than for Tillich, Niebuhr's God is "the actual structure

---

[64] See n. 40 above. On Reinhold Niebuhr's early pacifism see Gordon Harland, *The Thought of Reinhold Niebuhr* (New York: Oxford University Press, 1960), pp. 214 ff. Reinhold decisively rejected pacifism, Harland asserts, in 1932—the year of this exchange.

[65] "Man the Sinner," *Journal of Religion*, 15 (1935), pp. 279-80.

of things," the "God of things as they are," who is "inevitable and quite merciless." "He is the rock against which we beat in vain, that which bruises and overwhelms us when we seek to impose our wishes, contrary to his, upon him." But there is a dynamism in Niebuhr's concept of God, and a willingness to take history with utter seriousness, that I do not find in Tillich. He refers to the "real world" as "the total divine process," and implies that God is in action in "the actual processes of history." He places "that structure of the universe" in apposition with "that creative will." The kingdom of God is an "emergent," inevitably to be brought to fulfillment by God, but dependent for its completeness upon men's conscious turning aside from efforts to impose their will on history and to enter upon collaborative pursuit of the divine intentionality. And this God is *one*. "This same structure in things which is our enemy is our redeemer; 'it means intensely and means good'—not the good which we desire, but the good which we would desire if we were good and really wise."

We seem to detect in Niebuhr's account a movement from strictly impersonal, process-structural ways of speaking of God toward categories that might at the least be called "pre-personal." There is faithfulness—dependability and unswerving consistency—in the divine character, which expresses itself by requiring congruence from finite being, and exacting suffering when the capacity to rebel is exercised. The well-meaning, redemptive intention in the strict and implacable requirement of suffering is shown, paradoxically, in that the suffering exacted is most often imposed upon the innocent. But the key to that paradox, which is the realization that God himself participates in this redemptive suffering of the innocents, has not yet clearly appeared. Therefore while God is in action in history, that there is a personal character or personal agency in that action has not yet been claimed.

4. JESUS THE REVOLUTIONARY STRATEGIST

Our goal continues to be to understand the meaning of Niebuhr's conviction of God's sovereignty by examining its development in the formulations and imagery he used in speaking of it. Growth in a faith relationship, like growth in a love relationship, involves overcoming inhibitions. In his encounters with Tillich, with White-head, with crisis theology, and with Communist revolutionary strategy, we have seen Niebuhr overcoming in different ways various inhibitions to radical faith. We have observed him in the process of breaking through the limits of a theological frame of reference that subtly subordinated the independence, the reality, the primacy in power and value of God, to the service of finite ideals, interests, and powers. Positively put, we are observing Niebuhr in a process of development toward a mature *Christian faith-integrity*.

So far Niebuhr's characterizations of the sovereignty of God have come principally by way of philosophical and historical analyses. In light of the paper we are about to examine, the previous writings begin to appear as preparatory to a decisive new encounter with *the* pivotal figure in Christian history. It is as if Niebuhr's radical faith, developing by way of a secondary, mediated relation to the God of biblical faith, suddenly discovered its ground and depth through identification with the most authentic mediator and incarnator of radical faith in God, the Jesus of the New Testament. Of the unpublished papers H. Richard Niebuhr left, "The Social Gospel and the Mind of Jesus" is one of the most remarkable. It was read at a meeting of the American Theological Society in New York, on April 21, 1933,[66] and since it is not yet generally available I will quote from it extensively. Here we see Niebuhr's first substantive effort to interpret the faith of Jesus and the God of Jesus' faith. This paper also has major significance as a public contribution to the early criticism of the Social Gospel in America.

THE JESUS OF THE SOCIAL GOSPEL

Niebuhr's paper is divided into three parts, entitled somewhat playfully "The Mind of Jesus in the Social Gospel," "The Mind of Jesus *Not* in the Social Gospel," and "The Social Gospel in the Mind of Jesus." The first of these sections constitutes an overview of various pictures of Jesus and their significance as presented in notable books in the Social Gospel literature of the previous two

[66] Written in ink on yellow legal-sized paper, 23 pp.

decades. Among these are works by Walter Rauschenbusch, Francis G. Peabody, Shailer Matthews, Harry Ward, Kirby Page, Justin Wroe Nixon, and Reinhold Niebuhr. Niebuhr finds three distinct schools of thought among these writers: one that tends to identify the Christian gospel with utopian socialism or utopian communism; a second that interprets the gospel in "a liberal fashion and believes in the education of Christlike personalities active in social affairs"; and a third (a class of one constituted by his brother) that "finds values in the gospel which transcend both socialism and liberalism, social programs and personal ideals, but discovers in it no power adequate for the control of social life.[67] Despite this apparent variety, however, there is a common shared assumption that constitutes a point of fundamental agreement among these men: "The mind of Jesus in the social gospel is, on the whole, the mind of the liberal Jesus, of Jesus the moral idealist, the evolutionist, the indeterminist, the pacifist, the believer in personal values." [68]

Who is "the liberal Jesus"? Niebuhr devotes a paragraph to comparing the Jesus of the Social Gospel with the "classic liberal portrait of Jesus" in Adolf von Harnack's *What Is Christianity?* In this instructive paragraph, the only critique of Harnack I have found in Niebuhr's writings, he characterizes the Social Gospel vision as primarily a socialized version of the Harnackian individualistic value-idealism: "For Harnack the Kingdom of God is a state of the soul, for the social gospel it is a state of society; for Harnack the God of Jesus is the kind father of every individual, for the social gospel he is the father of humanity." [69] Save for the social extension of the ideas by the Social Gospel writers, Niebuhr contends, the mind of Jesus is interpreted in much the same fashion by the great German liberal and by the American Social Gospelers. Niebuhr's conclusion from this is really the prime thesis of the first part of his paper:

The first point is this, that the mind of Jesus according to the social gospel is the mind of a moralist, that is of a man who is interested

[67] "The Social Gospel and the Mind of Jesus," p. 2.
[68] *Ibid.*, p. 3.
[69] *Ibid.*, pp. 3-4.

above all in the conservation and realization of moral values, whether these values be regarded as human values or as eternal values.[70]

Here Niebuhr also gives a critique of Reinhold Niebuhr's interpretation of Jesus in *Moral Man and Immoral Society*. Despite the fact that this volume is often rightly viewed as the first dramatic departure from Social Gospel liberalism in this country, it is instructive to see that H. Richard views Reinhold as still belonging to the Social Gospel pattern in his interpretation of Jesus and Jesus' ethical teachings. He acknowledges that Reinhold Niebuhr's Jesus is, unlike most of the other interpretations, not a utilitarian, concerned simply with the conservation of human values. Rather, he is a perfectionist "upon whose lips the most characteristic word is 'Be ye therefore perfect even as your Father in heaven is perfect.' But the perfection of God, as religion generally, and, we must assume, as Jesus also, imagines it (for Jesus in this book is the type of the religious mind) is the sum of human virtues raised to the nth degree." [71] So if Reinhold Niebuhr's Jesus is not a utilitarian, he is a moral perfectionist who teaches an absolute morality and has a transcendent perspective on life. Despite the differences between this and the other interpretations, "the God of Jesus the perfectionist, like the God of Jesus the utilitarian is a moral ideal and this moral ideal is conceived in terms of values, . . . in the case of Niebuhr in terms of [the value] perfect love." [72] H. Richard concludes his section on the Jesus of *Moral Man and Immoral Society* with a statement that reveals as much about his own position as it does about his brother's:

Niebuhr's perfectionist Jesus does not fit into this picture [the general social gospel picture of Jesus] save for these important points: that the God of this Jesus is also the moral ideal, and . . . that little if any aid may be expected from such a God in man's social struggles. Both the absolute ideal and the God who gives some sort of existence to this ideal Niebuhr seems tempted to regard as more or less splendid illusions. Were he to go all the way and include Jesus as probably on

[70] *Ibid.*, pp. 4-5.
[71] Niebuhr cites Reinhold Niebuhr, *Moral Man and Immoral Society* (New York: Charles Scribner's Sons, 1960), pp. 63, 52.
[72] "The Social Gospel," p. 7.

his side in this admission, it seems to the writer that he would come closer to the mind of Jesus which is not in the Social Gospel.[73]

What is this mind of Jesus "not in the Social Gospel"? Here we turn to the second, constructive part of the paper.

JESUS AND THE GOD OF RADICAL FAITH

"We may describe the mind of Jesus which is not in the social gospel as the mind of a God-centered, apocalyptic revolutionary strategist. The interpreters of the apocalyptic element in the gospel have left the liberal picture of the liberal Jesus in a hopeless state of disrepair." [74] Niebuhr goes on to give a cogent critique of some of the efforts to evade the jarring picture of the apocalyptic Jesus (especially that offered by Schweitzer). Liberalism generally tried to evade the apocalyptic Jesus by viewing the first-century mythos about him as a dispensable "frame" relative to its time and culture, from which the nineteenth-century picture of the moralist Jesus (who teaches presumably universally valid moral values) can be removed. This involves them in an inconsistency. Niebuhr also points out the inconsistency of making woodenly literalistic interpretations of biblical apocalyptic imagery, which confuses the symbols and their meaning, while on the other hand being perfectly willing to admit symbolism and hyperbole (without such confusion) into contemporary literature.[75] He concludes:

Penetrate through the apocalyptical symbol to its meaning and we find, not what the liberals or the social gospel want us to find, an ethical

[73] *Ibid.*, p. 9. This means closer to the view of Jesus which is Niebuhr's and which finds expression in the next section of the paper—the Jesus whose God is the judge and slayer before he is redeemer and bringer of life. For the passage referred to in *Moral Man*, where the "absolute ideal and the God who gives [it] existence" are called "splendid illusions," see p. 81 of that volume. (The colon and comma in lines 2 and 3 of this quote were added by the present writer.)

[74] "The Social Gospel," p. 9.

[75] A point similar to that made in the classic interpretation of the ethical teachings of Jesus by Amos Wilder, *Eschatology and Ethics in the Teachings of Jesus*, 2d ed. (New York: Harper & Brothers, 1950). See pp. 25 ff. (The first edition appeared in 1939.) Noting this similarity, I mentioned it to Prof. Wilder. The book had its origins in his Yale doctoral dissertation. He recalls that Niebuhr was one of ten or twelve Yale faculty who took part in his dissertation orals in the spring of 1933, the time "The Social Gospel" was written.

teacher, proclaiming humanitarian morality and relatively painless progress toward the Family of God, but a prophet of doom and deliverance
who sees impending in the events of his time a revelation of the
destructive God who is at the same time man's deliverer.[76]

The New Testament Jesus, Jesus the apocalyptic prophet, is not
a man absorbed with the moral questions "What shall I do?" or
"What help may I expect from God in doing what I ought to
do?" Rather his mind is directed "toward what God was doing and
what man ought to do in the light of God's doing. God's doing—not
what God ought to do in order that he might live up to the
expectations men had of him, stands in the center of Jesus' mind.
God for him is not the moral ideal but rather cosmic reality. He is
the God of Job rather than the God of Plato." [77]

Jesus sees God's doing in the totality of the natural and the
historic processes. Almost never does Jesus seem to equate the
divine activity merely with moral and spiritual matters.[78] Jesus
sees God's rule in nature where "the rain descends on just and unjust with a glorious lack of moral distinctions," and where "the
lilies and the life of the birds are instances of God's working." [79]
But even more evident than God's rule in nature, for Jesus, is his
rulership in the social-historic process:

[76] "The Social Gospel," pp. 10-11.

[77] *Ibid.*, p. 11. This is the first clear expression of the theme that receives
its fullest development by Niebuhr in the lectures that became *Responsible
Self*. Before recovery of "The Social Gospel" it was impossible to say with
certainty that the theme of response to God's action appeared in any developed
form before Niebuhr's agonizing wrestle with the question of God's involvement in the Second World War. See "War as the Judgment of God," *Christian Century*, 59 (May 13, 1942), pp. 630-33; "Is God in the War?"
Christian Century, 59 (August 5, 1942), pp. 653-55, and "War as Crucifixion,"
Christian Century, 60 (April 28, 1943), pp. 513-15. Also there is a very
important unpublished paper from this latter period entitled "A Christian Interpretation of War." Niebuhr's annotations on the typed manuscript date it
1943 "For Fed. Council Commission."

[78] "The Social Gospel," p. 11. Here Niebuhr is by no means denying
that the moral or spiritual process is a part of the divine activity. His concern,
rather, is to overcome the reductionism involved in interpreting God and his
actions solely in moral or spiritual terms. In "Man the Sinner" (1935) he argues
in the same manner against the reductionism involved in equating *sin* with
moral guilt.

[79] "The Social Gospel," p. 11.

It is here that the rule of God comes to be of decisive importance and the meaning of eschatology lies largely in this, that it represents history not as an indeterminate sequence of events where men may adjust themselves to a relatively stable environment and to each other, but as a driving, directional movement, ruthless so far as individuals and nations are concerned, almost impersonal in its determination. The God of history plays no favorites with the Jews; the children of the Kingdom may be cast into outer darkness. He does not even stop for women who are with child. . . . This God of history, to whom the mind of Jesus is directed, is not the head of a family endeavoring to cement its members together by infinite kindness. He is a destructive as well as constructive God. He is a rock which falls with crushing weight.[80]

The God of the liberal Jesus is the God who exists for the sake of human life and morality. The liberal Jesus knows only God the friend, the savior, the father. But the God of Jesus the Jew "is the God of Abraham, Isaac and Jacob—the reality *which is that which it is*, he is the God of Amos, Isaiah and Micah, terrible in his judgments. He is not the synthetic unity of Goodness, Truth and Beauty, nor a First Cause, but a faithful, that is unswerving, reality with laws that can only be broken at the price of life." [81] The proper response to the manifestations of God's rule does not first call for celebration and rejoicing, but for fear and repentance.[82]

But the God of Jesus' faith is not only the impersonal, awesome destroyer understood in prophetic faith. For Jesus is not only Jesus the Jewish prophet; he is also Jesus the pious Jew. "The greatness of Jesus lies here probably as much as anywhere—that he does unite, not in an unresolved paradox or tension or compromise, but in a true synthesis the fear of God and the love of God, the knowledge of God the enemy and the knowledge of God the deliverer." [83] If the showing forth of God's rule in history calls for repentance and fear, it also calls for rejoicing and confident trust. For the God with whom we have to do is *one*. The judge and slayer is also the redeemer and bringer of new life. "It is one and the same process which damns and saves—not a righteousness

[80] *Ibid.*, p. 12.
[81] *Ibid.*, pp. 12-13.
[82] *Ibid.*, p. 12.
[83] *Ibid.*, p. 13.

which condemns and a love which redeems—but one God with one faithful working." [84]

Because Jesus has his mind centered on the revolutionary actions of God in history he is a revolutionary. He is impressed with the discontinuities in past and present rather than with the continuities, whether long-term or short-term. "A revolution," Niebuhr states in an important passage,

is an event which has end character, not as the "*telos*" toward which men strive, but as the "eschaton" which terminates striving, not by fulfillment but by complete denial. In that sense death is the great revolution in the life of the individual; the end of a national existence, the end of a civilization is the great revolution in the life of social groups. Jesus' mind is directed toward such an end, an "eschaton" in the existence of his people. Jerusalem will be destroyed, its inhabitants scattered. And like the prophets before him he does not seek merely to read moral meaning into this impending catastrophe; he accepts it rather from the hands of God and reads the meanings that are in it.[85]

But destruction and doom are not the last word. Jesus the revolutionary Jew sees that judgment and termination are not an absolute end but also a new beginning. "Let men accept the end as judgment and the new beginning as mercy, let them yield to it

[84] *Ibid.* The affirmation of the oneness of God was implied in Niebuhr's reply to his brother in "A Communication: The Only Way into the Kingdom of God." But here it is stated explicitly for the first time. Recall the instances in 1920 ("An Aspect of the Idea of God in Recent Thought") and in 1925 ("Back to Benedict?") where Niebuhr struggles with the ethical implications of philosophical monism and theological monotheism versus dualism or pluralism. See also the conclusion of "Religious Realism and the Twentieth Century" where Niebuhr sees the liabilities of German realism (especially those of crisis theology) as "dualism, agnosticism, pessimism and dogmatism." The liabilities of American realism he takes to be its "optimism, monism and rationalism" ("Religious Realism," p. 428). Here in "The Social Gospel" the issue has been resolved in the kind of monism that is present and normative for all Niebuhr's subsequent work. This passage from *Meaning of Revelation* (1941) states it well: "He [God] met us not as the one beyond the many but as the one who acts in and through all things, not as the unconditioned, but as the conditioner. The oneness of the person was the oneness of a will directed towards the unity of all things in our world. . . . He is the one who ties all our world together by meeting us in every event and requiring us to think his thoughts after him in every movement" (pp. 183-84).

[85] "The Social Gospel," p. 14.

as those who accept; let them have faith and they may enter into the Kingdom of God." [86]

Because of his radical attention to the discontinuities of the coming eschaton, Jesus the revolutionary was not a moralist but a strategist. The moralist's stance insists either on an ideal end to be striven for, with a determination of means by the end, or on strict obedience to transcendentally valid moral rules. Over against both these moralistic approaches, Jesus adopts the stance of the strategist, alert and expectant, prepared to respond faithfully and creatively to the new possibilities which the divine revolutionary process will bring.[87] In contrast to the teleologist, who views the kingdom of God as an ideal toward which to strive, for Jesus the kingdom was a *hope*. "To act in the light of an assured hope is not to engineer a direct road toward the 'telos' but rather to prepare oneself for a gift, so that one will not miss its possibilities. The strategic approach to life . . . consists in such preparations for taking advantage of gifts which the situation gives and in adjusting ends to means rather than means to ends." [88]

If there is a marked contrast between the revolutionary strategist and the teleologist, the strategist also differs from the followers of every perfectionistic morality that obligates persons despite the transcendence and unattainability of its norms. Niebuhr explicates this contrast in a passage that indicates in an important way some of the normative ethical content of the idea of the kingdom of God.

---

[86] *Ibid.*, p. 15.

[87] Anyone familiar with *Responsible Self* (1963) will see in this 1933 interpretation of Jesus as the revolutionary strategist an embryonic statement of the argument of chap. 1 of that work. There Niebuhr sketches the outlines of the teleological ("Man the self-maker") and deontological ("Man the citizen or self-legislator") ethical stances in order to contrast them with an ethics of response to the action of God. Consider also the parallels between this 1933 position and that of Dietrich Bonhoeffer in his *Ethics* (trans. Neville Horton Smith, New York: The Macmillan Co., 1955), especially Bonhoeffer's insistence that the norm of Christian ethical action is not "that I should become good, or that the condition of the world should be made better by my action, but that the reality of God should show itself everywhere to be the ultimate reality" (*Ethics*, p. 55). Bonhoeffer develops this position, more statically than does Niebuhr, in the rest of chap. 2, and especially in chap. 6, where he writes about "The Structure of Responsible Life," *Ethics*, pp. 194 ff.

[88] "The Social Gospel," p. 15.

It also makes clear the direction of his interpretation of the ethical significance of the Sermon on the Mount:

Jesus does not demand that men love their brethren because from a transcendent perspective all men are equal, but because the God of the historic and cosmic process is one who avenges all lovelessness, all lack of forgiveness because selfishness, self-assertion lead to destruction. The laws of God are not the laws of moral perfection, but the laws of reality. The Sermon on the Mount does not tell men what to do in order that they may live up to the moral ideal, but what to do in a world where hatred as well as murder, lasciviousness as well as adultery have terrible destructive consequences. The morality of the Sermon on the Mount does not stand on its own bottom, it stands upon the foundations of reality. The cosmic God rather than the moral God is the presupposition of that counsel, but certainly a cosmic God whose laws have been apprehended and partly set forth, though incompletely, in the Mosaic laws of morality.[89]

Niebuhr ends this central section with a paragraph that sheds further light on the character of a Christian revolutionary strategy. Here the question of Niebuhr's pacifism—which for him means forgiveness and nonresistance—receives further clarification:

The strategy of Jesus, the Jewish revolutionary, centers in the principles of repentance, faith, forgiveness and innocence suffering for guilt. It is impossible for man to take the Kingdom by violence, by self-assertion; he has no means adequate to this purpose. But it is possible for him, in repentance, to anticipate the judgment, to give up the attempt to preserve or extend the dying system and so to hasten its destruction.[90]

But unless there is faith that sees deliverance and new life beyond the judgment, such repentance is impossible. "Forgiveness and non-resistance are essential to this strategy because without them men electing themselves as instruments of divine vengeance and judgment simply supplant one kingdom of man by another and fail to appropriate the rule of God." If there is to be any cessation of the vicious cycle of self-assertion versus counter-self-assertion, "the suffering of innocence for guilt is the only strategy possible." [91]

[89] *Ibid.*, p. 16.
[90] *Ibid.*, p. 17.
[91] *Ibid.* In "The Inconsistency of the Majority," Niebuhr makes it clear that such a strategy calls the pacifist to suffer willingly and innocently: "A

Perhaps, he concludes, "we may be allowed to interpret [Jesus']
march upon Jerusalem and the invitation of death as a great symbolic action used to interpret this truth which Jesus had apprehended, as the old prophets had illustrated their insights by demonstrations and symbolic actions." [92]

ANSWERING SOME OBJECTIONS

In the third and final section of "The Social Gospel and the Mind
of Jesus" Niebuhr anticipates some of the criticisms that this radical reinterpretation of Jesus and of the God of Jesus' faith seems
likely to elicit. He freely admits that it is possible that his interpretation is as relative to the present, with its disillusionment and
sense of catastrophe, as the Jesus of liberalism was relative to the
optimism and burgeoning expansionism of its seminal era. But he
believes that such is not the case. For, he contends, his interpretation grows out of the historical studies that recaptured the eschatological thrust in Jesus' life and teaching. It requires the omission of
no major section of the biblical documents, as does liberalism's
embarrassment with the apocalyptic sections. Further, there seems
to be greater similarity between the troubled present and the situation of Jesus than between his situation and that of the nineteenth
century. Finally, the interpretation of Jesus as revolutionary strategist does not have to reject as self-deceptions what many other
ages have seen and responded to as authentic in Jesus.[93]

Christian pacifism or, better, a Christian non-resistance . . . knows that there is a
divine teleology, and that the aggressiveness of the righteous runs counter to it
as often as does the aggressiveness of the unrighteous. It sees that the characteristic deed of Jesus was not enacted in the temple but on Golgotha and understands that he did not say: 'Love your enemy in order that you may convert him
to your point of view,' but 'Love your enemies in order that ye may be sons of
your Father in heaven who maketh his sun to shine on the evil and the good.'
It will understand that the grand word 'reconciliation' has been employed by
Christianity in connection with the shedding of blood, not with the shedding
of words, and that the connection was not with the shedding of the blood of the
evil but of the innocent. This Christian pacifism will also understand that there
can be no exemption for pacifists, and it will seek none." (*World Tomorrow*,
17, January 18, 1934, p. 44.)

[92] "The Social Gospel" p. 17.

[93] *Ibid.*, p. 18.

To the possible objection that the position taken in this paper is a return to fundamentalism or millenarianism Niebuhr asserts that the old liberal-fundamentalist controversy is a thing of the past. "Fundamentalism consisted in the substitution of symbols for that which they meant; liberalism is the substitution of new meanings without changinng symbols—as in the case of Kingdom of God which was used to mean brotherhood of man. We are interested in what we believe to be the old *meanings* and reject the deification of such symbols as Christ, Bible, cross, virgin birth." [94]

But there is another, more serious dual objection: that "acceptance of the cosmic God and of the eschatological Jesus" leads to "individualism in Christian ethics and a passive attitude in social strife." To the first of these lines of objection Niebuhr's response involves four points: (1) In Paul's reinterpretation of it the eschatological thrust in Jesus' teachings *did* undergo an individualization. "The strategy of faith, repentance, the acceptance of grace, forgiveness, was found eminently successful in dealing with the revolution in the individual life." [95] But (2) "there was *a social gospel in the mind of this Jesus*. He was sent to the lost sheep of the house of Israel, he was concerned about Jerusalem; he spoke less of the death of the personal individual than of the judgment on the social individual. If he prepared a remnant for the future he did not do it as one who plucks brands from the burning but as one who forms a new party for the reception of a new dispensation." [96] (3) Contemporary Christians are more able to grasp this social element in Jesus because, like the Jews, we think in terms of social rather than personal individuals, "and because we, like the Jews again, take time seriously." [97] And (4) "the dualism of soul and body, of this world of matter and the other spiritual world—into which individuals can be saved one by one—has had to yield again . . . to a monistic view like that of the Jews who could not think in terms of an immortal soul inhabiting a mortal body but had

[94] *Ibid.*, p. 19.
[95] *Ibid.*, pp. 19-20.
[96] *Ibid.*, p. 20.
[97] *Ibid.*

91

to use the symbol of the resurrected body to express their faith in the conservation of personal values." [98]

To the charge of ethical passivity and quietism Niebuhr responds by saying, essentially, that if his position were like that of "Barthianism" the charge would be justified. For in the Barthian faith God so far transcends history as to become a mere transcendent point, a static conception of bare perfection, empty of normative content. But where God is in history, in the center of the process of becoming with its emergencies and emergences,

> there is indeed no room for self-appointed avengers and Messiahs. "Vengeance is mine" says this Lord. But neither is passive waiting possible. Activity is inescapable. The only activity which man cannot exert is God's activity. But he cannot evade the necessity of acting in the interim before the judgment, of preparing for death and for life. . . . This day the Lord sets life and death before him. Such interim ethics are not the ethics of quiescence. Precisely because God is moving man cannot sit still." [99]

Niebuhr concludes the paper with a forceful summary of the position he has developed: "To recapture the faith of Jesus is to recapture faith in the God of the creative process, the dynamic urge in the moving universe which brings death and destruction to those who will not yield to its universal, faithful working, which heals and forgives and makes even new beginnings possible." [100] Jesus had faith, and a hope grounded in faith, that "earth shall be fair and all men glad and wise." But unlike the Social Gospelers he knew that "gladness and wisdom are gifts bestowed, not ends for engineers and that they wait upon our willing obedience to the inevitable ways of a power not ourselves that makes for a Glory that is not human glory." [101] Apparently arguing against the kind of realism his brother propounded, Niebuhr continues: Jesus "saw that the strategy of the nations and classes who sought rough justice through the assertion of interests led to their quick destruction if they were weak, and to their slower but no less certain destruction

[98] *Ibid.*
[98] *Ibid.*
[99] *Ibid.*, pp. 21-21a.
[101] *Ibid.*

92

if they were strong, for both the strong and weak are weak before the power that moves in creation." [102] The strategy of Jesus was one based on a faith and hope that did not evade but moved through judgment and death; "on a faith which did not deny the destructiveness of the cosmic God but included it." The social gospel in the mind of Jesus was built on this faith and hope. "And on it alone, we believe, the only adequate social gospel can be built." [103]

JESUS' FAITH AND NIEBUHR'S

At the beginning of this section I spoke of the development of Niebuhr's faith in a sovereign God, revealed in part by his expressions of it in 1930–33, as an overcoming of inhibitions. Positively I characterized the development we are observing as a movement toward a *Christian faith-integrity*. Both observations may have sounded a little pretentious at the beginning. I hope that after this thorough report on "The Social Gospel and the Mind of Jesus" what those statements intended to convey is clearer.

On the matter of overcoming inhibitions, I need hardly comment on the boldness of this paper. It expresses a dramatic reappraisal of the person and meaning of Jesus. It portrays with great power the character of the God in whom Jesus' radical faith centered. Niebuhr's audacity shows in his implicit identification of his own growing faith-consciousness with that of Jesus. For it is always clear that in expounding "the mind of Jesus" Niebuhr was also expounding the content of his own growing faith stance. It may be argued, rightly, that Niebuhr has transformed Jesus the hero of the moral ideal of liberalism into Jesus the hero of faith and faithful response. Christologically, though there is a continuity in the heroism and in the stress on the humanity of Jesus, it must be granted that a real transformation has occurred and that its major advance is in the new doctrine of God that correlates with it.

On the matter of *Christian faith-integrity* all three terms are

[102] *Ibid.*
[103] *Ibid.*

important. In this paper Niebuhr does not deny or omit his philosophical, historical, and sociological critical background, but there is
a real sense in which this paper represents a new kind of *post-critical*
development in his thinking.[104] The standpoint is unapologetically
Christian. Niebuhr identifies his stance explicitly with that of Jesus.
The case unabashedly rests on *faith*. Outside of faith—a relation
of trust in and loyalty to God—the "knowledge of God" that comes
to expression in this interpretation of the mind of Jesus can only be
viewed from what Niebuhr will call the standpoint of "external
history." [105] From that standpoint the "knowledge of God" can
only be the recovery of an archaic mythos, important as the formative myth of Western culture, but perhaps no longer capable of
sustaining contemporary personal or communal integrity. But from
the standpoint of "internal history," speaking out of an identification with and a dwelling in the faith of Jesus, it can become—as
it did for Niebuhr in this period—"the story of our lives."

From what has just been said it should be clear that I view this
unpublished article as a kind of culmination, a kind of completion,
in the developing shape of Niebuhr's belief in the sovereign God.
As I read and interpret his later writings I see no marked departure
from or augmentation of the *substance* of the faith-conceptualiza-
tion of the relation of God and dependent being that we have seen

[104] I am indebted to Michael Polanyi's *Personal Knowledge: Towards a
Post-Critical Philosophy* (Chicago: University of Chicago Press, 1958) for the
phrase "post-critical." As used in this context I mean it to characterize a willingness to radically rely upon one particular faith orientation, as expressed in a
set of particular, finite, relative symbols and concepts, while knowing of that
orientation's historical relativity and being existentially aware that there are
genuine alternatives to it. One accepts, elects, or identifies with by embracing a
faith orientation that is post-critically held. Erik Erikson suggests something
like the meaning I have in mind here when, in his discussion of "Ego Integrity," he writes: "Although aware of the relativity of all the various life
styles which have given meaning to human striving, the possessor of integrity is
ready to defend the dignity of his own life style against all physical and economic threats. . . . The style of integrity developed by his culture or civilization
thus becomes the 'patrimony of his soul,' the seal of his moral paternity of
himself." See *Childhood and Society*, 2d ed. (New York: W. W. Norton &
Co., 1962), p. 268.

[105] For Niebuhr's distinction between external and internal history see
Meaning of Revelation, chap. 2.

cumulatively emerging in and through the writings from 1930 to this 1933 statement on the faith of Jesus. To be sure, Niebuhr's clarification and articulation of this position in subsequent years show movement and growth. His development of the ethical implications of such faith-knowledge will lead him to differentiate and expand on elements in this vision in complex and elaborate fashion. Also he will give much attention to understanding the process by which one comes to faith in such a God. Yet it remains true to say, I believe, that with "The Social Gospel and the Mind of Jesus" all the basal elements in Niebuhr's mature theological-ethical position can be counted as implicitly present in his thought.[106]

[106] It will undoubtedly be asked: If "The Social Gospel" has the kind of significance suggested here, why did Niebuhr not choose to publish it? I have been able to find no clue on which to base a solid answer to this question. Because of its continuity with published writings before and after it, however, I have no reservations about ascribing to it the significance given it here. One can only conjecture that such a straight, undiluted expression of radical faith must have met with the same incapacity to comprehend and unwillingness to accept, when given in 1933, that it would encounter in a gathering of university theologians today. It does seem likely that Niebuhr recognized it as a new plateau in a process of reinterpretation of, and identification with, the faith of Jesus. Perhaps he sensed that nothing of lasting significance in it would be lost in his subsequent work. (Reference has already been made to the foreshadowings of themes in *Meaning of Revelation* and *Responsbile Self* in this paper. The statement on Christ in *Christ and Culture* (pp. 11-29) owes much to the interpretation of Jesus given here, as does Niebuhr's understanding of the sovereignty of God in its threefold meaning in the history of American Christianity as expressed in *Kingdom of God*. In his unpublished works on faith, Niebuhr's effort is to show how it is that a self can be enabled to make the transition from suspicion of and rebellion against God to trust in him and loyalty to his cause. There Jesus as the pioneer and perfector of faith—and as the mediator of faith—bears a close relation to this Jesus of "The Social Gospel."

Chapter III
Radical Faith

1. MAN, SIN, AND THE CHURCH IN BONDAGE

Niebuhr's key writings of the years 1934–37 show him employing and consolidating the theological position we have seen emerging in his writings from 1930 to 1933. In this chapter it is our purpose to show and discuss Niebuhr's transition from a theology of the primacy of God that serves a primarily *critical* function, to an interpretation of God's sovereignty as a *constructive* principle. To achieve this purpose it will be necessary (1) to describe Niebuhr's analysis of the bondage of the church to idolatrous culture faiths; (2) to attend to the first explicit development of his doctrine of man and of sin; (3) to trace the emergence of a new richness and dynamism in his articulation of the transforming process that marks men's responses to revelation; and (4) to suggest how his reinterpretation of the central theme in three hundred years of American Christianity is expressive of a certain kind of culmination in the development of his fundamental conviction and its theological-ethical expression. As a beginning let us look at Niebuhr's approach to reform of the church from the standpoint of radical faith in a sovereign God.

"The time called particularly for the reformation of the church, and I was among those for whom this was the special task. As a convinced Protestant (not an anti-Catholic) who saw the sovereignty of God usurped by the spirit of capitalism and of nationalism I felt strongly, that the times called for the rejection of 'Culture Protestantism' and for the return of the church to the confession of its own particular faith and ethos." [1] This is the way H. Richard Niebuhr, writing in 1960, characterized the perceptions and motivations that led him, with two co-authors, to write *The Church Against the World* (1935).[2] In this tract for the times Niebuhr applied his growing apprehension by faith in a sovereign God to the question of how the church might regain its integrity. In a sermon the previous year, Niebuhr had forcefully argued that the time was past when the church could ask, What must we do in order to achieve the ideal of a warless world? or, What must we do to increase human brotherliness and kindness? "Our question now," he wrote, "is not the question of builders of the kingdom of God on earth but the question of Cain. The blood, the pain, the misery of our brothers cries up to heaven against us. What must we do to atone for this brutal common life of ours?" [3] The question of the

[1] H. Richard Niebuhr in Fey, ed., *How My Mind Has Changed*, pp. 74-75.

[2] Niebuhr, Wilhelm Pauck, and Francis P. Miller, *The Church Against the World* (Chicago: Willett, Clark & Co., 1935). Niebuhr's contributions are entitled "The Question of the Church" and "Toward the Independence of the Church," pp. 1-13, 123-56. References to Niebuhr's text quoted here refer to the reprint of them found in Sydney Ahlstrom, ed., *Theology in America* (Indianapolis: Bobbs-Merrill, 1967), pp. 590-618.

[3] "What Then Must We Do?" *Christian Century Pulpit*, 5, no. 7 (July, 1934), pp. 145-47.

church has to be "What must we do to be saved?" Niebuhr states in *The Church Against the World*. This is not a selfish question, concerned with mere institutional survival—which is likely to continue in some form anyway. Rather it is "the question of a responsible self," [4] facing the seriousness of its trouble and earnestly desiring to be set right. Any society grounded in the conviction that to seek life is to lose it, as is the Christian church, has to be aware of the foolishness of any effort to preserve its life merely for the sake of living. "Like any Christian individual faced with death, the church then realizes that the important question is not how to save its life but rather how to keep its soul, how to face loss, impoverishment, and even death without surrendering its self, its work, and its service." [5]

The threat against the church, Niebuhr contends, is not that posed by its harsh critics from without, though a faithful church will know that God will use the opponents and critics of Christianity as instruments of his judgment.[6] Nor is the threat primarily that posed by a rapidly changing social order, rendering outmoded the teachings and ministry of a lethargic church.[7] The real threat against the church comes from its own overadaptation to the world —its too great success in keeping pace with and offering legitimating sanction for the patterns of economic and political interaction that perpetuate poverty, exploitation and imperialism. "The church has discovered that it belongs to the crucifiers rather than the crucified. . . . It knows that it has been on the side of the slayers rather than the slain." [8] Standing convicted of this sin the church is not at all certain it has found out how to resist similar temptations in the future.[9] But it is coming to understand the

---

[4] "Church Against the World" (Ahlstrom, ed.), p. 593. This is the first published use of the term "responsible self," which is the title given Niebuhr's posthumously published Robertson Lectures given at the University of Glasgow in 1960.

[5] *Ibid.*, p. 596.

[6] *Ibid.*, p. 592.

[7] *Ibid.*, pp. 596-97.

[8] *Ibid.*, pp. 594-95.

[9] *Ibid.*, p. 595.

judgment with which it is being judged and the threat by which it is threatened:

The "cracks in time" which now appear are fissures too deep for human contriving, and reveal a justice too profound to be the product of chance. The God who appears in this judgment of the world is neither the amiable parent of the soft faith we recently avowed nor the miracle worker of a superstitious supernaturalism; he is rather the eternal God, Creator, Judge and Redeemer, whom prophets and apostles heard and saw at work, casting down and raising up. He uses all things as his instruments, but resigns his sovereignty to none. Hence the fear of the church is not inspired by men but by the living God, and it directs its question not to the changing world with its self-appointed messiahs but to its sovereign Lord.[10]

To Niebuhr the times called for a strategic withdrawal by the church. In a remark that foreshadows the analysis of *Christ and Culture*, he observes that the relation of the church to civilization must of necessity be a varying one, "since each of these entities is continually changing and each is subject to corruption and to conversion. The history of the relationship is marked by periods of conflict, of alliance and of identification." [11] In his periodization of present history Niebuhr judges that the only prospect for a new permeation or conversion of civilization by Christianity lies in a withdrawal which can "save the church and restore to it the salt with which to savor society." The present generation's task, he writes, "appears to lie in the liberation of the church from its bond-

---

[10] *Ibid.*, pp. 597-98. As was indicated earlier, this writing is the first in which Niebuhr actually employs the term "sovereignty" and "sovereign Lord." That this is the case leads me to two observations: (1) The substance, the meaning, the faith commitment, and the conviction of what Niebuhr later referred to as "the sovereignty of God" preceded his use of that phrase to express it. This means that in speaking of Niebuhr as a theologian of the sovereignty of God, we have to let his richly evolved content fill that old phrase in its own distinct way rather than pressing his stance to fit our stereotyped understanding of it. This is why I devote so much attention to this seminal period in the development of Niebuhr's ground conviction. (2) That Niebuhr now and later describes "what is for me fundamental" with this phrase reflects a conscious identification with a historic line of march in Christian thought that dates, I judge, largely from 1934-37. Principal figures in that line include especially Edwards, Calvin, and Augustine. Niebuhr's own list of these figures, given retrospectively in "How My Mind Has Changed" (p. 74) includes Edwards, Pascal, Calvin, Thomas Aquinas, and Augustine.
[11] "Church Against the World," p. 598.

age to a corrupt civilization." Such a strategic withdrawal is not surrender and flight, but rather renewal and reorganization in preparation for a new aggression.[12]

When he turns to the task of characterizing the "corrupt civilization" and the nature of the church's bondage within it, Niebuhr adopts an approach that deserves some explanatory comment. Earlier we examined Niebuhr's interpretation of Troeltschian value theory, and his own employment of a similar approach in the ethical analysis and prescription at the conclusion of *Social Sources*. There we saw that Niebuhr concurred with Troeltsch in affirming that any adequate Christian ethic would move beyond Kantian formalism to deal seriously with the concretely real and obligating values created by and necessary for culture—religion, the state, economic life, art, science, etc. In *Social Sources* Niebuhr's concern for Christian unity grew in large measure out of his conviction that only the transcendent ideal of a unified Christianity could provide the necessary synthesizing principle for the threatened values of Western culture.[13]

In the writings of 1930–33, however, we can observe an eclipse in value language and conceptualization. The reason for this is clear. A primitive layer in Niebuhr's fresh grasp of the reality and primacy of God was the recognition of God's radical transcendence of every finite value. We have seen that Niebuhr never lopsidedly affirmed God's "otherness" or radical transcendence of mundane values as the sole or even dominant meaning of his primacy. Rather, as did Tillich, he sought to hold together the poles of God's radical transcendence and his presence in values and actions in history. But it was still imperative that any vestige of the kind of thinking that allowed for too smooth a continuum between values in history and culture and the divine being be excised. Therefore the stress in the materials of 1930-33 falls on the discontinuities between the reality of divine being and intent and the transient, abortive

---

[12] *Ibid.*, p. 599. This insistence that the withdrawal is a strategic one, *for the sake of a new aggression*, is often ignored by interpreters who want to emphasize the positive importance of Barth's influence on Niebuhr.

[13] See *Social Sources*, p. 268.

character of autonomous finite striving. The emphasis falls on God's being and doing and its revolutionary consequences in and for human history, rather than upon proximate realizations of divine reality and intent in the structures of human meaning and value.

Because of this eclipse in value language and conceptualization it is significant that in analyzing the bondage of the church to a corrupt culture in 1935, Niebuhr returns to a value analysis. As in *Social Sources*, he again finds the church involved in idolatrous attachments to cultural values, good in themselves, but pernicious and destructive when allowed to become the gods of cultural faiths —capitalism, nationalism, and anthropocentrism.[14] But whereas in 1929 he was struggling to discern or recover a supreme value-synthesizing ideal, in 1935 Niebuhr is perfectly clear about the One from whom all value and meaning proceed, and before whom all finite centers of value are relativized. This clarity enables him to diagnose with considerable precision the root cause of the disease of which idolatrous faiths and the misvaluing of goods are major symptoms.

SIN AS FALSE WORSHIP AND WRONG LOVE

In diagnosing the root infection of church and society, Niebuhr offers us his first explicit statement of his doctrine of man and of sin. It comes in a tightly argued paper, prepared and presented as part of a symposium on the Christian doctrine of man.[15] The doctrine of human sinfulness, Niebuhr contends, is as central in any Christian strategy of life as is the doctrine of class struggle in Marxian strategy.[16]

[14] "The essence of worldliness is neither civilization nor nature, but idolatry and lust. Idolatry is the worship of images instead of what they image; it is the worship of man, the image of God, or of man's works, images of the image of God. It appears wherever finite and relative things or powers are regarded as ends in themselves. . . . It is desire desiring itself, or desire stopping short of its true object, seeking satisfaction in that which is merely the symbol of the satisfactory" ("Church Against the World," pp. 599-600.)

[15] "Man the Sinner," *Journal of Religion*, 15 (1935), pp. 272-80.

[16] *Ibid.*, p. 272. Note the continuing reference to parallels between Communist theory and praxis and radical Christian thinking and living.

To believe in the Christian doctrine of sin means "that in dealing with ourselves and with our neighbors, with our societies and our neighbors' societies, we deal not with morally and rationally healthy beings who may be called upon to develop ideal personalities and to build ideal commonwealths but rather with diseased beings, who can do little or nothing that is worthwhile until they persist in acting as though they were healthy, succeed only in spreading abroad the infection of their lives." [17]

The believer in this Christian doctrine of sin will not be impressed by theories that recognize a moral elite over against certain other individuals or classes in whom it is supposed evil is concentrated. He will not be moved by the Romantic idea that men individually are good, but that evil resides in institutions. Nor will he adopt the evolutionary theory that regards evil as the result of cultural lag and immaturity. Each of these theories of evil has a corresponding strategy for overcoming it. But none of them appear sound or sufficient from the standpoint of the Christian account. Though it may seem that the Christian doctrine of sin is more pessimistic than these others, Niebuhr contends that on the contrary it is fundamentally more optimistic. This is because the Christian doctrine of sin presupposes the doctrine of creation—which "implies that man's fundamental nature, obscured and corrupted though it is, is perfect." Man's restoration to health "is not a far-off achievement . . . it is rather the underlying datum of life." [18] Perfection is the true potential of man, according to this view.

But perfection, as Niebuhr speaks of it here, is not to be construed narrowly as *moral* perfection. Nor is the doctrine of sin to be reduced to a purely moral category:

To say that man is a sinner is not equivalent to the statement that he is morally bad. Modern moralism has subordinated all other value categories to those of the morally good and the morally bad. It has regarded these as somehow final and not in need of further definition,

[17] *Ibid.*, pp. 272-73.
[18] *Ibid.*, p. 273.

while it has reduced the value categories of truth, beauty and holiness, of intellectual, aesthetic and religious evil to their moral "essence." [19]

This moralizing reductionism, especially characteristic in religion, issues in the conception of God's perfection in terms of moral perfection and in the conception of sin as moral guilt. This leads, Niebuhr points out, to the mistaken conception of sin as a "composite term made up of a moral core and secondary accretions," such as when it is construed as meaning "moral guilt plus emotional overtones due to the religious feelings." [20]

The major reason why it is mistakenly arbitrary to reduce the idea of sin to moral terms is that this overlooks the fact that moral judgments are relative judgments—that moral principles of rightness and wrongness are relative to the *standard* of morality presumed by them. That standard, Niebuhr contends, is prior to morality and its source is always religious:

It depends upon what man finds to be wholly worshipful, intrinsically valuable—in other words upon the nature of his god or gods. The "chief good" of man is not the object but the presupposition of his moral choices, and his possession of a chief good is the presupposition of all moral judgments which he or another passes upon him.[21]

[19] *Ibid.*, pp. 273-74.

[20] *Ibid.*, pp. 274-75.

[21] *Ibid.*, p. 275. These two sentences express the theological and psychological basis for Niebuhr's approach to ethics through the metaphors developed out of valuation—valuing and being valued. Note the explicit influences of Luther and Edwards here. Luther wrote: "A god is that to which we look for all good and where we resort in time of need; to have a god is simply to trust and believe in one with our whole heart. As I have often said, the confidence and faith of the heart alone makes both God and idol. If your faith and confidence are right, then likewise your God is the true God. On the other hand, if your confidence is false, if it is wrong, then you have not the true God. For the two, faith and God, have inevitable connection. Now, I say, whatever your heart clings to and confides in, that is really your God." (Quoted from the "Larger Catechism" in Hugh T. Kerr, ed., A *Compend of Luther's Theology*, Philadelphia: The Westminster Press, 1966, p. 23.) Niebuhr's use of the term "chief good" suggests Edwards' distinctions between "chief end" and "ultimate ends" in "Dissertation Concerning the End for which God Created the World" (*The Works of President Edwards in Eight Volumes*, Worcester, Mass.: Isaiah Thomas, June, 1809, vol. 6, pp. 9 ff.), and the implicit understanding of *will* here, which sees it as the *expression* of one's possession of (or by) a chief good or goods is Edwardsean.

This passage makes it clear why Niebuhr will brook no subordination of religion to morality. Not only *should* morality derive its standards from a more primal source which is always religious, it necessarily *does* have such a derivative character, and it is an aberration and an illusion to deal with morality as though it were the primary rather than the derivative datum.

If, therefore, sin is primarily a religious category, and if it only secondarily and derivatively refers to moral attitudes and behavior, then how is sin to be defined? Niebuhr points out that efforts to characterize sin as "creatureliness" or as selfishness and sensuality miss the mark. The counterpart of the majesty of God is not human sinfulness. Neither creatureliness nor the flesh nor the self is sinful per se. Only on the basis of faith in a God who is the supremely worthful One and who is the origin of all being and value is it possible to understand the Christian doctrine of sin. For, writes Niebuhr, "the religious concept of sin always involves the idea of *disloyalty*, not of disloyalty in general but of disloyalty to the true God, to the only trustworthy and wholly lovable reality. Sin is the failure to worship God as God." [22]

But failure to worship God is not merely the *absence* of loyalty to God. "It is not possible for men to be simply disloyal; they are always loyal to something. Disloyalty implies a false loyalty and disloyalty to God always includes something that is not God but which claims deity. Sin therefore is . . . wrong direction, false worship." [23] And this means that sin necessarily has the character of rebellion against God. "To make a god of the self, or of the class, or of the nation, or of the phallus, or of mankind, is to organize life around one of these centers and to draw it away from its true center; hence in a unified world, it is to wage war against God." [24]

---

[22] "Man the Sinner," pp. 276-77.

[23] *Ibid.*, p. 277. Whenever Niebuhr employs the term "loyalty" to express that part of faith that implies value commitment, we are led to recognize the important influence upon him of the writings of Josiah Royce, especially *The Philosophy of Loyalty* (New York: The Macmillan Co., 1908); and *The Sources of Religious Insight* (New York: Charles Scribner's Sons, 1912), esp. pt. 5.

[24] "Man the Sinner," p. 277. In this long paragraph, a composite of Niebuhr's formulations, we see spelled out in complete if preliminary form the

But how can sin be called rebellion against God if sinful man is not conscious of his disloyalty and if he does not consciously *will* it? To Niebuhr, this kind of question misses the point on two counts. First, Christianity is not primarily concerned with assessing blame and assigning guilt, but rather with understanding the true character of man's situation and its cure. And second, to equate sin with conscious choice to rebel, and say that therefore it is productive of moral guilt, is an interpretation that rests on a dubious doctrine of freedom. "The starting point of the doctrine of sin is not man's freedom but man's dependence; freedom accounts for the fact that man can be and is disloyal, [but] not for the fact that he ought to be loyal." [25] To misunderstand this is to fall into the mistaken belief that by the exercise of his "free will" man can overcome his disloyalty and rebellion and put aside his sin. To Niebuhr, who here clearly follows Jonathan Edwards, the idea that the human will is the source of all good and evil is a mistaken myth—itself an outgrowth of the sin that denies man's complete dependence upon God. Men are completely impotent to rescue themselves from false loyalties and their consequences:

The will is always committed or it is no will at all. It is either committed to God or to one of the gods. "The will is as its strongest motive is." Man cannot transfer his loyalty from one of the false gods to God by exercising his will, since that will is loyal to the false god. . . . So long as man is loyal to himself, or to his nation, or his class, or to his moral standard based upon a self-chosen highest good, his efforts to rescue himself will be determined by his loyalty. The consequence is that he involves himself more deeply in disloyalty to God.[26]

---

foundations for all the essays and lectures, covering a span of years from 1943 to 1957, which Niebuhr published in 1960 as *Radical Monotheism*. Also present, but largely unaddressed as yet, is the problem of the nature of faith as trust in and loyalty to God, on which Niebuhr wrote extensively in the forties and fifties. Much of his best material on faith has not yet been published (see chap. 5 below).

[25] "Man the Sinner," p. 277.

[26] *Ibid.*, p. 279. The quote within the quote is from Edwards' work *Freedom of the Will* and appears to be a composite construct, not identical to any, but expressive of all, the several formulations by Edwards in section 2 of pt. 1 of that treatise. In the Yale edition, ed. Paul Ramsey (Yale University Press, 1957), this section is on pages 141-48. Compare a similar statement by Niebuhr on the will in *Kingdom of God* pp. 102-3.

The consequences of sin as disloyalty to the One "Creator and . . . essence of Being," [27] are conflict and death—personal and societal. Not to cleave to the One is to be divided by conflicting loyalties to the many values that lay claim to ultimacy. "Idolatry leads inevitably to polytheism and polytheism is conflict." [28] Such conflict, if not superseded by loyalty to the genuine overarching source and center of value, eventually leads to death—the disintegration of selves, and the destruction of societies by strife. And while sin is not primarily to be understood as moral wrongness, it does issue in moral (or immoral) consequences: "The moral consequences of sin—man's inhumanity to man, cruelty to beasts, exploitation of nature, abuse of sex, greed, commercial profanation of creation and its beauty—these are no less patent." [29]

TOWARD RESTORATION AND RECONCILIATION OF MAN TO GOD

Our look at Niebuhr's analysis of the captivity of the church led us into his fresh account of the root cause of idolatry in men and communities—the enmity toward and alienation from God that is sin. Let us sum up what we saw there. Not "knowing," and therefore not trusting, the supreme source of all being and value, men become entrapped in parochial systems of meaning and value that center in proximate goods and proximate causes—valuable in themselves, but productive of personal and intercommunal conflicts when elevated to ultimate status and explicitly or implicitly ascribed deity. To speak of sinful man as "entrapped" in his idolatrous systems of meaning and value is a rather precise description. For the will, as a lever of change and extrication, is totally depen-

---

[27] "Man the Sinner," p. 277.
[28] *Ibid.*, p. 278. In "The Church Against the World" (p. 605) Niebuhr refers to the church's bondage to the amalgam of "faiths" centering in capitalism, nationalism, and anthropocentrism as "our modern polytheism."
[29] "Man the Sinner," p. 279. Note the concern for nonhuman being that comes to expression in this passage. This is one of several places where Niebuhr articulates an ecological loyalty to animal and inanimate being as a correlate of faith in God the creator and source of being and value. In "Value Theory and Theology" (*Nature of Religious Experience*, p. 109) Niebuhr expresses a similar concern: "Only in occasional instances are the values relative to animal life included in a system of values." See also *Kingdom of God*, pp. 116-17.

dent upon the fulcrum of the self's (or the community's) organizing commitments. The will can only serve its "gods." Transformation and liberation come when the heart and mind get drawn away from and beyond the old gods to loyalties that are wider in scope and less focused on the defense or security or aggrandizement of the self or the association.

According to Niebuhr's view, the kind of critical, prophetic inquiry that exposes the idolatrous attachments and parochial loyalties can play a part in the movement of men's minds and hearts toward the true ground and source of value. But most important in the process are those developments in history that either expose the transiency and insufficiency of the limited goods or, more dramatically, crush them in the meshing of movements and catastrophes that is the historical process.

In *Social Sources* Niebuhr had offered a critical, prophetic inquiry that exposed the extent to which the churches' divided wills were shaped by allegiances to partial goods. Missing from that trenchant analysis, however, was a vision of true godliness to which the loosened, idolatrous affections might be drawn. His experiences and writings of the next four years (1930–33) show that it is only in the experience of the failure and destruction of our false gods that the visage of true godliness may be apprehended. And then it is first as the destroyer, the slayer, and the enemy that we apprehend it. In a time when the practical "polytheism" of the cultural faiths still has life, despite the threats to them, the theologian of the sovereignty of God works at a "theoria of God the enemy," pointing to the source, character, and meaning of the "judgment" that is in process. Such a theoria of God the enemy is the main thrust in Niebuhr's writings up to and including *The Church Against the World* and "Man the Sinner."

But there is a subtheme steadily growing in strength in these years, that gets called to the fore as a result of Niebuhr's new grasp on the meaning of sin and the character of the will's bondage. It points to the necessity, if redemption from sin is to occur, of a reconciliation with true godliness that works a transformation in the mind and heart, and in the commitment that anchors will.

In "Man the Sinner" Niebuhr merely touches on this subtheme: "Redemption from sin is possible only by a reconciliation to God, which cannot be initiated by the disloyal creature." [30] In that article, instead of elaborating on the process and agent of reconciliation, he concludes with a statement of the necessity, due to the reality and pervasiveness of sin, for restraint of evil in any responsible Christian strategy.[31]

But in *The Church Against the World* he speaks of the necessity and process of reconciliation with a clarity that links the theoria of God the enemy with what has been a more muted theme—a theoria of God the redeemer and reconciler. In order for the church to revolt successfully against its cultural bondage and its patterns of sin it must return to loyalty to God. "There is no flight out of the captivity of the church save into the captivity of God." To be sure, reestablishment in that loyalty is not possible by the church's own initiative. Yet, "through the destruction of our idols and the relentless pursuit of our self-confidence God is driving us, in the church and in the world, to the last stand where we must recognize our dependence upon him or, in vainglorious rebellion, suffer demoralization and dissolution." [32] In its drivenness the church must soon make that "last appeal beyond all finite

[30] "Man the Sinner," p. 279.

[31] *Ibid.*, pp. 279-80. In a paragraph that suggests a turn from Niebuhr's earlier nonresistant pacifism—a turn which is part of his transition from critical to constructive Protestantism—he gives the characteristics of a Christian restraint of evil: (1) Christian restraint knows itself to be the restraint *of* sinners *by* sinners. The restrainers know that their perception of the moral law is dim at best, and that they are linked to the restrained in an "equality of sinfulness." (2) Christian restraint will avoid the temptation to destructive moralism. It is medicinal rather than vindictive; if it must use force it will use it to conserve, for it knows "that force cannot redeem but only prevent some external consequences of sin." (3) A Christian strategy of restraint will be wholly subordinated to the strategy of reconciliation. "The doctrine of sin is meaningful only as it presupposes the doctrine of creation and furnishes the presupposition of the doctrine of redemption." (In his class lectures on Christian ethics Niebuhr regularly dealt with the acceptance of restraint by others and the exercise of restraint on others under the rubric "Response to the *Governing Action* of God." See chap. 4 below.)

[32] "Church Against the World," pp. 615-16.

109

principalities and powers . . . an appeal to the right of God." Such
an appeal to the right of God, says Niebuhr,

> means an appeal to the right of Jesus Christ. It is an appeal not only
> to the grim reality of the slayer who judges and destroys the self-
> aggrandizing classes and nations and men. Such an appeal would be
> impossible and such a loyalty out of the question were not men per-
> suaded that this reality, whose ways are again evident in historic pro-
> cesses, is a redeeming and saving reality, and did they not come to some
> understanding of the manner in which he accomplishes salvation. But
> such persuasion and such revelation are available only through the event
> called Jesus Christ. . . . When this memory of Jesus Christ, the
> crucified, comes fully alive it will not come as a traditional formula or
> symbol, reminding men only of the past, but as the recollection of a
> most decisive fact in the present situation of men.[33]

So far but no farther does Niebuhr take us toward an encounter
with the one in whom the persuasion and revelation requisite for
reconciliation are available. He ends his appeal for the independence of the church with a memorable testimony to the importance
of theology as a "theory of the Christian revolution," [34] and with
the counsel that while the church must be independent and aggressive in faithfulness to "the divine determinism," it must also
follow a dual strategy of alert and responsible participation in an
unrevolutionized world.[35]

Having attained considerable clarity about the character and
modes of judgment of "God the enemy," Niebuhr, through his
process of growth and his sensitivity to the needs of a demoralized
church and society, was presented with the problem of understanding and communicating how God the slayer is also God the re-

---

[33] *Ibid.*

[34] *Ibid.*, p. 617. Niebuhr continues to see the strategy of the church as
paralleling Communist revolutionary strategy. On the necessity for solid
theological theory he writes, "The revolters in the church . . . have learned
from the communists that years spent in libraries and in study are not necessarily wasted years but that years of activity without knowledge are lost years
indeed."

[35] *Ibid.*, pp. 617-18. He says of the church: "It is a revolutionary community in a pre-revolutionary society. Its main task always remains that of understanding, proclaiming and preparing for the divine revolution in human life.
Nevertheless, there remains the necessity of participation in the affairs of an
unconverted and unreborn world."

deemer and restorer. His adaptation of an Edwardsean doctrine of will made it clear with new vividness that judgment and destruction represents only half of the divine revolution. The other half must be constructive. It must be a response of the self or the community, bereft of its idols, to a new vision of the beauty, power, love, and comprehensive oneness of the source and ground of all being and value. For this constructive revolution there must be mediation and revelation. It should not be a matter of surprise, then, that in Niebuhr's classic study of the history of the idea of the kingdom of God in American Christianity and culture, the major advances in his own thought seem to come in relation to the centrality of revelation for any constructive strategy grounded in faith in the sovereign God.

2. THEOLOGY AS HISTORY

In order to see the culmination of the development of Niebuhr's thinking in the years 1930–35 we look not to a treatise in systematic theology, but to a book that is ostensibly a historical study. Given as lectures in 1936 and 1937, the chapters that became *The Kingdom of God in America*, Niebuhr tells us, grew out of his teaching classes and seminars at Yale on "The Ethical Ideal of American Christianity." [36] In Niebuhr's eyes this book was a sequel to and corrective for his earlier book *The Social Sources of Denominationalism*. Speaking of the letter volume, with its account of the influences of social factors on faith, Niebuhr expressed dissatisfaction with it for several reasons:

Though the sociological approach helped to explain why the religious stream flowed in these particular channels it did not account for the force of the stream itself; while it seemed relevant enough to the institutionalized churches it did not explain the Christian movement which produced these churches; while it accounted for the diversity in American religion it did not explain the unity which our faith possesses despite its variety; while it could deal with the religion which was dependent on culture it left unexplained the faith which is

[36] *Kingdom of God*, p. xvii.

111

independent, which is aggressive rather than passive and which molds culture instead of being molded by it.[37]

So it is the faith basis of American Christianity, its undergirding dynamism and formative power, that Niebuhr set out to discern and explicate in this second book.

Only the reader who has attended with some care to Niebuhr's writings between *Social Sources* and *The Kingdom of God in America* can know how much significance to give the following statement in Niebuhr's preface: "This may seem to be an effort to present theology in the guise of history, yet the theology has grown out of the history as much as the history has grown out of the theology." [38] This may be read in at least three ways. We may simply accept the implication of the author that this inquiry is a scholarly investigation having as its aim the identification and clarification of the central theme, with its variations, of American Christianity. In that context Niebuhr's statement may be understood simply as a claim to objectivity for the treatment.

In a second sense, however, the claim that "the theology has grown out of the history as much as the history has grown out of the theology" is a powerful expression of Niebuhr's conviction that history—not as account but as *process*—is the *real*-ization of the rule of God. So he writes, "The history of the idea of the Kingdom of God leads on to the history of the kingdom of God." [39] To Niebuhr, American theology, at its best, arose out of discernment of God's active presence in that history, and, as faithful response to it, became a dialectical force in the process of the kingdom.

But there is also a third interpretation, which comprehends and includes both the others while going beyond them. To me, a sensitive reading of Niebuhr's 1930–35 writings makes this third interpretation unavoidable. When one has read those writings one

[37] *Ibid.*, pp. ix-x.
[38] *Ibid.*, p. xiii.
[39] *Ibid.*, p. xvi.

can see how much Niebuhr's incisive reinterpretation of the theological armature of American Christianity owes to the core of conviction winding in his own mind and heart during these years. Except in the veiled hint given in the statement we are discussing, Niebuhr nowhere suggests the degree to which his own personal history, with its experience of the kingdom, provided the hermeneutical lenses which brought the core faith of American Christianity into such vivid focus.[40]

In subsequent years Niebuhr comes to speak of all faith and all knowing as having a triadic structure.[41] Here, in his own relation both to the faith of American Christianity in a sovereign God and to that God, we have a beautiful illustration of the triadic structure of faith-knowing. Though it grossly oversimplifies, the accompanying diagram and its explanation show the relations I am suggesting in this third interpretation:

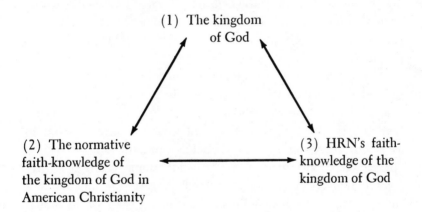

(1) The kingdom of God

(2) The normative faith-knowledge of the kingdom of God in American Christianity

(3) HRN's faith-knowledge of the kingdom of God

[40] In his explanation for why he decided to try to interpret American Christianity with the idea of the kingdom of God Niebuhr attributes the suggestion to "recent European writers," and to the examples of K. G. Kirk's interpretation of Catholic ethics under the rubric of *The Vision of God*, and James Truslow Adams' interpretation of United States history with the idea of the "American Dream." *Ibid.*, pp. x-xi.

[41] See "The Triad of Faith," *Andover Newton Bulletin*, 47 (1954), pp. 3-12; *Christ and Culture*, pp. 249-56; *Responsible Self*, chap. 2; "On the Nature of Faith," in Sidney Hook, ed., *Religious Experience and Truth* (New York: New York University Press, 1961), pp. 98-100.

The reciprocal movement between (3) and (1), some of the documentation of which we have examined in Niebuhr's writings from 1930 to 1935, created in (3) a sensitivity to and congruence with content in (2) that had in large measure been lost. In the recovery of that lost content of (2) with its meaning and power, the grasp of (3) on (1) was deepened and confirmed. Reciprocally, (3) was drawn to heightened identification with (2), and through giving an explication of the contents and meaning of (2), (3) itself came into clearer focus and expression.[42]

In the previous paragraph I have tried to show how Niebuhr's statement that "the theology has grown out of the history as much as the history has grown out of the theology" also refers to Niebuhr's personal history and his personal theological development. This means that in all three of the senses I have suggested *The Kingdom of God in America* may properly be termed "an effort to present theology in the guise of history." The fact that the book's content grows out of this remarkable confluence of personal experience and its central principle doubtless helps account for its greatness.

My insistence on the importance of Niebuhr's own new theological and faith stance for his resonance with the core meaning of American Christianity is not intended to detract from his claim that as a historian he is dealing with what is "there." I want to avoid any suggestion that in Niebuhr's interpretation we have a "projection" rather than an extrapolation from reliable data. My point is that Niebuhr's emerging theology gave him unique sensitivities to the internal impulse and meaning of the faith he sought to interpret, and that his interpretation also involved an expression and clarification of his own position.

---

[42] The actual development I have abstractly and somewhat crudely depicted here is further complicated by the fact that the growing apprehension by (3) of (1) that began the cycle was in significant measure formed and nurtured by (2) as well as by traditions and sources in quite the other faith-knowledge triads to which Niebuhr belonged. The identification that happened for Niebuhr between (3) and (2) also reflects the fact that back of (3) and (2) is a long line of common root sources.

RADICAL FAITH

How did Niebuhr himself understand the relation between the "theological history" that is *The Kingdom of God in America* and his own theology? I cannot answer this question conclusively. His introduction deals with methodological questions, gives notice of his intent in writing the book, and astutely anticipates and blunts the objections from the then powerful school of thought that viewed religion and ideas generally as mere epiphenomena of economic and social class relations.[43] Niebuhr's intention of taking seriously those elements in the religious history of America that resist reduction to epiphenomenal status is couched in terms of the demands of a Diltheyan *verstehende* historiography. "Every movement, like every person," he writes,

needs to be understood before it can be criticized. And no movement can be understood until its presuppositions, the fundamental faith upon which it rests, have been at least provisionally adopted. The presuppositions may not be our own; we may find good reason for rejecting them in favor of others; but we cannot understand without occupying a standpoint, and there is no greater barrier to understanding than the assumption that the standpoint which we happen to occupy is a universal one, while that of the object of our criticism is relative.[44]

The advantages of his taking this approach and stating it clearly at the outset are immediately obvious. Niebuhr does not have to play the critical game of interspersing exposition and criticism, subjecting every element of the world views under study to scrutiny from an extraneous standpoint. But more important and more strategically significant is the fact that he can insist on attending to the integrity of the views of reality and power, as well as of the self-understanding, expressed by representatives of the tradition he is studying. Without himself seeming to become an apologist he

[43] *Kingdom of God*, pp. 4-9. In the course of this argument he gives a very convincing case *for* the reductionist interpretation of religious ideas and institutions. His statement of the functions religion has served in American society is particularly acute. He grants, as only the author of a study like *Social Sources* could do, that the social determinist argument "is so clearly the true interpretation of so much that happens in religion that the student is ill at ease in seeking to exempt from its scope any part of faith" (p. 6).
[44] *Kingdom of God*, p. 13.

115

can (and must) provide the best apology for a theology of the kingdom of God that it could have—a firm, empathetic, and artistically powerful portrayal of its content and rationale. So he can say, not in his role as a loyalist to the kingdom of God, but as a loyalist to the historiography of understanding:

We make an arbitrary choice when we substitute the dogma of economic determinism or of human self-determinism for the dogma of divine determinism. Moreover it is a choice which bars us from understanding the thought of the divine determinists and which denies from the beginning the validity of their interpretation of themselves and their world. This-worldliness may seem more objective than other-worldliness to those who have never faced their own presuppositions. When they do face them they become aware that their ultimate dogma is at least as much a matter of faith as is the dogma of the other-worldly man.[45]

Furthermore he can write a literary masterpiece that powerfully expresses his own faith position even as it offers a determinative interpretation of American Christianity, and can achieve both things without having to appear in the book as an advocate for either. To me there is little doubt that Niebuhr followed a consciously evolved strategy in taking this approach. That he apparently did so indicates, I think, an awareness that his audience is a much wider one than just churchmen. He is writing also for the despisers of religion, all of whom are "cultured" to some degree by the core of faith that is the subject matter of the book.

This strategy of *The Kingdom of God in America* reflects a transition in Niebuhr's focus of attention from the predominantly *critical* development of the implications of radical faith in God's sovereignty, to a concern with the *constructive, formative* resources of that faith. It also represents a transition, I believe, from the emphasis, in *The Church Against the World*, on the disengagement, independence, and renewal of the *church*, to an engagement with the problems of renewing and reforming an American *society*, the original intentionality of which, Niebuhr now sees, has much in common with the revolutionary faith of the church. Important

[45] *Ibid.*, pp. 13-14.

in both aspects of this transition is Niebuhr's growing confidence in the conviction that national history is, no less than churchly history, part of and subject to the kingdom of God.[46]

The Kingdom of God in America is so richly compact and speaks for itself so eloquently that here I shall only indicate the ways in which Niebuhr's account seems to consolidate and extend his own theology of the sovereignty of God. This will mean following his effort to explicate the constructive thrust of radical faith in the kingdom of God. It will also mean attending to his fresh apprehension of the process of transformation that ensues from the encounter of suspicious, mistrustful persons with the persuasive mediator of faith, Jesus the Christ. Pursuing such a course should enable us to begin to draw together the multiple dimensions of what "the conviction of the sovereignty of God" has come, by 1937, to mean to Niebuhr. By the end of this chapter it will be possible in relatively brief space to sort out the rootage, in Niebuhr's fundamental theological principle, of the three major normative approaches in his theological ethics.

THE PROBLEM OF CONSTRUCTIVE PROTESTANTISM

I find it significant, in light of the unfolding pattern of Niebuhr's thought from 1930 to 1935, that the first chapter of *The Kingdom of God in America* centers on what Niebuhr calls "The Problem

[46] It may not be going too far to suggest that in *Kingdom of God*, Niebuhr wrote, as Robert Bellah did on a more modest scale thirty years later in his article "Civil Religion in America," a normative theology of American Civil Religion (in Donald R. Cutler, ed., *The Religious Situation*, 1968, Boston: Beacon Press, 1968, pp. 331-56). In doing so Niebuhr frequently seems to write about American society as though it had churchly norms, obligations, and functions. Recall Niebuhr's articles of the early twenties, where we noted a tendency not to differentiate clearly between church and society. In the twenties articles, however, the tendency to conflate church and society grew out of a supposed congruence of ends and values that was a characteristic of liberalism. In 1937 it grows out of the conviction of a unity in reality and history due to the comprehension of both church and society in the sovereignty of God. Structurally the positions are much the same. Dynamically, the mature position encompasses tragedy, conflict, and apparent disunity in a way the earlier tendency did not, and it sees the relation between cultural values and the valuing of God as a *tension* in which the former are being judged and transformed.

117

of Constructive Protestantism." [47] Having grasped so clearly the critical, prophetic side of what he will later call "radical monotheism," Niebuhr, working in the midst of a society sundered with conflict and threatened again with war, recognizes with equal clarity that something more than protest is needed. Following biblical precedent, and the precedent of the Christian community in other perplexing times, he turns to the past to interrogate it for insight and guidance.[48] Since he is (in his own terms) a "convinced Protestant," [49] for Niebuhr the most immediately relevant past begins with the struggle of the earliest Protestant movements to find practical patterns of personal, social, and institutional life in which to incarnate the heart of Protestant Christian faith—"its fresh insistence on the present sovereignty and initiative of God." [50]

The Protestant movements set great currents of liberation and individualization in motion. "Insofar as Protestantism was a movement of protest," Niebuhr writes,

its principle of the kingdom of God was very effective. In the name of the kingdom it would challenge the absolute claims of every relative power. . . . The institutional church was required to give way to the living word of God, conceived . . . in a prophetic sense. In the light of the coming judgment the relativity and temporality of the feudal-hierarchial order were revealed. . . . The pall which hung over the world, the sense of the indefinite continuation of present goods and

[47] Six years earlier, in a book which Niebuhr read and learned from (*Die Religiöse Verwicklichung*, 1930), Tillich considered the problem of "The Formative Power of Protestantism." In abstract terms he stated the problem of constructive Protestantism with great clarity: "Formative power is the power of creating a form; Protestantism is the attitude of protest against form. How can they be united? . . . We raise the question as to how formative power and protest against form can live together in a church, how form and protest against form can create a new, over-arching form." (See Tillich's *Protestant Era*, p. 206.)

[48] "Christians of the twentieth century," he wrote, "are like the biblical Israelites who needed to remind themselves in every period of crisis of their deliverance from Egypt, of their wanderings in the desert and their ancient covenant with Jehovah, not only that they might have consolation but even more that they might find direction" (*Kingdom of God*, p. 1).

[49] *How My Mind Has Changed*, p. 75. See also *Kingdom of God*, pp. 27-28 n.

[50] *Kingdom of God*, p. 17.

118

evils among which men needed to prepare themselves for a remote heaven, was lifted. . . . Protestantism furnished a revolutionary philosophy to the new forces which were stirring in the political, economic and racial world.[51]

In those liberations from tradition, authority, and old patterns of social and economic relations that were fructified by the Protestant movement, it was inevitable, Niebuhr observes, that some anarchial tendencies should emerge. Likewise it was inevitable that the vacuum of economic and social control should draw into itself individuals bent on establishing new absolutisms. Protestantism faced the problem of developing and gaining the adherence of individuals, societies, and states to a new discipline in place of the old. In this, Niebuhr points out, the Protestant revolution faced no unique problem. Every revolutionary movement opens the way for turmoil and anarchic conflict in the wake of the old order's passing. If its leadership has a sufficient will to power, a clear enough sense of direction, and the requisite force and ruthlessness to impose it, order can be reestablished on the new basis. But just here Niebuhr exposes the nerve of the dilemma of Protestantism as a constructive movement:

It had no will to power and in view of its positive principle could have none, for supreme power belonged only to God and evil resulted from every human arrogation of his dominion; it had no definite idea of the end toward which it was travelling and could have none, since the future lay with the free God; and it could not be ruthless since it had the inhibiting commandments of the gospel ever before it.[52]

In the sphere of morality and the faithful structuring of everyday lay life, the Protestant ethics of perfection in faith and love offered none of the casuistic comprehensiveness and particularity possessed by the ethical teachings of medieval Catholicism. In politics and economics the negative principle that all authority is subject to the will of God could readily be applied, but Protestantism found it difficult to say with specificity how the will of God intended

[51] *Ibid.*, pp. 28-29.
[52] *Ibid.*, p. 30.

119

commerce and industry to be reorganized. Especially in the church the dilemma of a community that must renounce its power in acknowledgment of the sovereignty of God became plain. Simply to say, "Let the Word of God rule the church" solves very little. Who shall interpret that word, and how? How shall it be applied and enforced? [53]

In his exposition of these various aspects of the Protestant dilemma Niebuhr's setting of the problem is not of merely historical interest for him. In his more hopeful moments he sees parallels between that emergence of radical faith in God's sovereignty that erupted in the Reformation and the present signs of God's revolutionary winnowing and renewal of the church in the period of this writing. Even when he is pessimistic about the likelihood of a new permeation of the culture by faith in the sovereign God, he is still clear that radical faith calls for formation of total life in the church—personal and communal—in accordance with the valuing and will of God. The dilemma of constructive Protestantism is personally and existentially real for Niebuhr.

AMERICAN PROTESTANTISM AGAINST ITS EUROPEAN BACKGROUND

As necessary background for looking at America as "an experiment in constructive Protestantism" [54] Niebuhr devotes a brief section to the three major variant strategies of the early European Protestant movement. In his characterizations of the Lutheran, Calvinist, and sectarian Protestant developments, and their strengths or liabilities as constructive viewpoints, his analysis largely parallels that of Troeltsch, whom he cites.[55] The Lutheran strategy, centering in faithfulness to the sovereignty of God "as exercised by his Word over the spirit of man," tended to see the civil law and

[53] *Ibid.*, pp. 31-34.

[54] "Whatever else this America came to be, it was also an experiment in constructive Protestantism." *Ibid.*, p. 43.

[55] See Ernst Troeltsch, *The Social Teaching of the Christian Churches,* trans. Olive Wyon (Torchbooks; New York: Harper & Brothers, 1960). (Originally published in German in 1911 and in English in 1931). On Luther and Lutheranism see vol. 2, pp. 461-575; on Calvinism, vol. 2, pp. 576-655; on what Niebuhr calls "separatism" see vol. 2, pp. 656-729.

existing political and economic orders as divinely ordained. To Luther, Niebuhr wrote, "only God can rule the spirit of man and only the spirit is really important." Hence, he concludes, "the Protestantism which stems from Luther has continued to concentrate its energies upon maintaining the freedom of the Word and has been inclined to yield to political and economic forces in what seem to be purely temporal matters." [56]

Niebuhr's brief look at "separatism in all its varieties" maintains the same ostensive descriptive (as contrasted to evaluative) stance he assumed in his analysis of Lutheran ethics. But, as in the account of the Lutheran position, it is clear that as a constructive principle separatism, in Niebuhr's eyes, has little to recommend it. Like Lutheranism and Calvinism, separatism "believed that only God had the right to absolute sovereignty and that man was ultimately responsible to him alone." [57] But if Lutheran dualism allowed for too complacent a compromise with the conditions of the political, economic, and social status quo, the separatists with their heightened consciousness of the imminently coming kingdom, their withdrawing concern for purity, or their occasionally violent revolutionary effort to supplant the old order with the direct rule of Christ, evaded all compromise and therefore all social responsibility.[58]

Niebuhr's look at the constructive tendencies of Calvinism is, like that of Troeltsch, more favorable. Calvin's realism about the

---

[56] *Kingdom of God*, p. 38.

[57] *Ibid.*, p. 41.

[58] On the whole, in this brief summary Niebuhr seems to follow Troeltsch's tendency to see the separatist revolutionaries as spiritualists who were bound by none of the restraints on "enthusiasm" that controlled Lutherans and Calvinists. Troeltsch counts the revolutionaries among the mystics and sees in them a dangerous tendency toward erratic behavior, untempered by anchors in scriptural and churchly authority. Sociologically and constructively they have little positive significance. (See Troeltsch, *Social Teaching of the Christian Churches*, pp. 741-45.) Niebuhr consistently expresses disfavor with the separatist strategy because in its withdrawing tendencies it implicitly denies the actual, present sovereignty of God in every sphere of life and history; and in its revolutionary impulses it presumes to be the vindicator or establisher of the divine kingdom, a stance plainly ruled out by radical faith in a sovereign God. (See "The Social Gospel," pp. 21-21a.)

necessity for restraint of evil and for limitations on the power of all human agencies, coupled with his recognition that restraint is not a positive step toward the attainment of the good, laid a basis for a theological ethic with formative power for all life under the sovereignty of God.[59] From this realism, grounded in the conviction of God's sovereignty, there stemmed two other constructive principles: (1) a *constitutionalism* that sees church and state as equally subject to the will of God declared in Scripture and nature, and as separated in function but bound in common loyalty to the kingdom of God; and (2) a *universalism* that comprehends all of life and history under the predestinating will of God. Because only God predestines his creatures, the Calvinists refused to exclude any part of human life as outside the hope of redemption.[60] "Lutheranism," Niebuhr writes in conclusion, "shared these ideas [with Calvinism] in principle but in practice tended to give up the area of 'natural things' as beyond the scope of the Word; separatism tried to withdraw from the established social life; but Calvinism insisted with the thoroughness of the Hebrew Prophets that God was king over every creature." [61]

This grasp of the kingship of God, interpreted dominantly in accordance with the Calvinistic constructive principles, Niebuhr sees as the theological faith basis of the American experiment in constructive Protestantism. As he studied its formative effects in the history of American Christianity he found it necessary to distinguish in it three major themes, each of which, while inextricably bound to the others, successively subordinated the other two. One of his own summaries of the thesis puts it best:

The Christian faith in the kingdom of God is a threefold thing. Its first element is confidence in the divine sovereignty which, however hidden, is still the reality behind and in all realities. A second element is the conviction that in Jesus Christ the hidden kingdom was not only revealed in a convincing fashion but also began a special and new

[59] Note the parallels with Niebuhr's own position in "Man the Sinner," pp. 279-80.

[60] *Kingdom of God*, p. 39.

[61] *Ibid.*, p. 40.

career among men, who had rebelled against the true law of their nature. The third element is the direction of life to the coming kingdom in power or to the redemption of the self-sufficient world.[62]

The first theme—that of the sovereignty of God—dominates in classical American Puritanism. The kingdom of Christ theme came to the fore in the Great Awakening movements of the eighteenth century, with their vivid recovery of the revolutionary power of Jesus Christ to reconcile persons with the God who is both judge and redeemer. The theme of the coming kingdom, present in each of the other periods, emerged to primacy in the nineteenth century's welter of religious and social efforts to press into the kingdom of Christ, making it real in the present. Each of these is a variant expression of the core faith in the kingdom of God. Each was present and essential, though muted, in the periods dominated by the others.

FAITH IN THE SOVEREIGNTY OF GOD

In Niebuhr's exposition of the early Puritans' faith in the sovereignty of God, it is the God of Jesus' faith in "The Social Gospel and the Mind of Jesus" that we meet.[63] Their faith in the kingdom of God was a faith in the "living reality of God's present rule, not only in human spirits but also in the world of nature and human history." [64] Their God was not a composite projection of human ideals, but rather "that last being which crowns with destruction the life which proceeds from it." [65] They were not and could not be utopian, "for they did not share the fundamental presuppositions of utopianism—the beliefs that human ills are due to bad institutions, that a fresh start with good institutions will result in a perfect commonwealth, and that human reason is sufficiently wise, or human will sufficiently selfless, to make the erec-

[62] *Ibid.*, p. 88.
[63] It is also the God of "The Grace of Doing Nothing," "A Communication: The Only Way into the Kingdom of God," and "What Then Must We Do?"
[64] *Kingdom of God*, p. 51.
[65] *Ibid.*

tion of a perfect society possible." [66] The Puritans' kingdom of God "was not something to be built or to be established nor something that came into the world from without, it was rather the rule which, having been established from eternity, needed to be obeyed despite the rebellion against it which flourished in the world." [67] Loyalty to this kingdom as a positive commitment was what made of these men (whose ranks also included Quakers and Baptists) nonconformists, dissenters, protesters, and independents. In this central positive allegiance, despite variations and conflict over subsidiary themes, they were all united. From this common loyalty, Niebuhr contends, flowed three constructive corollaries of the sovereignty of God to which, in varying modes and degrees, they all subscribed: Christian constitutionalism, the independence of the church, and the limitation or relativization of human sovereignty.[68]

In his development of these three corollaries Niebuhr weaves new emphases in with echoes of themes already touched on in the writings from 1930 to 1935 that we have examined. Under "Christian constitutionalism" he discusses the authority of Scripture—as the history and medium of revelation—for the early Protestants. He stresses the polar character of their life between God's self-revelation in Jesus Christ and the active, present initiative of God as governor and as enlivening Holy Spirit. For Puritans and Quakers the principle of Christian constitutionalism was "the principle . . . that the revelation of God in Christ was the test which needed to be applied in every case to the answers reason or spiritual experience gave to the question, what is the will of the sovereign Lord for men in this present situation?" Niebuhr concludes the discussion of Christian constitutionalism with a reference to the interrelationship of this idea with its secular counterpart, political constitutionalism.[69]

[66] *Ibid.*, p. 49. Compare Niebuhr's "Man the Sinner," pp. 272-73.

[67] *Kingdom of God*, p. 56.

[68] *Ibid.*, p. 58.

[69] *Ibid.*, pp. 65-66. Here Niebuhr disagrees with interpretations that see the former as dependent on the latter. He sees a real mutuality of influence. This

When Niebuhr turns to the corollary of the "independence of the church," themes made familiar in *The Church Against the World* emerge. Positively stated, this corollary is "the principle of the dependence of the church on God's kingdom." [70] The essence of the church is its conscious dependence upon and loyalty to the kingdom of God: "For what is the church save the assembly of people before God, or the movement of those who, abandoning all relative and finite goals turn toward the infinite end of life?" [71] The church lives with a dual strategy of service in and to the world, but this is coupled and in tension with an independence of (literally a refusal to depend upon) everything less than God.[72] On the corollary of the "limitation of power" Niebuhr stresses its rootage in theocratic rather than democratic ideas. God's will and law are supreme. All finite authority is subject to divine authority; therefore human individuals and institutions must have their proclivity to usurp sovereign authority firmly limited. This principle of limitation applied to every finite reality and not just the state. It led then to the principle of the separation of church and state.[73] Finally, God's kingship limits conscience—which is not in itself an

---

brief allusion forecasts a major strain in Niebuhr's later writings in which the idea of constitutionalism is traced to its rootage in the idea of covenant. This development shows that for Niebuhr constitutionalism refers not only to the regulative function of scriptural revelation (as is the main stress in *Kingdom of God*), but more importantly to the convenantal structure of reality and of God's relation to his creatures. See "The Idea of Covenant and American Democracy," *Church History*, 23, no. 2 (1954), and "The Protestant Movement and Democracy," in J. W. Smith and A. L. Jamison, eds., *The shaping of American Religion* (Princeton: Princeton University Press, 1961).

[70] *Kingdom of God*, p. 66.
[71] *Ibid.*, p. 67.
[72] *Ibid.*, pp. 69, 72-75.
[73] *Ibid.*, pp. 80-82. This theme too forecasts a number of papers and lectures in Niebuhr's later writings. Among these is a lecture manuscript, typed, entitled "The Limitation of Power and Religious Liberty." (A note at the end identifies this 16-page lecture as "Address given at the Institute of Human Relations at Williamstown, Mass., August 27, 1939." He adds in pencil, "Some of this published in *The Protestant* without my consent.") Also in continuity with this theme is another unpublished lecture, 30 pp., handwritten with an outline preceding it, entitled "The Idea of Original Sin in American Culture." (Notations on the first page read, "Princeton University—Program of Studies in American Civilization. February 24, 1949.") In many ways this is an extension and application of the position developed in "Man the Sinner."

125

absolute but is shaped by apprehension of the kingdom. "Not conscience but the reality which conscience apprehended was absolute." [74] With these three principles, then, Niebuhr characterized the constructive norms and implications for society, the state, the church, and the individual conscience, of the conviction of the sovereignty of God. By employing rather extensive documentation I have tried to suggest how these formulations are in continuity with developments of his own position in both earlier and later writings.

We noted in the discussion of "Christian constitutionalism" Niebuhr's frontal attention to the centrality of revelation. In his chapter on the second great variation of the theme of the kingdom of God, "The Kingdom of Christ," the focus on revelation both deepens and widens toward an explication of the transforming power and revolutionary process of change that true revelation works in persons and groups. It is in this chapter that the influence of the great Evangelicals, especially Jonathan Edwards, becomes apparent.[75] And it is in this chapter, in my judgment, that we see the most signs of the growth and enrichment of Niebuhr's own position. It contains some of the most stirring passages in all his writings.

Niebuhr begins the chapter with an interpretation of the meaning of Jesus Christ that has a very contemporary thrust. With Jesus Christ, the American Protestants believed, a new revolution in history was inaugurated:

The common conviction was that whereas before the revolution of Jesus Christ men, with some exceptions, had to be kept in order and had to keep themselves in order by fear and restraint and were without hope, they now had experienced or could experience the "expulsive

[74] *Kingdom of God*, p. 84. Niebuhr's statement seems to reflect the position of William Ames, whom he quoted on p. 83. Niebuhr's concern is to stress the objective character of the rule or right of the kingdom which is subjectively (and therefore partially) apprehended in human conscience.

[75] Recall the importance of Edwards' doctrine of the will in Niebuhr's restatement of the Christian doctrine of man and sin in "Man the Sinner."

power of a new affection" which made a life of freedom possible. The new relation to God established by Jesus Christ meant that an order of liberty and love had been substituted for the order of regimentation and fear.[76]

They did not conceive the "order of liberty" thus inaugurated, however, in primarily political terms (though Niebuhr points out that "freedom in Christ" did give impetus to church democracy and thence to political democracy).[77] Rather it meant first a liberation from the bondage to sin. Freedom was its goal, and it saw that there is no genuine or lasting or truly beneficial freedom that is not "the liberty of men who had been brought somehow to fall in love with a universal goodness and to love it for its own sake alone." [78] For this freedom a "cleansing of the inner parts" and an elimination of internal conflicts is required.[79] The education of the intellect alone cannot bring this about. "A complete rebirth of the whole man was required, a revolution in the will to power or in the will to live." [80] And in a formulation that anticipates central themes in *The Meaning of Revelation* (as do many in this chapter) Niebuhr states, "The Protestants of the seventeenth century were consciously embarked upon a permanent revolution which was to continue until complete freedom was brought in by the 'Order of Glory.' " [81]

The kingdom of Christ with its revolutionary implications be-

---

[76] *Kingdom of God,* p. 90. Cf. Jürgen Moltmann, "The Revolution of Freedom: The Christian and Marxist Struggle," in Thomas W. Ogletree, ed., *Openings for Marxist-Christian Dialogue* (Nashville: Abingdon Press, 1968), pp. 47-71.

[77] *Kingdom of God,* pp. 96-98: "What needs to be emphasized . . . is that the whole outlook on life which lay back of church democracy was one which definitely looked toward liberty in all the relations of life" (p. 98).

[78] *Ibid.,* p. 98.

[79] *Ibid.,* p. 91.

[80] *Ibid.,* p. 99.

[81] *Ibid.,* p. 98. In *Meaning of Revelation* (pp. ix, 118 ff.) Niebuhr links the term "permanent revolution" with *metanoia* (repentance, turning about, conversion) to characterize the continuing process of transformation that life in radical faith involves.

came the dominant theme in American Christianity, Niebuhr contends, with the Great Awakening movements of the eighteenth century. For over a century—until the Civil War—its theme of personal regeneration was central in American Protestantism.[82] The Evangelicals' preaching of the kingdom of Christ, however, was rooted deep in their faith in the sovereignty of God.[83] They knew (as Edwards' theology best expresses it) "that the human will is always committed to something and that so long as it is not committed to the universal good it is attached to the relative." [84] Only the action of God can bring about the transfer of the will's loyalty from the relative (which by claiming absoluteness becomes demonic) to the truly absolute. Therefore "the divine sovereignty stands at the gate of the kingdom of Christ." [85] Divine sovereignty is fundamental to the Awakeners in these further respects: it is God's action in Jesus Christ that has brought the revolution that opens to men the kingdom of liberty and love; and the reconciliation that marks the revolutionary process "is reconciliation to Being, to the divine reality, which man cannot but consider to be his enemy so long as he is intent upon promoting his own will and life." [86] Niebuhr summarizes his point about the dependence of the teaching of the kingdom of Christ on the conviction of God's sovereignty by continuing the analogy between radical Christian faith and Communist theory: "In these ways the proclamation of the kingdom of Christ was solidly based upon the conviction of God's kingship, more solidly, if possible, than the communist doctrine of revolution is based upon the materialist theory of his-

---

[82] *Kingdom of God*, pp. 99-101.

[83] *Ibid.*, p. 101. Niebuhr writes, "Jonathan Edwards, the greatest theologian of the movement, comes to mind at once as one in whom faith in regeneration was solidly founded upon a supreme conviction of the reality of divine sovereignty." And he says of Wesley, Whitefield, the Tennents, Archibald Alexander, and Finney, "Faith in the divine sovereignty was the platform on which they stood as they preached the kingdom of Christ" (pp. 101-2).

[84] *Ibid.*, p. 103. Here Niebuhr shows again the rootage in Edwards of the understanding of will we saw developed in "Man the Sinner."

[85] *Kingdom of God*, p. 103.

[86] *Ibid.*, pp. 103-4.

tory or the art of healing upon the knowledge of anatomy and the conviction of nature's dependable uniformity." [87]

What is the character of the rule of Christ? How is it expressed and made effective in the lives of men? Only a reading of Niebuhr's text can reveal the immense power, the multidimensional subtlety, and the fine balance of his account of the kingdom of Christ as "above all a rule of knowledge in the minds of men." [88] In this rich account it is Edwards who more than any other illumines the way Niebuhr chooses. Moving, as Edwards himself did, between the poles of a rationalism that acknowledged the faith character of its presuppositions, and a critical empiricism that looked to experience for verification and insight into the truth of the gospel, Niebuhr exposes the combination of rational conviction and affectional confirmation that hallmarks true faith-knowledge: "The Evangelicals," he wrote,

made effective and explicit the Protestant principle that God and faith belong together, or that a knowledge of God which is conceptual only and not axiological is not really knowledge at all, or that, to use a different symbolism, a knowledge which is that of the head and not of the heart is of little importance in religion. At the same time they understood that this knowledge which is faith, or this faith which is knowledge, is available to the common man as readily as to the scholar living in his conceptual world. . . . The kingdom of Christ remains then a rule of knowledge. To be a member of this kingdom is to be one who sees the excellency and the beauty of God in Christ, and so loves him with all his heart for his own sake alone.[89]

[87] *Ibid.*, p. 104. But note how the understanding of the divine revolution is being modified to mean dominantly the revolution in personal and communal loyalty rather than, as in "The Grace of Doing Nothing," focusing in the destruction of all patterns of self-assertion and aggression by the judgment of the God who is the process-structural Reality. Niebuhr does not drop the negating, judging side of his understanding of the divine revolution, but here and in *Meaning of Revelation* the major emphasis is on the revolution in *personal* faith from false loyalties and suspicion to loyalty to, and trust in, true Being.

[88] *Kingdom of God*, p. 105.

[89] *Ibid.*, p. 112. Out of his encounter with the Evangelicals, and most especially Edwards, there begins to emerge—as in this passage—a use of the metaphor of "seeing" to express the experience by which such faith-knowledge is formed or transformed.

129

I have to read this passage as not only an epitomization of the evangelical understanding of faith-knowledge, but also as an expression of Niebuhr's own "convinced Protestant" understanding of the nature of faith.[90]

Linked with the view that "the will is as its strongest motive is," and that a man's God is that, or those things, which he values absolutely, is the Edwardsean view that "a man's actions are the most proper test and evidence of his love." [91] In this view genuine love of neighbor depends upon a genuine love of God. Most ostensible love for the neighbor or altruism is in reality an extension of self-love. The extension of self-love from the narrowness of the actual self to the self widened in the family, or nation, or humanity, or life "still leaves it attached to its root and so makes it exclusive at the same time that it seeks to be inclusive." [92] Niebuhr, walking with Edwards, sees only one way to break the destructive bondage of human self-love:

What if man could see that the universal, the eternal, the fountain and center of all being is their true good? What if they could learn to love their neighbors not insofar as they are persons, lives, minds, but because they are creatures of God and sacred by relation to the ultimate Being who is also man's true good? That is precisely the possibility that has been opened in Jesus Christ. In him the intention of the universe, to speak anthropomorphically, has become apparent; in his fate, even more than in his teaching, it has been made manifest that God is love. Through his life, death and resurrection it has become possible to love the "Enemy" who seemed to destroy all his creatures but now is shown to be seeking their redemption.[93]

[90] In *Meaning of Revelation* (pp. 22-37) he develops a position that makes clear the valuing dimension in any adequate knowledge of God. There he refers again to Luther on God and faith and cites Schleiermacher and Ritschl as building their theological approaches on a conception of faith that makes the axiological dimension central.

[91] *Kingdom of God*, pp. 113-14, quoting Edwards, *Christian Love as Manifested in Heart and Life*, from Edwards, *Works*, 6th ed., Philadelphia, vol. 7, p. 337.

[92] *Kingdom of God*, p. 114.

[93] *Ibid.*, pp. 115-16. Though we will devote much effort to saying how this is the case and what it means, we have here, in its essential characteristics, Niebuhr's Christology and soteriology.

The new vision of a God, beautiful in his loyalty to persons and all dependent being, as shown forth in the life, death, and resurrection of Jesus Christ, was the foundation of neighbor love and that regard for nature miscalled humanitarianism.[94] To Niebuhr the

> dynamic result of Calvinism as of revival was a validation of the theory which lay back of both. This theory was that human power to do good did not need to be generated but needed only to be released from the bondage to self and the idols, from the conflict in which divided loyalty involved man and in which power inhibited power. . . . Deliverance, atonement, hope came from reconciliation to God and from faith in his forgiveness. So when Christians found themselves short of good works, of genuine love to their fellows—as indeed they constantly did—they did not try to whip up their wills by admonitions, threats and promises. They sought to cleanse the fountains of life. In penitence and longing they turned to worship, to self-examination in the presence of God, to the contemplation of the cross of Christ.[95]

Without introducing the term, Niebuhr is here describing the phenomenon of *metanoia* which, along with the new vision that elicits it and makes it possible, is a constituent element of faith's "permanent revolution."

In concluding his chapter on the kingdom of Christ, Niebuhr points out the Evangelical movement's tendency toward individualism and its only indirect effects on or engagement with politics.[96] Yet the revival movement did result, he suggests, in the foundation of many humanitarian societies and institutions in the early nineteenth century—the anti-slavery movement, colleges, secondary schools, the Sunday school movement, missions societies, temperance, peace, prison reform, and charitable enterprises of all kinds. And, Niebuhr points out, because they preached the kingdom of

[94] *Ibid.*, pp. 116-17.
[95] *Ibid.*, p. 118.
[96] *Ibid.*, pp. 123-24. "In some respects the men who had come under the sway of the kingdom of Christ seemed less interested in political liberty than their Puritan ancestors had been. Wesley was a tory in politics, Jonathan Edwards seems scarcely to have been aware of the political problem" (p. 123).

Christian liberty, with its permanent revolution toward a community of love, the "struggles for a limited liberty profited." [97]

CONCLUDING REMARKS

Our analysis has carried us through Niebuhr's account of the kingdom of Christ as the central emphasis of the great early evangelical phase of this nation's history. In Niebuhr's phrase, that movement was "our national conversion." [98] We may say that the material we have just surveyed is also expressive of Niebuhr's personal conversion.

The latter part of the book preserves the same stylistic brilliance and synthetic power that characterize the earlier part. But there is less of Niebuhr in it. Unless my judgment fails me, it is more directly a historical overview and account and less a co-expression of still burning fires of new apprehension and comprehension than is the earlier part. Dealing with that failure of the evangelical hope that brought the Civil War, and with the routinization and secularization of that hope's revolution in the later Social Gospel, the account is—as the history itself may be—anticlimactic. And, it may be pointed out, Niebuhr does seem to end with considerable pessimism about the apparently inevitable tendency toward ossification and rigidity in institutions built to conserve the values generated by movements.

3. THE THEOLOGY OF GOD'S SOVEREIGNTY: METAPHORS AND DYNAMICS

This section provides an opportunity to draw out of the previous two chapters a model by which to help clarify the pattern and dynamics of Niebuhr's mature theological-ethical thought. In what

[97] *Ibid.*, p. 124: "In America as in England the Christian enlightenment stood beside the rational enlightenment in the battle for democracy, and it furnished ten soldiers to the cause where the latter furnished one, for it dealt with the common men about whom the rationalists wrote books."
[98] *Ibid.*, p. 126.

follows I am looking both backward and forward from our temporary vantage point of 1937. This conceptual representation of Niebuhr's way of thinking would be an overinterpretation at some points were it based solely on the 1930–37 writings. I will be drawing out implications and patterns that might not be suggested or justifiable simply on the basis of retrospective looking. Nevertheless, in letting the contours of Niebuhr's subsequent thought guide this tentative interpretation, I do not believe that I am imputing to the 1930–37 writings any elements that are not there or in the process of emerging.

THE FORMAL MEANINGS OF THE SOVEREIGNTY OF GOD

Preliminary to the effort to set forth the content and dynamics of Niebuhr's apprehension of and by the sovereignty of God, it is possible and necessary to indicate several mainly formal meanings he intends with that phrase. Over against all theories that directly or subtly represent God as the projection of individual or group consciousness, Niebuhr asserts the *reality* of God. Niebuhr's God is the *really* real as opposed to a merely "actual" ideal representation. And as *the* reality with which man has to do, this God is powerful, often harsh in his judgments.

In this supreme reality and power God is sovereignly *independent* in at least a twofold sense. God is literally not dependent on that which issues from him. He is not bound by or forced by the actions of persons. In the second, epistemological sense, God is independent of or "other than" every effort by dependent being to capture him in concepts and to "know" him as he is. In relation to the subtle tendency of an advanced liberalism to identify God as the guarantor and perfection of human moral values, Niebuhr too could utter a decisive "Nein!"

In his reality and independence the sovereign God is *one*. The slayer and destroyer, set over against all human self-assertion and all efforts to impose human projects on the will of God, is also

133

the redeemer and initiator of reconciliation. The apparent dualities or plurality of a seemingly chaotic world mask the underlying unity of a will and purpose and power working its way in the natural and historic processes.

These several characteristics of God—reality, power, independence, otherness, and oneness—are all aspects of the *primacy* in *being, value,* and *power* that constitutes the sovereignty of God. If these formal characteristics exhaustively expressed the meaning of this phrase for Niebuhr, there would be little that is distinctive or particularly interesting to study in the remainder of his work. It is the constructive content and the dynamic movement in Niebuhr's positive understanding of the sovereignty of God that make his theology unique and intriguing.

THE CHARACTER AND ACTION OF THE SOVEREIGN GOD:

GOD AS PROCESS AND STRUCTURE

Analysis of a listing of every important reference to the character and action of God in the writings of 1930-37 shows that there are three major underlying metaphors implicit in Niebuhr's emerging mode of theological expression. By "metaphors" here I mean images or analogies drawn from human experience that, taken together, are made to bear the weight of conveying the substantive meanings of the sovereignty of God. With the modifier "underlying," I mean to indicate that Niebuhr, in these writings at least, registers no self-consciousness about the varying metaphors he is laying hold of to organize and express the faith working in him and its implications.

Formally stated, the first of these metaphorical images to be encountered in the 1930–37 writings is the one which speaks of God's mode of being and action in terms of *the intentional structure in the processes of reality.* We can observe the beginnings of the convergence of the ideas of structure and process in the appropriation of Tillich's and Whitehead's ideas in the writings of 1930–31.

In the 1930–31 writings the two ideas are sometimes juxtaposed but not yet truly synthesized. Consider, for example, Niebuhr's 1930 programmatic characterization of the kind of historical realism he found needful in theology:

> The way . . . appears to lie only in a realism which will apprehend in all their stubborn actuality the facts of history and the fact of God . . . and which will not replace the God with whom the soul struggles, God the enemy and God the ultimate reality, with some man-made deity.[99]

Read "facts of history" and "God the enemy" as pointing to *process* and as deriving from Whiteheadian influences. Read "the fact of God" and "God the ultimate reality" as implying *structure* and as deriving from Tillich. The polar unity of the two ideas begins to come into focus in another programmatic sentence from the last of the 1930–31 articles. There Niebuhr speaks of theology as being "the theory of an immanence which is present [structure] and which yet must be attained [process]."[100]

The real wedding of the ideas of structure and process begins in "The Grace of Doing Nothing." And it seems to occur there, in part, through Niebuhr's appropriation of Marxist philosophy of history with its process-structural determinism. The Christian believers in God—a real God—Niebuhr writes in that article, are "like the communists . . . assured that the actual processes of history will inevitably and really bring a different kind of world with lasting peace."[101] Such radical Christians rely upon "forces which often seem very impersonal . . . as impersonal and as actual as machine production, rapid transportation, the physical mixture of the races, etc., but as parts of the real world they are as much a part of the total divine process as are human thoughts and prayers."[102] But this action of God in and through the seemingly

---

[99] "Can German and American Christians Understand Each Other?" p. 915.
[100] "Theology in a Time of Disillusionment," pp. 21-22.
[101] "The Grace of Doing Nothing," p. 379.
[102] *Ibid.*

impersonal processes of history has an intentionality that is inseparable from a certain order and reliability—even inevitability— in the processes. In his response to his brother's critique of "The Grace of Doing Nothing" Niebuhr wrote:

God, I believe, is always in history; he is the structure of things, the source of all meaning, the "I am that I am," that which is that it is. . . . That structure of the universe, that creative will, can no more be said to interfere brutally in history than the violated laws of my organism can be said to interfere brutally with my life if they make me pay the cost of my violation.[103]

And then, in a passage that foreshadows the consummation of Niebuhr's uniting of the ideas of structure and process as modeled on the radical faith of Jesus, he writes, "But this same structure in things which is our enemy is our redeemer; 'it means intensely and means good.' " [104]

This polar view of God as the process-structural reality finds its culminating expression in this formative period in "The Social Gospel and the Mind of Jesus" (1933). It is well to remind ourselves that in this paper Niebuhr seems to identify with his exposition of the radical faith of Jesus in the sovereign God so that it may also be taken as a normative expression of his own faith. The God of Jesus is "the destructive God who is at the same time man's deliverer." [105] Jesus was directed "toward what God was doing and what man ought to do in the light of God's doing." God, for Jesus, is "cosmic reality." [106] God's rule was apparent to Jesus in both the natural and historic processes, but especially in the latter. "It is here [the social historic process]," Niebuhr writes,

that the rule of God comes to be of decisive importance and the meaning of eschatology lies largely in this, that it represents history not as an indeterminated sequence of events where men may adjust

[103] "A Communication: The Only Way into the Kingdom of God," p. 447.

[104] *Ibid.*

[105] "The Social Gospel," p. 11.

[106] *Ibid.*

themselves to a relatively stable environment . . . , but as a driving, directional movement, ruthless so far as individuals and nations are concerned, *almost impersonal* in its determinism.[107]

Jesus' faith unites in a true synthesis "the fear of God and the love of God, the knowledge of God the enemy and the knowledge of God the deliverer." [108] His God is "a faithful, that is unswerving, reality, with laws that can only be broken at the price of life." [109] The laws of this God are the laws of reality. "The morality of the Sermon on the Mount . . . stands upon the foundations of reality." [110] But over against his lawfulness the God of Jesus' faith is "the God of the creative process, the dynamic urge in the moving universe which brings death and destruction to those who will not yield to its universal, faithful working, which heals and forgives and makes ever new beginnings possible." [111]

In the writings we have examined here, the twin images of God as process and as structure are interwoven. There is almost an equilibrating alternation between them in Niebuhr's effort to express Jesus' understanding of God's character and action in nature and history. It is not clear to me that structure and process are polarities so far as logic is concerned; but conceived in the polar relationship of tension and unity we have seen here, they become indispensable in Niebuhr's effort to grasp and portray the relationship of the sovereign God to nature and history.

As we followed the convergence of the two ideas and the emerging polar synthesis they produced, we were also observing a gradual process of *personalization* of the process-structural concept of God. Though not in the main a personalization in the direction of anthropomorphism, in the course of full emergence God, the process-structural reality, became God the enemy and then God

[107] *Ibid.*, p. 12. (Italics added.) Contrast "almost impersonal" here with "impersonal forces" in "The Grace of Doing Nothing."

[108] "The Social Gospel," p. 13.

[109] *Ibid.*, pp. 12-13.

[110] *Ibid.*, p. 16.

[111] *Ibid.*, p. 22.

the deliverer, toward whom, respectively, fear and love—personal attitudes—are appropriate. "Impersonal forces" become "almost impersonal," and it becomes quite natural to speak of "God's doing" and of "the destructive God who is at the same time man's deliverer." I want to try to be clear about this point: there is, in the total pattern of this metaphor's emergence, a tendency to move from terminology more expressive of *fatefulness* to formulations conveying something like personal agency and will (*though avoiding direct anthropomorphism*). The tendency is not without reversals, but is, I judge, indicative of growth or transition in Niebuhr's own faith and its expression. This tendency parallels the Whiteheadean formula about religion as evolving from God the void to God the enemy, and from God the enemy to God the companion—which also describes a movement toward personalization of the God metaphor.

GOD AS SOURCE OF BEING AND NORM OF VALUING

The emergence of the second major implicit metaphor is really the reemergence of an earlier central theme in Niebuhr's thought. This is the metaphor built around value-valuation. Put in formal terms, it sees God as *source of all being and norm of all valuing.* We need not rehearse here what was said earlier about Niebuhr's appropriation of value theory from Troeltsch, Macintosh, and others. Nor need we do more than refer to the reappearance of value language and conceptualizations informed by the positions of Luther and Edwards in "The Church Against the World" and "Man the Sinner." The important thing to be grasped is how Niebuhr takes a universal and fundamental (indeed primitive) aspect of man's moral experience and expresses through it the meaning and reality of God in his sovereignty. God is the "Creator and . . . essence of Being." [112] He is man's proper "chief good." [113] God is "the only trustworthy and wholly lovable reality." [114] His

[112] "Man the Sinner," p. 277.
[113] *Ibid.,* p. 275.
[114] *Ibid.,* pp. 276-77.

perfection is not reducible to merely moral terms,[115] for he is "the universal, the eternal, the fountain and center of all being" and man's "true good." [116]

We have seen how Niebuhr's first explicit statement of his doctrine of man and of sin was built around this value-valuation metaphor in "Man the Sinner." I think we have to say that this metaphor is really the primitive one in Niebuhr's thinking, by virtue both of its early role in his thought and of its pervasive presence in every decade of his teaching and writing career. We may also observe that it is the first of the metaphors to become explicit for Niebuhr. When he developed his first published statement on man and sin around this theme, it represented a new level of self-consciousness about his own emerging doctrine of God. It also revealed the presence of a hitherto implicit *co-relational* metaphor for man: he is man-the-valuer and man-the-misvaluer. (There is, of course, also a co-relational metaphor for man that corresponds with the process-structural metaphor. We will look at these co-related anthropological metaphors later.)

THE GOD WHO COVENANTS AND REDEEMS

If we try an inductive approach to the third major metaphor, it is impossible to be as confident or specific as we have been about the metaphorical form of the first two. It is hard to name this third one. Viewed inductively, it seems in some ways to be really an amalgam of the first two, personalized, but this time in an anthropomorphic—or, better, incarnational—direction. But we can be quite clear about its content and its function in relation to the other two. This is the God who *covenants*. This is God the faithful self-binder, who commits himself in loyalty to the beings that issue from him. This is God the redeemer and self-revealer, who initiates reconciliation with estranged or misvaluing man. The metaphorical rootage here points toward the central figure of the New Covenant, though he and it are to be understood in relation

[115] *Ibid.*, pp. 273-74.
[116] *Kingdom of God*, p. 115.

to the covenanting Suzerain and Father of the Old Covenant. *It is in this metaphorical arena or dimension of the sovereignty of God that the kind of revelation occurs which can illumine, clarify, and tiansform man's consciousness of God in the two other metaphoric modes.* In Jesus Christ, Niebuhr writes in *The Kingdom of God in America,*

> the intention of the universe, to speak anthropomorphically, has become apparent; in his fate, even more than in his teaching, it has been made manifest that God is love. Through his life, death and resurrection it has become possible to love the "Enemy" who seemed to destroy all his creatures but now is shown to be seeking their redemption.[117]

This third metaphorical image includes the "right of God" which must be seen in the light of the "right of Jesus Christ," by which men become persuaded that the destructive reality "evident in historic processes, is a redeeming and saving reality." [118] We could do worse than identify God in this implicit metaphor as *the covenanting person* and *faithful Being.*

The important point about this third implicit metaphor is that it is the locus for the transforming encounter with revelation. When we come to consider the interrelation of these three metaphors in Niebuhr's emerging theology, we shall see that the movement tends to evolve toward this third metaphorical arena. Then with revolutionary effect the impulses from the decisive encounter with revelation work back transformingly on the other two metaphors.

MAN IN RELATION TO GOD: THE CO-RELATED METAPHORS

In considering the three major images Niebuhr employs to depict God's being and action in relation to man, history, and nature, it is important to bear in mind that Niebuhr's use of these implicit metaphors was not systematic in any self-conscious way. This analysis, therefore, is an effort to disclose patterns and metaphors

[117] *Ibid.,* pp. 115-16.
[118] "Church Against the World," pp. 615-16.

underlying Niebuhr's thought, thereby making explicit a structure of which Niebuhr himself would not necessarily have been aware.

It would be a distortion of Niebuhr's thought not to point out that these representations of divine being and action do not try to speak of God as he might be in himself. Niebuhr is both a Kantian and faithful to the Old Testament in maintaining that God as he is in himself is not a possible object of human knowledge. We can only know God *in relation* to life and history.

Because God is sovereign, the fundamental fact about humans is their relation to God. Therefore when we ask, What is man? or, What should man do? or, What is man's true end? we again have in view a relational object—*man in relation to God.* Though Niebuhr explicitly developed his doctrine of man in terms of only one of the three metaphors of God's relation to man in the 1930–37 period, it is clear that corresponding to each of the others there are implicit *synecdochic analogies* for man in his relation to God.[119]

We have already mentioned that co-related to the metaphor of God the *source of all being and norm of all valuing* is the image of *man-the-valuer* or *man-the-misvaluer*.[120] It is important for an understanding of later developments in Niebuhr's thought to recognize here that for Niebuhr both true selfhood and salvation involve, among other things, having the person's formerly conflicting, polytheistic value-commitments ordered and subordinated in an overarching loyalty to the one true center of being and value. And that this is only possible—or the response to God as supreme value and center of loyalty is only possible—when man comes to understand and experience *his being valued by God.* Therefore man is also *self-valuer;* and the transformation in his valuing that

---

[119] "Synecdochic analogy" is Niebuhr's own term. (See *Responsible Self,* chap. 1, esp. p. 56.) A synecdochic analogy or metaphor for man takes an aspect of human being and activity and generalizes from it to form an image that tries to sum up what man in his wholeness is or does.

[120] Just as there is an implicit doctrine of man corresponding to each of the God metaphors, there is also an implicit characterization of sin as well as of the goal of saving action or relation corresponding to each one.

faith brings begins with a revolution in his self-valuation and its basis.

Co-related to the metaphor of God *the intentional structure in the processes of reality* is the implicit synecdoche of man *the "patient" and counter-actor*.[121] Man is being acted on, limited, ordered, driven. He responds in accordance with his interpretation of the meaning or intentionality in the forces acting upon him. His action resists or cooperates with, counters or embraces, such intentionality as he discerns in his field of force. The integrative effect of radical trust in the sovereignty of God comes through the audacious faith that there is unified purpose and power, working with redemptive intent for us and for all being, subordinating and utilizing all the various forces acting in our lives and in the life history of creation. In the relation to God depicted by this metaphor a person can understand himself as *man the victim* or *man the heroic protagonist* against the powers that be. He can also be *man the discerner and responsible co-worker*.

The metaphor for man co-related to God seen as the *covenanting person and faithful Being* is *man the fiduciary being*. English makes the verbal form of "faith" awkward—"to faith" or "faithing." Therefore we shall speak of *fiduciary being*. As *fiduciary being* man can mistrust and distrust as well as invest trust in another. As *fiduciary being* man can betray and be disloyal, as well as keep faith with and be loyal to another. He can also *be* betrayed and be the sufferer of disloyalty. To say that man is *fiduciary being* is to say that he is moral being—he defines himself by promises and commitments. His sin grows out of his inability to trust. In his distrust he breaks promises and shirks commitments. Revelation is the experience in which man's distrust of the cosmic other, his suspicion of Being, is turned around. Through having the faithfulness of the covenanting One disclosed—a faithfulness unto redemptive death—our distrust is turned to trust and we respond with

[121] In using the term "patient" I am borrowing from Prof. Richard R. Niebuhr. In this somewhat archaic usage the term denotes the self as the object or recipient of action upon it. As "patient" the self both "endures" and "enjoys" God's action as process-structural reality.

142

loyalty to the cause to which the covenanting One is faithful. We dare to trust that there is a fiduciary texture to reality, that there is an utterly faithful other whose covenant is its constitution.

Figure 1 gives a summary representation of our discussion of the three co-related metaphors. This will remind us that the God whose action and being in relation to man, history, and nature is expressible in three metaphorical modes, is *one*. Moreover, the three corresponding synecdochic images for man represent complementary characteristics of supposedly every human actor.

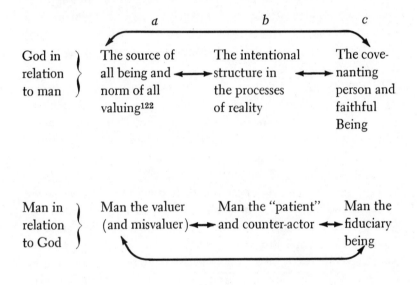

Fig. 1. The co-related metaphors implicit in Niebuhr's emerging theology of the sovereignty of God

---

[122] Because I judge the value-valuation metaphor to be the primitive one in Niebuhr's thought, I have placed it at the arbitrary beginning point of what is really an organic system.

TO SEE THE KINGDOM

So far we have worked at constructing a conceptual model that will help us understand the interrelations of various elements in Niebuhr's thought as they emerged in 1930–37. From my study of Niebuhr's later writings, I have come to believe that the three underlying metaphors we identified above represent major permanent poles in his theological-ethical thinking. In my judgment, therefore, if we can understand rightly the unity that underlay these elements at the point of their emergence, and if we can grasp the somewhat complex dynamics of interaction between them implied in Niebuhr's account, we shall have moved a long way toward solving some of the riddles that otherwise make interpretation of his later work difficult.

In this section it is our task to try to clarify what might accurately be called the *evolution* and *revolution* of faith-consciousness in Niebuhr's doctrine of the sovereignty of God. Before saying why it is not rhetorical redundancy to speak of both evolutionary and revolutionary changes in faith-consciousness, let me try to stipulate the limits of the action model we are presenting here. "Faith-consciousness" is really the delimiting term. *Here we are concerned primarily with how a person experiences the action of God and conceptualizes it, and with how that conceptualization undergoes alterations and transformations in the course of a person's encounter with revelation.* The behavioral and therefore ethical analogies of faith-consciousness in its various stages will be dealt with in the next chapter.

Now to the matter of evolutionary and revolutionary change in faith-consciousness. It is clear from the literature we examined from the 1930–37 period that the formation of radical faith represents a revolution or a transformation in faith-consciousness. We have seen so many references to that kind of change that we need not document it further at this point. The question of evolutionary change in faith-consciousness, however, is not quite so clear-cut. Niebuhr's appropriation of the Whitehead formula, by now thoroughly familiar to us, leads him at points to write as though

144

prior to and in preparation for revelation a gradual movement toward personalization of the God concept in faith-consciousness occurs. It is as though Niebuhr sees a growth in man's "natural religion" paralleling the process of differentiation and clarification of the self concept over against others and reality. Like a kind of Wesleyan "prevenient grace" or Bultmannian *Vorverständnis*, it tends to direct the consciousness toward the expectation that what is over against us is at least an intentional reality (whether it intends well or maliciously for us). Though I cannot prove the operation in Niebuhr's mind of this nascent theory of the evolution of religious consciousness, neither can I convince myself that it is not there. Therefore, trusting my hunch, I will speak of evolutionary change, prior to revelation in faith-consciousness. Taking this seriously at least allows us to affirm what is certainly true of Niebuhr—that he takes seriously the pre-Christian, and quasi-Christian, faith-consciousness, and that he sees the revolution or transformation that Christian revelation brings not as a discarding of the old forms of consciousness but as their conversion, transformation, and fulfillment.[123] If there is such a nascent evolutionary dynamic in Niebuhr's theory of faith, its parallel with the Whitehead formula might be depicted as shown in figure 2.

	a	*b*	*c*
Evolving consciousness of God in relation to man	The (indeterminate) source of all being and value ⟶	The process-structural reality (limiter and destroyer— almost impersonal) ⟶	The cosmic person

(God the void) ⟶ (God the enemy) ⟶ (God the companion)

Fig. 2. The nascent theory of an evolution in
faith-consciousness in Niebuhr's theology

[123] These matters will receive extensive treatment and clarification in chap. 5 below.

In figure 2, the content of the implicit metaphors has been changed somewhat from figure 1 to indicate that the experiences of *valuing* (*a*), or of *limitation* (*b*), or of *unified agency in reality* (*c*), *prior to revelation* have a different content than they have after it has worked its transformation in faith-consciousness.

We have the necessary elements before us now to offer a diagrammatic representation of the conceptual model I find implied in Niebuhr's emerging theology of the sovereignty of God (figure 3). By employing this model here, I will try to depict the evolutionary and revolutionary changes in faith-consciousness that we find in Niebuhr's account. The understanding of the principal poles and their interrelatedness in Niebuhr's doctrine of God's sovereignty which this model represents, opens the way for our analysis of the ethics he builds on these bases. In order to grasp what figure 3 tries to depict, take note of these explanatory remarks:

1. It has been our concern in this part of our study to try to make explicit and overt an organic structure which seems to underlie Niebuhr's theological formulations as they emerge from 1930 to 1937. Let it be clear that Niebuhr's development and employment of these formulations does not show awareness on his part of the underlying structure we are trying to bring into view. Therefore, the schema offered here must be understood as a merely heuristic model, necessarily deceptive in its tidiness, which may nonetheless be helpful in summarizing our analysis of the implicit patterns and dynamics of Niebuhr's maturing theological thought.

2. The *content* of the co-relational metaphors in rows I and II is derived from Niebuhr's analyses of the faith-consciousness of sinful man—man prior to the clarification and restoration that revelation brings. One of the points of the diagram is to show that the metaphorical *forms* seem to remain constant while the *content* they hold undergoes changes as faith-consciousness is transformed.

3. What is depicted here as a simultaneous, comprehensive, "once for all" process is by no means that in reality. The kinds of changes in faith-consciousness suggested here do not occur without pain, disruption, and struggle. Often there are reversals.

The movements forward always risk becoming static, complacent, and idolatrous. Rows III and IV should be represented as open-ended because they can also be frozen and become inimical to real faith. They should be taken, not as states to be attained, but as directions for pilgrimage. Revelation, and its transformation through repentance and forgiveness, keeps on happening.

4. Start in the upper left corner of the diagram. The dotted lines indicate the movement of the *evolution of religious consciousness* leading to readiness for the decisive personal encounter with revelation. The broken lines issuing from the revelation encounter indicate *the direction of revelational impact* on the faith-consciousness. The solid *lines* indicate the *directions of the revolutionary processes*. (Read the unidirectional solid lines as "becomes.")

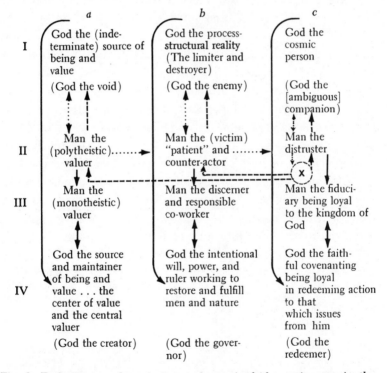

Fig. 3. Evolutionary and revolutionary change in faith-consciousness in the conceptual model of the sovereignty of God implicit in Niebuhr's theology

TO SEE THE KINGDOM

The previous discussion and the diagram in figure 3 have put before us the three principal dimensions in which Niebuhr sees God acting in relation to man, nature, and history, The three underlying metaphors he employs to image those dimensions of God's action were identified by a process of induction from the 1930–37 writings. It would be less than honest, however, not to say plainly that I was prompted to look for them there in part by the approach to normative ethics which Niebuhr consistently took in his Yale lecture course on ethics from at least 1946–47 on to the end of his career.[124]

Niebuhr usually began the course with an introductory section entitled "The Function and Field of Christian Ethics." Following that he devoted a substantial amount of class time to discussing "The Structure and Dynamics of the Moral Life." [125] In part three under the title "The Principles of Christian Action" he undertook a historical-comparative and constructive approach to the normative bases of Christian ethics. There he would present the two major classical principles which Christian ethical thinkers have "converted" [126] from philosophical ethics—the teleological and deontological approaches. After suggestively characterizing the varying versions or types of teleological and deontological thinking in Christian ethics, he would offer penetrating critiques of each. Then in an exposition that incorporated the strengths of each of the two classical positions he offered his own normative approach under the rubric "The Principles of Response to Divine Action":

---

[124] I have reliable student notes and course outlines for Niebuhr's "Christian Ethics" of 1946–47, 1952–53, 1953–54. Prof. Richard R. Niebuhr has kindly made available his father's own lecture notes from spring, 1961. With those are individual lectures on various of the topics treated in the course from as far back as 1945.

[125] For the subheadings under each of these refer to the Appendix.

[126] In his lectures of 1946–47, Niebuhr is quoted as saying: "The Christian moralist is always converting a philosophy in his theology. . . . Many of the disputes between Christian ethicists arise out of the fact that they convert different philosophies" (p. 5).

Our action is response to something which has happened to us. This is not in automatic response but a response to an interpretation of what is happening to us. . . . Christians see the action upon them as divine action, and God is present in all action. How shall we respond? We must respond to the divine in all actions upon us.[127]

Then follows Niebuhr's discussion of the character of God's action and of the principles by which it is to be discerned, interpreted, and responded to. This substantial section of the course came under the headings "Response to the Creative Action of God (A Christian Theory of Value)," "Response to the Governing Action of God" (Niebuhr sometimes spoke of this as "The Theory of Self-Denial"), and "Response to the Redemptive Action of God" (which he sometimes subtitled "The Theory of Freedom" or "God's Liberating Action"). Note that in figure 3 the faith-consciousness as transformed by the revelation event comes to perceive the divine actor as *God the creator, God the governor,* and *God the redeemer* (see row IV).

The usefulness of the tri-metaphorical analysis offered in this section seems to find confirmation when we look in detail at that major part of Niebuhr's ethics course in which he dealt successively with response to God as creator, governor, and redeemer. There is no denying that in Niebuhr's writings we never see him reflecting systematically on the way these three clusters of metaphors relate to each other and hang together. It does seem important, however, to point to the apparent constancy of this underlying structure in his subsequent thought. And we may hazard the judgment that, had Niebuhr lived to write his *Ethics,* very likely he would have had to bring into explicit and systematic relationship the three poles in his thought which the present analysis has identified. The next chapter shows how these three metaphorical modes come to expression in Niebuhr's ethics of response to divine action.

[127] *Ibid.,* p. 20.

Chapter IV
To See the Kingdom

Such merit as the action model offered in the previous chapter (figure 3) has lies in its ability to help us hold in simultaneous focus several of the principal structural and dynamic elements of Niebuhr's thought. It enables us to see in their interrelatedness the three central metaphoric forms Niebuhr employs for imaging God-before-man and man-before-God. It suggests the direction of evolutionary development in the individual religious consciousness. And it depicts the dramatic transformations in faith-knowing that issue from ongoing encounters with revelational event and revelational person. Despite the dangers of oversimplification and reification, this action model does seem to take us "inside" Niebuhr's thought and to put us in the midst of the tensions, polarities, and movement that give it its life and power.

In this chapter I want to show the relationships between Niebuhr's emergent theology of the sovereignty of God and the subsequent major thrusts of his theological-ethical teachings. I will try to offer what Niebuhr himself never gave us in written form, namely, a comprehensive overview of his theological-ethical thought viewed as a whole. The structure and much of the content for this chapter depend on notes from Niebuhr's lecture course on Christian ethics,[1] for in the sweep of that extensive course the direction and pattern of Niebuhr's thought most fully found expression. But an effort has also been made here to point to and draw on his post-1937 published and unpublished writings, and to indicate how they fit into the total pattern of his thinking.[2]

1. MAN THE RESPONDER:
THE TRIADIC STRUCTURE OF OUR LIFE IN RESPONSE

In the last chapter we saw that, correlated with the three metaphoric forms which Niebuhr employs to convey the character of divine being and action in relation to man, there are three synecdochic analogies for man: man the valuer and self-valuer; man the "patient" and counter-actor; and man the "fiduciary being." Each of these analogies denotes a dimension of human experience and action in which the person is impinged upon by other persons, by events, relations, objects, and claims to which he must respond, and in confrontation with which he initiates actions. Each of these analogies denotes a dimension in which the person is impinged upon by divine action. The student of Niebuhr's ethics makes a significant step when he recognizes that these three central analogies in his doctrine of man are unified under the more comprehensive synecdoche "man the answerer" or "man the responder."

---

[1] See chap. 3, n. 124. See also the Bibliography, p. 283, and Appendix.

[2] Readers may find it useful to compare the present chapter with James M. Gustafson's "Introduction" to *Responsible Self*, pp. 6-41, which is the only other attempt I know to show the direction of Niebuhr's thought as revealed in his classroom lectures. The other available interpretations of Niebuhr depend almost totally upon his published writings.

The phrase "the responsible self" is the most suggestive and complete formulation of this analogy.[3]

Niebuhr describes four characteristics of "the form of personal existence we call responsible." [4] The first of these is that *personal action is responsive* action: "It is like the action of one who *answers, responds* to another; it is reaction to action." [5] But in order to be the action of a self or to be moral action it must be a response to *interpreted* action. This is the second characteristic of human responsive action: it "occurs in accordance with the *self's interpretation* of the deed and the power to which it reacts. . . . We interpret events that force themselves upon us as parts of wholes, of sequences, as symbolic of larger meanings. . . . It is these larger patterns in our understanding that guide . . . our response to action upon us." [6] The third characteristic of responsible action is *accountability:* "Our deeds are responsible not only insofar as they are reactions to interpreted actions upon us, but also insofar as they are made in anticipation of answers to our

---

[3] The phrase was used first in Niebuhr's contribution to *Church Against the World* in 1935 (see *Theology in America*, p. 593). A detailed accounting of the role of the idea of responsibility in Niebuhr's thought would be a book in itself. The major source is *Responsible Self*. There is also a typed unpublished manuscript of 24 pp. delivered at Cambridge University, May 25, 1960, entitled "On the Meaning of Responsibility." For important earlier employments of the idea see "The Christian Church in the World's Crises" in *Christianity and Society*, 6, no. 3 (1941), pp. 11-17; three *Christian Century* articles: "War as the Judgment of God" (vol. 49, May 13, 1942); "Is God in the War?" (vol. 59, August 5, 1942); "War as Crucifixion" (vol. 60, April 28, 1943). See also "The Responsibility of the Church for Society" in Kenneth Scott Latourette, ed., *The Gospel, the Church, and the World* (New York: Harper & Brothers, 1946, pp. 112, 114 ff.); *Christ and Culture*, p. 247; *The Purpose of the Church and Its Ministry*, pp. 91, 116; *Radical Monotheism*, pp. 47-48. From at least as early as 1946–47 Niebuhr presented his own constructive ethical approach in his lecture course under the rubric "The Principles of Response to Divine Action." For a recent study of he idea of responsibility in religious ethics, which includes a discussion of Niebuhr, see Albert R. Jonsen, *Responsibility in Modern Religious Ethics* (Washington: Corpus Books, 1968). On Niebuhr see pp. 132-52.

[4] "On the Meaning of Responsibility," unpublished manuscript of address given at Cambridge University, May 25, 1960. See p. 10.

[5] *Ibid.*, p. 10. See also *Responsible Self*, p. 61.

[6] "Meaning of Responsibility," pp. 12-13. (See *Responsible Self*, pp. 61-63.)

answers." [7] This forward-looking component makes explicit the element of accountability, understood as action in anticipation of reaction, brings into view the question of the time and the history in which selves act. Our responses to actions upon us differ because our interpretations vary but also because the time spans into which we fit our acts change." [8] Finally, accountability within a time span implies a community in which responsive-responsible action takes place. For Niebuhr (who here follows Royce, Buber, and George Herbert Mead) there is no selfhood apart from community. The self is dependent upon the faithful response of others in community in order to form a reliable sense of identity, to shape its dominant interpretative images of the real, and to develop conscience and conceptions of moral value.[9] The self's social existence is triadic in structure: "The movement of response, and interpretation, and anticipation in accountability of future reactions, seems always to be triadic." [10] It is not going too far to say that for Niebuhr the self is never alone as a knower, valuer, initiator, or responder. Man's relations to objects, other persons, to ideas, are always qualified by his relations to companions— co-knowers, co-valuers, and co-interpreters in communities of interpretation.[11]

To be the action of a responsible self, in sum, an action must be a *response* to action upon me, in accordance with my *interpretation* of the action upon me, and in *anticipation* of answering responses to my response, all in a continuing *community* of interpretation-action.[12] To be a responsible self is to be responsible *to* others and *for* others: "In the religious setting," Niebuhr writes,

---

[7] "Meaning of Responsibility," pp. 16-17. (*Responsible Self*, pp. 63-65.)

[8] "Meaning of Responsibility," p. 18.

[9] See *Responsible Self*, chap. 2; "The Ego-Alter Dialectic and the Conscience," *Journal of Philosophy*, 42 (1945), pp. 352-59 (also longer, unpublished version); and "The Triad of Faith," *Andover Newton Bulletin*, 47, pp. 3-12.

[10] "Meaning of Responsibility," p. 21.

[11] See chap. 5 below.

[12] Cf. *Responsible Self*, p. 65.

I am responsive-responsible to my companions for my responses to God; I am responsive-responsible to God for my reactions to my companions. Bur response and responsibility in this double interaction seem to run through the whole of personal existence even when our total or ultimate environment is not in view. It runs through my activity as knower, as citizen, as soldier, as teacher, as husband and father.[13]

It is not Niebuhr's aim to urge persons to "be responsible." To be a self *is* to be responsible. The crucial questions, rather, are the following: (1) From among all the actions and impingements upon me to which ones will I shape my responses? (2) From among all the actors in my field of action to which shall I respond? (3) By what community's interpretative constructs shall I construe action upon me, and in what time perspective? (4) In my responses to action upon me *to* whom and *for* whom am I accountable? These questions arise in each of the dimensions of man's life in response—in his life as valuer and self-valuer, in his life as "patient" and counter-actor, and in his life as fiduciary self. To be a self is to have developed some consistency of interpretation and response in each of these dimensions of impingement, and to have achieved some interdimensional intergration of one's interpretations and response.

From the standpoint of radical faith in the sovereignty of God it may be asserted: There is one Actor in all the actions upon you. "God is acting in all actions upon you." And from this indicative flows an imperative: "So respond to all actions upon you as to respond to his action." [14]

In order to respond thus to the action of God there must be discernment—eyes that see with the vision of faith. It is for the guidance of such discerning that Niebuhr develops his ethics of response. He does so in three major sections, each of which centers around one of the metaphorical images for the relation between God and man that we have brought into view.

[13] "Meaning of Responsibility," p. 22.
[14] *Responsible Self*, p. 126.

2. RESPONSE TO THE REDEEMING ACTION OF GOD: REVELATION AND LIBERATION

In the action model of faith-consciousness given in chapter 3 we saw that it is predominantly in the third metaphorical dimension that explicit revelational encounter occurs. The effects of revelation then work back transformingly on the two other metaphorical modes of faith-seeing. In this effort at an overview of Niebuhr's ethics of response to divine action it is to our advantage to reverse his usual pattern of presentation in his lecture course on ethics and to begin with the topic he generally dealt with last: *the redeeming action of God.* By beginning at this point we can subsequently approach the discussions of the *governing* action of God and the *creative* action of God without having to recount the transformation dynamic shown in the last chapter. When giving account of response to God's governing and creative action, I will presuppose a faith-consciousness already decisively shaped, illumined, or being restored to trusting, by experience of the redemptive action of God. Therefore, we begin here with Niebuhr's teaching about God's redemptive action. This path leads us into the heart of Niebuhr's understanding of revelation, of reconciliation, of the mediation of faith, and of his philosophy of history. This means involvement in his christological teachings and a further examination of his doctrine of man.

"We come now to the greatest theme in Christian Ethics; it is the most distinctive, and yet the most difficult. . . . It is the Christian principle of the love of Being, that love is at the very core of existence." [15] With these words Niebuhr opens his lectures on response to the redemptive action of God. In the introduction he points out that the God who impinges on life and history as redeemer is not different from the God who is creator and governor. In his creating and ruling/judging, the God of Christian faith-consciousness acts redemptively—with loyalty and faithfulness, with

[15] Class lecture, April 21, 1952, as transcribed by Robert Yetter *et al.*, p. 132.

conserving, restorative intention—on behalf of that which issues from him.

There is a double character to God's redemptive action as Niebuhr understands it. On the one hand it is the *quality* of God's impingement on man and being, through the entropy-defying, continuing creation and through the process-structural intentionality that express divine love and faithfulness to dependent being. On the other hand it is that specific mode of impingement on human consciousness by which man's distrust and hostility toward the Cosmic Other are turned around. It is that relation in which man's suspicion and mistrust of Being are transformed toward the freeing perception that, in that Other, supreme power is wedded to supreme goodness, and that the disposition of God toward dependent being is love, even a suffering love. In order to do justice to this double theme in Niebuhr's thought we shall range beyond his lectures into some of his published and unpublished writings.

THE WISDOM OF SURVIVAL AND THE LOGIC OF THE CROSS

Man's natural religion is a *polytheism in valuing* and a *logic of survival in response to the claims and limitations of life* upon selves and nations.

The first principle of our thinking is this premise: we are perishing. We often start at a slightly lower point, saying that self-preservation is the first law of life. This is a way of saying that we believe that if we do not preserve ourselves we will not be preserved. What is back of this idea is evidently another one, namely, the conviction that our frustration, our annihilation, our death is a law of the behavior of all that surrounds us.[16]

In this conviction that "perishing" is the label stamped on our being, we develop a "wisdom of survival." With the aid of this wisdom we build defenses, construct and apply schemes for seizing and securing our share of the scarce, perishing goods of life, and set about the central task of outliving foes and friends.[17]

[16] "The Logic of the Cross," unpublished sermon from 1950s, p. 2.
[17] *Ibid.*, pp. 3-4.

From this wisdom of survival there issues an ethics of death that may take several forms. In its Epicurean form it faces its gloomy fear of reality with a struggle to discover how to blot out our fear of the future and to maximize present happiness. In its form as obsession with survival, it subordinates every interest to the destruction or neutralization of (perceived) enemies and to surviving longer than that which threatens. In another form it may express itself in that kind of noble resignation that seeks immortality by investment in the service of those things which promise to survive—the world of ideas, ideals, and essences.[18] From the point of view of this wisdom of survival, it seems absurd to take seriously the life and faith of one who died on a cross:

It is nonsense that we who need to survive should direct all our thought toward One who was not a survivor. The wisdom of survival can study the strategy of an Augustus Caesar, the genius of the Roman Empire, the shrewdness of Caiaphas—all of whom were able to outlive Jesus. But what can it learn from One who was not able to maintain himself in life against Roman, Jewish, and ordinary human wisdom of survival? [19]

Yet it is the cross of Jesus that calls into question the foundations of our wisdom of survival. The cross does not entirely deny the premise that we are perishing, but it raises the question of its sufficiency. "The cross . . . raises the question whether we do not need a presupposition beyond the one we have adopted. Not whether we come from nothing and go to nothing but whether beyond that nothing there is not Being." [20] The cross and resurrection suggest a new hypothesis: "We are being saved."

We are indeed coming through disaster, but we will not be lost. The cross does not deny the reality of death. It reinforces it. It denies its finality. . . . We may ask how it is that from the cross we come to raise this question and make this great assumption: We are being saved. How are we enabled to move from the first statement, "We are perishing" to this other one, "We are being saved"? However we explain

[18] Class lecture, April 21, 1952 (Yetter, p. 133).
[19] "Logic of the Cross," p. 5.
[20] Ibid., p. 8.

the transition . . . the *cross has been and is that demonstration of the power of God whereby that conversion of the first principle of our thought is accomplished.*[21]

Of course it is not the cross that brings about this change, but the one whose faith led to it and whose faith was ratified and confirmed by a radical act of redemption and restoration from death. "It seems most strange that by the recollection which we have of the betrayal and the disastrous end of the one who trusted in the Power of Being as utterly faithful to him, we should have had introduced into our lives a little ability to trust."[22] The faith of Jesus came to the end of its historic existence with the cry "My God, my God, why hast thou forsaken me?"

There was faith in the cry: My God. But it is the uttermost cry of faith, at the edge of nothingness. If at this point in the central tragedy in our history there had occurred the demonstration of the power and glory of the God in whom he trusted . . . then might not faith as universal loyalty and universal trust have been reconstructed among men?[23]

It did not happen that way. Elijah did not return; the cry ended in a choke and darkness came. "But something else has happened, something that is very ordinary and very strange, something over which we wonder." Niebuhr continues:

In consequence of the coming of this Jesus Christ to us we are able to say in the midst of our vast distrust, our betraying and being betrayed, our certainty of death and our temptations to curse our birth: Abba, Our Father. And this we say to the ground of being, to the mystery out of which we come, to the power over life and death. Our Father, who art in heaven, hallowed be thy name; I believe, help thou my unbelief.[24]

[21] *Ibid.*

[22] Chap. 6 of "Faith on Earth" (unpublished book manuscript from the 1950s, hereafter cited as *FE*), "The Reconstruction of Faith," p. 17. (This chapter is one of the most important christological statements in all Niebuhr's writings. We shall look at "Faith on Earth" in detail in chap. 5.)

[23] *Ibid.*, p. 16.

[24] *Ibid.*, pp. 16-17.

THE RECONCILING WORK OF JESUS CHRIST

When I examine "Faith on Earth" and other writings in which Niebuhr's understanding of the redemptive action of God in Christ comes to expression,[25] I find Jesus as the Christ being spoken of in three major roles. He is *the prototypical faithful man.* His trust in and loyalty to God "is trust in this Lord of heaven and earth as One who has bound himself to care for the apparently most despised beings, human, animal and vegetable in his creation. He trusts completely in the loyalty of the transcendent One and in his power, being certain . . . that nothing can separate men from the love of God." [26] With this trust in God "the Jesus Christ of our history" combines complete loyalty to men. Jesus spends himself for his fellowmen. While he does not trust them, he is wholly faithful to them, "even or perhaps particularly," Niebuhr adds, "when he chastises them for their disloyalty to each other and their distrust of God." In his character as supremely faithful man he is the image of our potential—he is true personhood:

It is the personal relation of a faithful, trusting, loyal soul to the source of its being which is the astonishing thing. This is a superhuman thing according to all our experience of humanity. Yet it is humanity in idea, in essence. This, we say as we regard him, is what we might be if we were not the victims and the perpetrators of treason and distrust.[27]

But Jesus as the Christ is not only the exemplar of faith, the prototypical faithful man, he is also *the mediator of faith.* It is not simply that Niebuhr's Jesus (somewhat like the Jesus of the liberals) is the Son of God by virtue of his faith and faithfulness. It is not merely that he mediates faith by being the hero of faith. Jesus Christ becomes the means whereby trust in and loyalty to God are evoked by virtue of his resurrection from the dead:

Jesus Christ was designated to be the Son of God in power according to the Spirit of holiness by his resurrection from the dead. It is through

---

[25] In addition to "Logic of the Cross" I refer to *Meaning of Revelation;* to *Christ and Culture,* pp. 11-29; and especially to a remarkable handwritten unpublished lecture from the 1950s entitled "The Mediation of Faith" (p. 23).

[26] FE, "The Reconstruction of Faith," p. 14.

[27] *Ibid.,* pp. 14-15.

the resurrection that the great demonstration is made that the Determiner of human destiny is the One in whom Jesus Christ had faith. The resurrection of Christ from the dead is the act in which God shows himself to be one who keeps faith.[28]

Niebuhr provides a fitting summary statement for these first two roles of Jesus as the Christ in his thought: "Jesus Christ going to crucifixion and ignominy is the revelation of human faithfulness, of its possibility. The resurrection of Jesus Christ from the dead is the demonstration of the faithfulness of God, by which the distrust of man is broken and his trust in the power and goodness, that is loyalty of God, [is] called forth." [29]

There is a third role of Jesus as the Christ implied and required by Niebuhr's position, though direct statements of it are not frequent. Jesus who is "Son of God in his faith" and is affirmed as Son of God in his resurrection, is also the *expression and symbol of a participation by God in the suffering of the beings dependent upon him*. Reconciliation of man to God involves a showing forth of God's faithfulness and love that converts man's distrust and enmity to trust and loyalty. Such a faithfulness and love is incredible unless there is a participating "pain of God." [30] The supposed union of supreme goodness and supreme power in God does not square with the suffering of innocence in a cosmic vicariousness unless (*a*) God has limited his sovereignty over the consciousness and actions of man, and (*b*) he too shares in the agonies and waste of being that result from human autonomy and divine lawfulness. Jesus Christ, simultaneously the prototypical suffering innocent and the faithful Son of God, symbolizes and is an expression of that participating pain of God which is an indispensable element in the reconciliation of man to God and in the reconstruction of faith.[31]

[28] "Mediation of Faith," p. 21.

[29] *Ibid.*

[30] I take this phrase from Kazoh Kitamori, *The Theology of the Pain of God*, trans. from the Japanese, *Kami No Itami No Shingaku*, 5th ed., 1958 (Richmond: John Knox Press, 1965).

[31] See especially "War as Crucifixion," *Christian Century*, 60 (April 28, 1943): "[The cross] . . . is a revelation, though 'in a glass darkly,' of the

In his analysis of Niebuhr's Christology, Hans Frei offers a concise set of standards which the tradition of faith imposes on any christological statement: "A Christology must indicate the Lord's consubstantiality with the Father according to his Godhead; his consubstantiality with us according to his humanity; the union of the two distinct natures; and the abiding distinctness and unconfusedness of these two natures in the one, unitary person." [32] Frei, on the basis of an analysis of Niebuhr's christological section in *Christ and Culture*,[33] sees Niebuhr as meeting these traditional standards in a way that avoids either a psychologizing of the unity between Jesus as the Christ and the Father, or at the other extreme, a spiritualizing of the Christ which disregards all questions of the historicity of Jesus. "He [Niebuhr] seeks to understand Jesus Christ as having his unity in his moral purpose, as being one in his moral being. . . . The unity of the person of Jesus Christ is embedded in and immediately present to his teaching and practice. . . . The teaching and acts of Jesus Christ, his moral virtues, themselves the direct clue to his being. In them one may find, by an historical and at the same time theological exegesis, in faith, hope and love, the unique moral Sonship to God of one who is completely at one with men." [34] Frei rightly asserts that this christological direction is a unique constructive contribution to contemporary theology. Drawing on additional materials, my presentation of themes in Niebuhr's understanding of Jesus as the Christ confirms Frei's

---

intense moral earnestness of a God who will not abandon mankind to self-destruction; it confronts us with the tragic consequences of moral failure. It does all this because it is sacrifice—the self-sacrifice of Jesus Christ for those whom he loves and God's sacrifice of his best-loved son for the sake of the just and the unjust. War (and the suffering of the innocent in it) is like the cross in this respect" (p. 514); "Interpreted through the cross of Jesus Christ the suffering of the innocent is seen not as the suffering of temporal men but of the eternal victim 'slain from the foundations of the world.' If the Son of God is being crucified in this war along with the malefactors—and he is being crucified on many an obscure hill—them the graciousness of God, the self-giving love, is more manifest here than in all the years of peace" (p. 515).

[32] Hans Frei, "The Theology of H. Richard Niebuhr," in Paul Ramsey, ed., *Faith and Ethics* (Torchbooks; New York: Harper & Row [1957], 1965), p. 115.

[33] *Christ and Culture*, pp. 11-29.

[34] Frei, "Theology of H. Richard Niebuhr," p. 115.

conclusions and, I believe, goes beyond them. What is offered here, however, only begins to mine the christological richness of "Faith on Earth," especially chapter 6. In the next chapter we will examine that work and its Christology more closely.

To speak of the relation between Jesus as the Christ and humanity as the relation in which our suspicion of being and our obsession with death are turned around is to speak of *revelation*. The disclosure of goodness and love at the heart of being relativizes our wisdom of survival and requires the adoption of new master images by which to interpret the actions that impinge upon us. Niebuhr's *Meaning of Revelation* is a carefully wrought but bold attempt to try to bring his readers and co-seers, through an evolution of thought and reflection upon their own experience, to the point where they can apprehend and be grasped by the oneness, power, goodness, and love of the sovereign God. Niebuhr wants to enable his readers to *see as faith sees*, and to *see what faith sees*. This means ultimately bringing the reader to the point where it becomes a possibility to "walk by him the man [Jesus] and thou comest to God." With Augustine, Niebuhr sees the center of God's redemptive action in Jesus as the Christ: "I do not say to thee, seek the way. The way itself has come to thee: arise and walk." [35] Around Jesus as the Christ arises a community of interpretation which, through his cross and resurrection, fixes on the premise "We are being saved." And in the transformation which that premise represents, the images of the heart that reason serves are converted from self-defensive, solipsistic images, or mechanical, impersonal images, to the image of One whose valuing is universal and whose power and goodness are the final reality.

In his lectures on the redeeming action of God, Niebuhr used what he called "parables" to epitomize elements in God's action as redeemer. He spoke of *reconciliation*, the making of peace where there had been hostility and wrath between man and God and between man and man. He spoke of *healing*, the restoration of health, wholeness, completeness through the removal of hostility,

[35] Niebuhr quoting Augustine in *Meaning of Revelation*, p. 191.

163

and overcoming the obsession with death. God's redeeming action involves *justice*, the restoration of right relations between man and God, man and man, and man and nature. It is a *rebirth*, a new beginning, man becomes a "new creation." And it is a literal *redemption*, a release of the captives from the bondage of sin and death, from shackled moral imagination, and from parochial images of community and responsibility.[36]

THE ETHICS OF RESPONSE TO GOD THE REDEEMER

What can we say of human action in response to the redemptive action of God? What are the ethical implications of faith in God the redeemer? Niebuhr's confessional phenomenology, grounded in the conviction of the sovereignty of God, leads to *a confluence of the indicative and the imperative in Christian ethics.* Insofar as faith, seeing through the clarifying lenses of revelation, discerns the contours of the kingdom of God—the actual present relation of sovereign God and dependent being—it shapes its responses and initiatives in accordance with that reality. To "see the kingdom," and to interpret actions in my action field in accordance with an image of divine action and reality, is already to grasp the imperatives under which I stand, at least in principle.

The *indicative* that comes to expression in Niebuhr's teaching about God's redemptive action might be stated this way: From a human point of view we are being slain all day long. But our interpretation of our life of response in accordance with that viewpoint has been decisively interrupted by the teachings and actions, the death and vindication of Jesus—who appeared in our history as a man, and who is present in the community of interpretation formed around him. As exemplar and mediator of radical faith in the faithfulness of the power by which we are, he has embodied a New Covenant which lays bare the fiduciary structure of the relation between God and man and between man and man, and which invites a conscious joining of a universal community of faithfulness. From the ability to trust, which Jesus as the New

[36] See class lecture, April 21, 1952 (Yetter, pp. 133-34).

Covenant inaugurates, flows a new master interpretative image for personal life and a new philosophy of history: *We are being saved.* *Ultimate power* in history and nature *is one with ultimate goodness;* both strain toward a restoration, fulfillment, and completion (perfection) of being.

And what of the *imperative* that arises for faith-consciousness when it begins thus to "see"? It might be put this way: So act as to express conscious membership in the universal community of faithfulness, to respond with hope to redemptive intent and power in all actions upon you, and to express trust in and loyalty to the cause of that One to whom and to whose cause Jesus the Christ is loyal.

If we depict diagrammatically the triadic structure of our life in response to the redemptive action of God, it might be represented as shown in figure 4.

Divine power and goodness loyal
to finite being

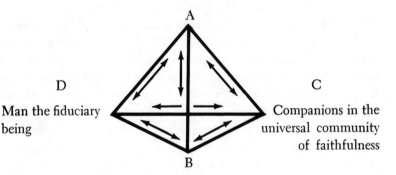

A

D
Man the fiduciary
being

C
Companions in the
universal community
of faithfulness

B

Jesus the Christ as reconciling
companion and mediator of faith
in the faithfulness of God

Fig. 4

Here the impingement of divine action upon human experience and consciousness comes as a disclosure of a unity and a personal character in the source and limiter of life and being, a personal character that loves that which issues from it. In that disclosing, for which Jesus as the Christ is our principal mediator, reconciliation to the divine character and to our companions in being—to whom he is also faithful—is initiated.

3. RESPONSE TO THE CREATIVE ACTION OF GOD: NIEBUHR'S VALUE THEORY

We come now to one of the most pervasive and complex dimensions in Niebuhr's mode of thinking and speaking of divine action and human response—his approach through value-valuation. We have already had occasion to refer to the early and prominent role of value-thinking in his emerging position. In the chapter on Niebuhr's relation to Troeltsch we noted the influences upon him of Troeltsch's value-thinking; that *knowing* is a matter that involves *valuing*; that practical ethics requires engagement with the real and diverse values that compete for people's loyalties; and that personal integrity and cultural coherence both require a synthesis of values that can only be achieved through an overarching religious commitment. In the chapter on Niebuhr's analysis of the cultural captivity of the church and man's bondage in sin, the centrality of value-thinking was patent. There Niebuhr's understanding of the human will was presented in value terms. Revelation and redemption were seen to grow out of the experience of being valued by God and of undergoing the transvaluation in valuing which that experience entails. And under the influence of Luther, Calvin, and Edwards (but also Augustine and many others), Niebuhr made it clear that true knowledge of God *is* value-knowledge. One responds to God's valuing with trust and loyalty; faith is a valuing.

CREATED BEING AND VALUE

It may be well at the outset to clarify the connection in Niebuhr's thought between creation—the divine creative action—and the idea of value-valuation. For in doing so we come face to face with the fundamental premise of the value-valuation dimension of Niebuhr's theological-ethical approach. That premise, formally stated, is: *"Being and value are inseparable."* Translated into more concrete terms: "Whatever is, is good." Though we will clarify the ground and implications of these cryptic formulations in detail, the heart of the matter can be stated briefly: Through the redemptive action of God, the faith-knower begins to trust the creative source or action by which he is and by which all that *is* (or has being) is. In this reconciliation to the Creator, the faith-knower knows himself to be valued being. The experience of being valued transforms his personal axiology. He begins to perceive that he and his companions-in-being are co-members of an inclusive commonwealth of being, and that this commonwealth is unified under the conserving, valuing regard of the One by whom it is and by whom it is faithfully sustained. To the Creator *all* being is valued being; all being is the object of redemptive care. From this standpoint, being (whatever is) cannot be separated from value (the worth of a being to Being); whatever is, is good.[37]

Having offered this preliminary statement of the relation between the idea of value and the creative action of God, I want to try to explicate this value-valuation dimension of Niebuhr's thought more fully. For the purposes of this analytic overview, it is useful to distinguish two levels or strata in Niebuhr's teaching about value-valuation. Though these elements are by no means separable in the actual dynamics of his thinking, it is helpful here to attend separately (1) to Niebuhr's epistemological dialogue with value theorists in theology and philosophical ethics, and (2) to his own practical theological ethics of response to the creative action of God.

VALUE THEORY AND THE KNOWLEDGE OF GOD

Earlier we observed that Niebuhr, at the beginning of the decisive formative period of his career, criticized the religious realism of his teacher Macintosh and other American theologians for its too

---

[37] To say, "Whatever is, is *good*," was to Niebuhr quite a different matter from saying, "Whatever is, is *right*." (His theory of the right is examined on pp. 174-75; 180-81 below.)

uncritical subordination of religion and God to the self-realization of man and to the conservation of human values. In "The Social Gospel and the Mind of Jesus" Niebuhr scored the image of Jesus in the Social Gospel theologies as being primarily that of a moralist —"interested above all in the conservation and realization of moral values." Yet during the same period Niebuhr found Barthian crisis theology deficient because it left an utter disjunction between God and human value-aspirations.

In his important 1937 paper "Value Theory and Theology" [38] Niebuhr tried to clarify the epistemological basis of a position that could incorporate value-valuation in its depiction of the relation of God and man, but do so without falling into the subordination of God to human standards of value. Niebuhr begins his paper with a thoroughgoing critique of value theologies. His first major point is that all the principal forms of the theological adaptation of value theory (he distinguishes three kinds) suffer finally from the same objectionable feature: "they assume that men have a knowledge of absolutely valid values which is not only independent of their knowledge of God but which is also in some way determinative of God." [39] This fundamental flaw expresses itself in three serious deficiencies of value theology: (1) When God is defined in terms of prior valuing, theology becomes an "interested" enterprise; it sacrifices its "objectivity" and loses its independence. "A theological science which is interested above all in serving the needs of men becomes a bad science incapable of supplying real benefits." But a theological science "that deals disinterestedly with its material may be of very great benefit indeed, as history indicates. For disinterested theology has been pursued at various times in the past, notably by the Hebrew prophets." [40] (2) Value theology falls into "religious unsatisfactoriness" because

---

[38] In *Nature of Religious Experience*, pp. 93-116.

[39] *Ibid.*, p. 95.

[40] *Ibid.*, p. 101. This deficiency Niebuhr characterizes as the "scientific inadequacy" of value theology. In a somewhat awkward way he is calling for a *disinterested interest* in the object of theology—an interest that loves God "for his own sake rather than for the sake of any value, high or low, material or spiritual, which he is conceived to conserve, promote or increase" (p. 102).

it tends to confuse the worship of God with the worship of the values in reference to which he is understood. This results in a reductionism in which only those elements of divine action considered to be relevant to the operative value standard are brought into view.[41] And (3) value theology gets involved in philosophical inadequacies. It is a mistaken tactic for theology to try to evade the dogmas of religion by basing itself on ethics. For every ethics finally rests upon a dogmatic—that is to say religious—basis: "Whatever may be true of the dogmas of metaphysics, the dogmas of ethics are religious. They are assertions of faith, confessions of trust in something which makes life worth living, commitments of the self to a god." [42] An even more serious philosophical inadequacy arises out of value theology's failure to face the relativity of its dogmatic value standards. Value theologies have spoken of values that are relative to *human* structures and processes as though they were the final values of reality "or, at least, as the standpoint whence the values of [the] universe become visible as an integrated system." [43] Values relative to animal life are almost never included in statements of human value systems. "It is not only possible but highly probable that human ideas of justice and goodness . . . are out of line, so to speak, with divine ideas of goodness and justice or with goodness and justice relative to the divine nature, so that conflict and tragedy rather than progressive integration are to be looked for." [44] Some of men's grandest illusions have grown out of the belief that values relative to men—to *some* men—fit together in an integrated harmony from which it is possible to extrapolate an overarching web of universal values.

Niebuhr's critique of previous value theologies sets the parameters for his own attempt at developing the basis of a more adequate position. At the outset he underscores the indispensability of the dimension of valuation in theology and ethics. Religion *is* an affair of valuation. There is no genuine knowledge of God that is

---

[41] *Ibid.*, pp. 102-3.
[42] *Ibid.*, pp. 105-6.
[43] *Ibid.*, p. 106.
[44] *Ibid.*, pp. 109-10.

not value-knowledge.[45] But how can valuation be incorporated into theology in such a way as to have its categories shaped in accordance with the being and valuing of God rather than on the basis of prior value assumptions or commitments?

Here, says Niebuhr, an adequate value theology must recognize the relativity of values, but do so without prejudice to their objectivity. This means interpreting values not as relative to conscious desires and needs—not as psychologically or emotionally relative, but rather "as relative to structure and organic needs." Value, he argues, cannot be abstracted from the relation between a subject and an object (or better, from the relation between beings). "Value has no existence save in valued beings, and they possess value not as an independent quality but by virtue of their character or constitution, as that which corresponds to a need." [46]

How can relational value theory speak of God—of that which has the value of deity for man? "The value of deity would appear . . . to be quite independent of human desire and consciousness of need, but not independent of the human constitution and its actual need." [47] A man's actual need for deity is not identical with his feeling of dependence or his sense of the numinous. Nor is it identical with his need for that which will conserve or justify his highest values. "The religious need," Niebuhr writes,

is the need for that which makes life worth living, which bestows meaning on life by revealing itself as the final source of life's being and value. The religious need is satisfied only in so far as man is able to recognize himself as valued by something beyond himself. . . . The valuation of which man becomes aware in religious experience is not first of all his evaluation of a being, but that being's evaluation of him.[48]

[45] *Ibid.*, p. 112.

[46] *Ibid.*, p. 113.

[47] *Ibid.* "The situation may be stated positively in the terms of Augustine, that God has created us toward himself and that our souls are restless until they find rest in him. It may be stated negatively by saying that, while the being men call God exists independently of the creatures constituted to need him, it is not possible to define his Deity without reference to his relation to his creatures."

[48] *Ibid.*, p. 115.

Religious experience, so understood, does include a response of valuing from man, but according to Niebuhr its more primary expression comes in the judgment "This is the being which values me or judges me, by relation to which I have worth or possibility of worth." Secondarily and reflexively it gives rise to the judgment "This is the being of supreme intrinsic value, which corresponds to all my deepest needs." [49]

"Such a value-experience is primitive and original. It deals with that absolute source of all value by relation to which all other things have their value." To describe it in preestablished categories is inevitably to lose sight of its fundamental character and to falsify it. "The experience of the ground and source of all value leads to the criticism and reconstruction of the ethical system rather than to the support of one which has been accepted as absolute prior to the experience." [50]

When one reads the conclusion of this paper, with its characterization of the "religious need" and its speaking of deity value in terms of that Being which can fulfill the religious need, it seems necessary to ask whether Niebuhr really escapes the dilemma of value theology he indicated at the outset. Has he not fallen into the same trap of defining God in terms of human need (albeit in terms of "objective"—structural or organic—need rather than psychological or emotional need)? Three points have to be made in answer to that question. First, though Niebuhr characterizes the religious need as "the need for that which makes life worth living, which bestows meaning on life by revealing itself as the final source of life's being and value," [51] the value-commitments implied in that statement are formal and transcendental. They are not content-specific. He counts on religious experience, the experience of revelation, to fill them with normative content. Second, this makes clear the confessional basis of Niebuhr's value theology. He has argued that every ethics has a dogmatic basis. Here we see a major aspect of his faith basis quite clearly. *He really does believe that revelation is*

[49] *Ibid.*
[50] *Ibid.*, pp. 115-16.
[51] *Ibid.*, p. 115.

real, and that the Other encountered in religious experience is real Being. And he clearly believes that the Other meets us in the revelation event in such a way as to transform, remake, and renew our categories of valuing, our master images of the heart by which we interpret action upon us, and our behavioral actions and responses to action upon us.[52] Third, Niebuhr believes that the transvaluation of valuing which religious experience brings, works toward the realization of the best (objectively speaking) interests of the self as well as of the commonwealth of being of which the self is a part. His point over against other value theologies, however, is that "what the best interests are cannot be decided prior to the experience of that which is the source of all value." [53]

THE CENTER OF VALUE

The other major statement in Niebuhr's dialogue with value theorists in theology and ethics came fifteen years later in an article entitled "The Center of Value." [54] In this article Niebuhr's position has not basically changed from what we saw of it in "Value Theory and Theology." Here, however, it is brought into dialogue with philosophical ethicists rather than value theologians, and it is brought into engagement with somewhat different issues. By 1952 Niebuhr has begun to call his position "objective relationism" to avoid the confusion of his kind of relativism with the psychological and emotional relativism of some intuitionists and emotivists and their opponents in philosophical ethics.

Niebuhr begins by reiterating the fundamental points of a relational theory of value. Value has no existence in itself. "Value is present whenever one existent being with capacities and poten-

[52] In these and many other ways this article points toward *Meaning of Revelation,* where Niebuhr describes in rich and stirring imagery the experience of revelation and of the transformations of valuing, interpretative imagery, capacity to trust, and moral action that revelation brings. See esp. chap. 3, "Reasons of the Heart," and chap. 4, "The Deity of God."

[53] "Value Theory and Theology," p. 115.

[54] Originally published in Ruth Nanda Anshen, ed., *Moral Principles of Action* (New York: Harper & Brothers, 1952). Quotations here are from the version in *Radical Monotheism,* pp. 100-13.

tialities confronts another existence that limits or completes or complements it. . . . Good is a term which not only can be but which . . . must be applied to that which meets the needs, which fits the capacity, which corresponds to the potentialities of an existent being. . . . Evil . . . is that which thwarts, destroys, or starves a being in its activities." [55] Value may be said to be "present objectively for an observer in the fittingness or unfittingness of being to being." [56] As he argued in 1937, Niebuhr repeats, "Such relational value theory is then relativistic, not in the sense that value is relative to emotion, hence private and irrational, but in the sense in which physical science is relativistic without loss of objectivity." [57]

To Niebuhr the relational theory, with its understanding of objective value, avoids many of the difficulties that beset the positions of both the intuitionists and the emotivists in ethics. The former tend to define value as *sui generis*—as distinct from any existence. In doing so, Niebuhr argues, they almost inevitably begin "to confuse [value] . . . with a certain kind of being, that of ideas for instance, and at the same time to deny value to non-ideal existence." [58] To do so is to confuse good with the idea of good, and so to bifurcate being and value. The emotivists (or subjectivists), on the other hand, in regarding the good as a function of desire, are involved in an even more serious split of being and value. By "relating value to only one sort of power and that an ultimately unintelligible one, [their approach] results in the irrationality of separating value judgments from fact judgments." This is an irrational result, Niebuhr contends, "since it leaves value judgments beyond the range of rational criticism and ignores the presence of value judgments in all fact judgments." [59]

In contrast, relational value theory is based on the understanding

[55] *Ibid.*, p. 103.
[56] *Ibid.*
[57] *Ibid.*, p. 106.
[58] *Ibid.*
[59] *Ibid.*, p. 107.

that being and value are inseparably connected. But it also understands "that value cannot be identified with a certain mode of being or any being considered in isolation, whether it be ideal or actual." In a summary statement Niebuhr writes:

> Value is the *good-for-ness* of being for being in their reciprocity, their animosity, and their mutual aid. Value cannot be defined or intuited in itself for it has no existence in itself; and nothing is valuable in itself, but everything has value, positive or negative, in its relations. *Thus value is not a relation but arises in the relations of being to being.*[60]

It is important to remind ourselves, however, that Niebuhr is speaking here of a "good-for-ness" that corresponds to the *real* entelechy or needs of the valuing being. Part of the function of ethics is to help in the development of "a rational non-participating, disinterested view of the relations of being to being" by which desiring and valuing can be educated to recognize the good as *its* good. Paraphrasing Kant, Niebuhr writes, "Desire without reason is blind; reason without desire is impotent." [61]

Relational value theory, Niebuhr asserts, provides a basis for distinguishing between the *good* and the *right* without either collapsing the one into the other or setting them up as two distinct principles.

> "Right" means that relation between beings, good-for-each-other, in which their potentiality of being good for each other is realized. It is that relation in which beings that are actually bound together in their interdependent existence consent to each other, actually further each other, in the realization of their potentialities.[62]

"Right" does become a part of the good as when right relatedness among parts becomes an element in the goodness of a whole for another being, Niebuhr acknowledges. "But in the interaction of being with being, right is not merely a means to the good; it is the goodness of relatedness in action." [63]

---

[60] *Ibid.*, p. 107. (Italics added.)
[61] *Ibid.*, p. 108.
[62] *Ibid.*
[63] *Ibid.*

Insofar as a value theory is relational (and Niebuhr contends that all value theories become relational when engaged with concrete problems), it must have a value center or central standard. "If one is to construct anything like a consistent system of value judgments and determinations of what is right . . . it is necessary to take one's standpoint with or in some being accepted as the center of value." [64] Most philosophical value theories, he suggests, have one or more such overt centers of value, and often these are coupled with one or more covert sources of value standards.[65] "In view of this necessity of beginning with a value-center," he writes,

it seems evident that every theory of value, so far as it is relational, is religious in character. Every such theory adopts as its explicit or implicit starting point some being or beings in relation to which good is judged to be good and evil evil, in relation to which also the rightness or wrongness of its relations to other beings is examined. The question of the goodness of this central being for other beings is usually not considered.[66]

Biblical faith, Niebuhr contends, is much more compatible with relational value theory than with essentialistic or spiritualistic theories. The radical monotheism of biblical faith results in a relativism like that acknowledged by relational theory: all being is of value in relation to the transcendent Being, and no finite being or value should be confused with God. Radical monotheism relativizes all the value standards of other relational theories and subordinates them to the most universalizing center of valuing. "Its starting point, its dogmatic beginning, is with the transcendent One for whom alone there is an ultimate good, and for whom, as the source and end of all things, whatever is, is good." [67] Mono-

[64] *Ibid.*, p. 109.

[65] For Niebuhr's examples ("English empiricism," Bergson's vitalism, Hartmann's neo-idealism) see *ibid.*, pp. 109-11.

[66] *Ibid.*, pp. 110-11.

[67] *Ibid.*, p. 112. These themes are most fully developed in the lectures that make up the main part of *Radical Monotheism*. There he utilizes a typology in which he contrasts *polytheism* (denoting trust in and loyalty to a variety of

theistic faith "no more begins by asking what God is good for than humanistic or vitalistic ethics begins by the inquiry what man or life is good for." But, Niebuhr concludes, "it has the great advantage over humanism and vitalism that it does not offer an evident abstraction of one sort of finite being from the rest of existence, with the consequent appearance of arbitrariness in the selection of finite centers of value that from any disinterested point of view have no greater claim to centrality than any others." [68]

THE ETHICS OF RESPONSE TO GOD THE CREATOR

Having examined the more formal statements of his value theory, I want to turn now to Niebuhr's development of his practical ethical thinking around the theme of response to the creative action of God. Where his lectures overlap with the material we have looked at, I will simply indicate the congruence. I will reserve critical questions that arise in relation to the ideas we have considered until the full contours of Niebuhr's position are before us.

"Moral life has a basis in the aesthetic." [69] With this sentence Niebuhr begins what must have been one of his favorite sections of his lecture course on ethics. Previously we have seen him insisting that it is a distortion to reduce the idea of perfection narrowly to moral perfection or the idea of sin to moral failure.[70] In both perfection and sin there is an aesthetic dimension. And in man's response to the creative action of God there is a valuing that includes but transcends moral valuing—a valuing that appreciates the beauty, the variety, the richness of all being, and approaches an aesthetically grounded understanding that "whatever is, is good."

Our usual form of response to the givenness of beings and

---

finite centers of value) and *henotheism* (denoting the ascription of supreme value to some one finite center or standard of worth) with *radical monotheism* (trust in and loyalty to God as the One supreme source and center of value).

[68] *Ibid.*

[69] Class lecture, March 26, 1952 (Yetter, p. 104).

[70] See "Man the Sinner," pp. 273-74.

events is to discriminate among them on the basis of some egocentric system of relational valuing. "We have," says Niebuhr, "a
perverted selectivity of what is important." We divide the world
into the good, the true, the important, and into that which ought
not to be: the bad, the ugly, the false, the unimportant. We tend
to respond as though a good creator is the power active in all the
good creatures. To the rest we respond as if it were either the rough
material on which the creator must still impress his pattern or as
if it were the product of a bad creator. In this *inversus a se* we
concentrate on the works of our own hands and treat the things
with which we come into contact with the attitude of utilitarianism:
How can we exploit this to our own use? How can I make this
instrumentally valuable? All human and animal worth becomes
subject to exploitation. Ultimately behind inhumanity is a lack of
the aesthetic.[71]

In contrast to the self-referencing perversions of our response
in sin to God the creator, the Christian response is quite different.
(Here Niebuhr makes reference to Psalm 8, Isaiah 40:26, Matthew
6:28-30, Luke 12:6-7.) "Man is of more value than the sparrows,
but the value of the sparrow is asserted." The reason they are to
be valued, he continues, is not because they have a human source
or because they can be used to any human end. "They are valuable
because they are the product of the infinite Creator." [72] In this
same lecture Niebuhr refers to Augustine's *Confessions*, the concluding chapters of book 13, in which "exegetical comments on
creation—adorational and prayerful rather than instructional—say
that surely whatever is, is good; for it is by the power of God that
they are present in the moment. All things are to be loved because
of their relation to him; they would not be if they were not good
in his sight." [73] St. Francis, Schweitzer, and Woolman are all
quoted as witnesses for a more universal valuing. But it is Jonathan

[71] This entire paragraph is made up of quotes or paraphrases from Yetter's
notes on Niebuhr's lecture of March 26, 1952 (pp. 105-6).

[72] *Ibid.*, p. 106.

[73] *Ibid.*

Edwards who has obviously been most influential on Niebuhr in this regard: "When we come to Jonathan Edwards we get the more adequate universalisitic view in which the participation of a thing in Being is the highest criterion of value and appreciation." [74]

One can approach the world of being with the attitude "whatever is, is good" only when "the deep distrust of the ground of being is changed by the *metanoia* [worked by redemption]; . . . only then do we know that the Creator is not a demonic being, that it is not chance that brought us into being." In our *metanoia*, Niebuhr continues, "we recognize that the Creator has something like personality. The recognition of this is the miracle which happens when we come into relation with the Son, whom the Father presents to us as Son and as his revelation of his nature." [75]

Under the impact of this *metanoia* our attitudes toward created being begin to change. We are not enabled to say, "Whatever is, is good" at once; nor do we respond responsibly to God the creator without the disciplines and preparations necessary to appropriate the graciousness of God's valuing of us that revelation discloses. Niebuhr sees five stages in this revolution in our value responses to God's creations.

First there is *acceptance*. As the experience of revelation begins with the experience of being valued, so acceptance begins with self-acceptance. In acceptance of self we come to say, "I am willed; I am accepted"; therefore I can will myself. Self-acceptance involves knowing the limits of my responsibility; it puts boundaries on both my pride and my despair. Turned outward, acceptance says, "Though there are beings I don't like and whose existence seems inimical to me, I will and can respect their right to be."

The second stage is *affirmation*. Affirmation asserts that "what

[74] *Ibid.*, p. 107.
[75] Class lecture, March 28, 1952 (Yetter, pp. 108-9). Characteristically Niebuhr goes on to say that we cannot claim exclusivism for this revelation; others than Christians "see the given stuff of existence as good." We can only say confessionally that we have this good news through Jesus Christ (p. 109).

is ought to be." Yetter quotes Niebuhr as saying, "My great act of distrust is to say: it would have been better if I had not been." Turned outward, distrust of Being leads to the bifurcation of reality and leads us to say of some of its parts, "That ought not to be." Christians are to affirm their enemy; even while they are at war with him, they affirm that he ought to be. Affirmation says, "Love your enemies." It believes that conflict will always be, but that strife can be creative when it conserves the ought-to-be-ness of the opponent.

The third stage in our response to God as creator—or to God in his creation—is *understanding*. Understanding is not only acceptance of the existence of the inimical or the strange; nor is it only the affirmation of its worth, despite its lack of appeal or supportiveness to me. Understanding says, "Let me look at it; let me try to understand it." Understanding undertakes the struggle to think the thoughts of the Creator after him and to perceive and appreciate the goodness that he has created.

The fourth stage Niebuhr speaks of in our response to the creative action of God is *cultivation*. Cultivation is the service and tending of created being. It is a response that serves the entelechy in the being served. "If understanding is response to the Creator," Niebuhr is quoted as saying, "cultivation and tending is response to the Redeemer." This is not to say that we are to tend all the tendencies in the beings we serve; cultivation requires selectivity, elimination, and transplanting. But it does seek to realize the best for being without reference to its utilitarian or instrumentalist value.

Beyond cultivation there is *mimesis*—mimesis is response to the creative activity of God by imitation—imitation, not of the products, but of the creative action itself: "The great human creator does not imitate the work of God, but rather he imitates the working of God. . . . We are created to be creative, to be mimetic. We must realize that we are limited; we cannot begin with nothing; our sense of novelty is small. But we can create. We can create in pride and to our destruction; or we can create in response to God, prayer-

179

fully. Thanks be to God that creation is not complete, but that it continues toward us and also through us." [76]

Before we conclude this section, two remaining questions must be dealt with briefly. First there is the question of Niebuhr's theory of the right. "Right," we saw earlier, "means that relation between beings, good-for-each other, in which their potentiality of being good for each other is realized." Right "is the goodness of relatedness in action." Right, says Niebuhr, "is never definable in the abstract but only by reference to the nature and relations of beings in interaction." [77] Reflection upon these comments about right points to some important implications for a proper understanding of his ethics: (1) *Right* for Niebuhr, like *good* or *value*, is a relational matter. In fact, *it is a particular kind of valuing relation* —one in which beings are so related as to mutually serve their objective (as opposed to merely perceived or desired) needs. (2) To value *rightly* is to value according to a universal standard and from a universal standpoint; it is to value as God values. (3) Through the experience of knowing oneself to be valued by God, the self's capacity to value other being as God values it is expanded; in the continuing revolution that is *metanoia* this capacity continues to expand. (4) The standpoint of monotheistic faith, radically centering in God as source and center of value, provides a *critical* standpoint by which misvaluing and wrong (unjust) valuing can be judged. And (5) by reference to the faith and love of Jesus, and of other incarnators of radically monotheistic faith, it offers general guidelines for the direction of right valuing. But (6) it does not offer much specific guidance in the selection and ordering of subsidiary centers or norms of valuing, and (7) it does not provide much concrete help in the task of choosing which among the incommensurate goods competing for our valuing deserve our preference.

On the basis of the foregoing reflections I think we have to say

---

[76] The discussion of these five stages in its entirety is drawn from *Ibid.*, pp. 109-12.

[77] "Center of Value," p. 108.

that, while Niebuhr offers the beginnings of that kind of theory of the right which one expects to find in a philosophical ethics, he does not develop it very far at that level. And so far as he has developed it, it is not clear that his position really does distinguish between the good and the right without collapsing the one into the other. It seems likely that futher development of his theory of the right at that level might have gone in either of two directions. He might, on the one hand, have developed an epistemology of right around the critical valuing of the God of monotheistic faith, somewhat in the manner of the venerable tradition of the "ideal observer" in philosophical ethics.[78] Or, on the other (and this seems the more likely tack for Niebuhr), he might have developed a theory of the right on a contractual model, synthesizing the themes of the commonwealth of being (triadically related to God as valuer and redeemer) and the universal community of faithfulness (triadically related to God as covenanting, faithful governor).[79] The themes of this latter approach are well developed in Niebuhr's thought, but he did not utilize them to develop a formal theory of the right or of justice.

The second issue I wanted to touch on is value preference. Niebuhr did not leave us entirely without guidelines. At the end of his classroom lectures on response to the creative action of God, he regularly addressed the question of how to choose from among the possible goods one might serve or pursue. He reviewed a representative selection of commonsense and philosophical-ethical value scales. Then he offered some guidelines for valuing in accordance with radically monotheistic faith: (1) The fundamental

[78] Niebuhr's important paper "The Ego-Alter Dialectic and the Conscience," *Journal of Philosophy*, 42 (1945), pp. 352-59 is a helpful exploration of this option.

[79] See Niebuhr's "Introduction to Biblical Ethics," in Waldo Beach and H. Richard Niebuhr, eds., *Christian Ethics* (New York: Ronald Press, 1955), pp. 17-21; *Radical Monotheism*, pp. 40-42; "The Idea of Covenant and American Democracy," *Church History*, 23, no. 2 (1954); and "The Protestant Movement and Democracy," in J. W. Smith and A. L. Jamison, eds., *The Shaping of American Religion* (Princeton: Princeton University Press, 1961), pp. 20-71.

value choice in this perspective is not between good and evil, but between a greater or a lesser good. (2) Do not serve yourself in your valuing, for you are being served. If you value in accordance with God's valuing, your needs will be served, for they are included in God's valuing. (3) Serve that value which is in greatest need of your service, not that which is considered highest. (4) Serve that which is at hand; serve the nearest. (5) In every choice of value one is making a sacrifice of something sacred. Vicarious suffering is in the nature of things; one good thing is sacrificed for another. This is made clear in the cross.[80]

In and through Niebuhr's discussion of response to divine creative action a vision of the kingdom of God—of how it actually is between God and dependent being—comes to expression. The vision itself is an indicative. From the indicative flows an imperative thrust. I conclude this section with an attempt to summarize both the indicative that comes to expression in Niebuhr's ethics of response to divine creative action and the imperative it implies. As in the previous section I will offer a diagram of the triadic structure of this dimension of man's response to God.

The *indicative:* The creative source of being and the entropy-defying power that sustains it and produces ever new novelties is One. The Creator (who is something like personality) is loyal to that which issues from him and he actively wills its fulfillment and completion. Because all that is, issues from him, and because he values it, whatever is, is good.

The *imperative:* So act in your pursuit of the good as to express faith in the one God as the source of all being and center of all value, refusing to ascribe highest trust in and loyalty to any other, lesser cause or center of value; make his valuing of being the norm of your valuing, and act so as to conserve and fulfill your companions in the commonwealth of being.

A diagrammatic representation of the triadic structure of man's response in and to the creative action of God may be shown as in figure 5.

[80] This version is compiled from p. 24 of the typescript of Niebuhr's lectures for 1946–47, and from p. 116 of Yetter's notes (lecture for March 31, 1952).

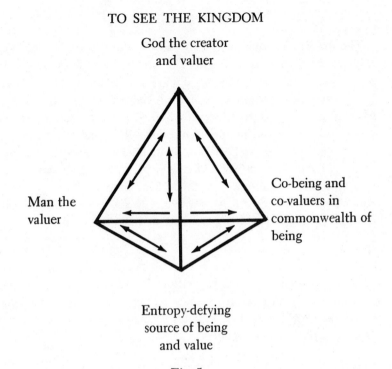

God the creator
and valuer

Man the
valuer

Co-being and
co-valuers in
commonwealth of
being

Entropy-defying
source of being
and value

Fig. 5

4. RESPONSE TO THE GOVERNING ACTION OF GOD: THE THEORY OF SELF-DENIAL

Niebuhr's ethics of response to the governing action of God was hammered out principally in the midst of crises in national and international life. It is built around what I have identified as the *process-structural* metaphor for imaging God-in-relation to man. Earlier we examined the emergence of this approach in Niebuhr's wrestle with the Japanese invasion of Manchuria in the thirties. There, and in his coming to terms with the prophetic faith and view of history held by "Jesus the revolutionary strategist," Niebuhr became clear that prior to asking, What must we do? in any given crisis situation, the Christian person or community must ask a prior question: What is God doing?

183

The massive international crisis and bloodletting of World War II pressed this question on Niebuhr with a forcefulness he could not avoid. If God is sovereign, if God is one in his power, love, and justice, and if God is sovereignly related to human history, what is his relation to this war? In his effort to discern God's action in the war, and to understand how Christians might respond so as to respond to God's action in it, Niebuhr came to a depth of insight and a clarity of vision which, in my judgment, stand in almost direct continuity with biblical prophecy. If we would understand Niebuhr's ethics of response to God's governing action it is to this theology of emergency that we first must look.

GOD AND WAR

As Niebuhr took stock of the efforts by Christian thinkers and groups to bring the war into theological perspective, he found some encouragement in the fact that all seemed to see the war as an expression of God's judgment:

> Something has been gained as a result of the very general recognition that God is judging the nations, the churches and all mankind in this great conflict and crucifixion. The conviction of sin, which the social gospel has brought about, and the old understanding of history, which Marxism has forced Christianity to remember, leave all Christians with a bad conscience in the presence of this struggle and with the recognition that men are reaping what they have sown.[81]

All the Christian groups seem resolved, he observes, to work for the achievement of a just peace—a peace that acknowledges the moral failings and wrongness of all parties to the war instead of trying to cloak the vanquished in exclusive guilt.

Niebuhr finds fault with all the approaches of Christian groups to the war, however, at the point of their failure to see that God's judgment in it requires a response to his action in the *present*. The pacifists, he points out, besides attending to the action of God in judgment, believe "Christians ought to attend to the bad actions

---

[81] "War as the Judgment of God," *Christian Century*, 59 (May 13, 1942), p. 630.

of all men who are making war and respond to the latter by refusal to participate in the conflict." Believing that men, not God, make war, the pacifists want to participate in the coming peace-making but refrain from all present involvement in war.[82] In contrast to the pacifists there are the patriots. They too regard war as the judgment of God. But in addition they see it "as a defense of our own country against the enemies not of God so much as of our country." This patriotic response seeks to keep separate the response of the Christian to God in war and the response of the Christian as citizen to the enemy.[83] A third group (which seems to include Reinhold Niebuhr) "makes a distinction between the absolute judgment of God to which all men must respond with penitence, and the relative judgments of men to which other relative judgments must be opposed." For this group "the war requires the double response of contrition for common sin and of confident assertion of the relative rightness of democracy in opposition to totalitarianism." [84]

Each of these approaches is involved in a *dualism* of response. In addition to responding to the action of God they are intent on responding to the action of the opponent as well. The dualism of double response "is an intolerable one; it makes us 'double-minded men, unstable in all our ways,' ditheists who have two Gods, the Father of Jesus Christ and our country, or Him and Democracy, or Him and Peace. Country, Democracy and Peace are surely values of a high order, if they are under God, but as rivals of God they are betrayers of life." [85]

I want now to try to state Niebuhr's position as it emerges in the several articles he wrote on God's involvement in the war. First it is important to note Niebuhr's own understanding of the point of view from which he speaks. A clear statement on this emerged in his response to a critic who asserted that Niebuhr was trying to understand the war "from God's point of view." Niebuhr

[82] *Ibid.*, p. 630.
[83] *Ibid.*, pp. 630-31. (The use of the term "patriots" is mine, not Niebuhr's.)
[84] *Ibid.*, p. 631.
[85] *Ibid.*

185

categorically rejected the charge. "I am trying to think about war and peace," he wrote,

from the only point of view available to me, which is that of a man whose thoughts are very far from being divine; but it is that of one who has been persuaded that if he is to make any sense out of his experience and life he must always try to discover the universal in every particular and respond to it. Further, it is the point of view of one who has been required to seek in every particular that universal being and action which Jesus called Father. My problem is . . . that of understanding how to stand in the presence of God as I stand in the presence of every individual event, good or evil.[86]

Looking to Jesus as the model of faithfulness to the mono-theistic God, Niebuhr decries the kind of subjectivism that locates and interprets God's action as an affair of the inner life and feelings: "I cannot begin, as religious subjectivism does, with the Fourth Gospel, but must start with the Synoptics and with a Jesus who finds God's action not within himself but in objctive, natural and historic events." [87] For Niebuhr, here, as in his reply to his brother's critique of "The Grace of Doing Nothing" ten years before, God is in history as that objectively real "structure in things," the "rock against which we beat in vain." [88] He is that One who incorporates impersonal forces[89] as well as the aggressive and self-serving actions of men and movements in history into the divine process and will.

From the standpoint of faith in God as one and as creative and redemptive in his power, what does it mean to say that war is the judgment of God? How is divine justice to be understood and its operation to be discerned? Neither the simple hypothesis that God executes primitive vengeance on wrongdoers, nor the more complex view that in the processes of history righteousness ultimately is vindicated, is adequate to interpret the workings of divine justice.

---

[86] "Is God in the War?" Niebuhr's response to a letter from Virgil C. Aldrich, Professor of Philosophy, Rice Institute, *Christian Century*, 59 (August 5, 1942). Quote is from p. 954.

[87] *Ibid.*

[88] "A Communication: The Only Way into the Kingdom of God," p. 447.

[89] "The Grace of Doing Nothing," p. 379.

The suffering of the innocents cries out against these extrapolations from human views of justice. It is not the leaders of nations who bear the brunt of suffering and loss in war; nor is it usually the most powerful aggressors among the nations who endure the worst trampling. Faced with these facts Niebuhr proposes an alternate interpretative master image: "Wars are crucifixions." [90] The question must arise for Christians, "whether that understanding of cosmic justice which the crucifixion of Jesus Christ discovered to men must not and may not be applied to war, as it must and may be applied to many personal events that are unintelligible save through the cross. Is war, then, crucifixion?" [91]

I find Niebuhr's explication of how war and crucifixion are alike applicable to the United States' protracted entanglement in Indochina in recent years. War is very much like crucifixion, Niebuhr suggests, in that in both events justice and injustice are strangely intermixed, both on the side of those who regard themselves as upholders of the right, and on the side of the vanquished. Niebuhr has in mind that three were crucified on Golgotha: two supposedly guilty (though one of them recognized the relative justice of his punishment), and a third who was innocent of the charges made against him (yet ambiguously so since his kingdom held unknown dangers for Roman order and Jewish law). The crucifiers were no less mixed in their justice and injustice: they were "soldiers who did their duty in obedience to their oath, priests who acted according to their lights . . . a judge who failed in his duty, citizens who were devoted to the sacred values of Jewish culture, a mob overborne by emotion. They knew not what they did. War is like that—apparently indiscriminate in the choice of victims and of victors, whether these be thought of as individuals or as communities." [92]

War is like Crucifixion in a second sense. Both are occasions for the revelation of "the sublime character of real goodness." The cross demonstrates "the intense moral earnestness of a God who

[90] "War as the Judgment of God," p. 631.
[91] "War as Crucifixion," p. 514.
[92] *Ibid.*

187

will not abandon mankind to self-destruction; it confronts us with the tragic consequences of moral failure. It does . . . this because it is sacrifice—the self-sacrifice of Jesus Christ for those whom he loves and God's sacrifice of his best-loved Son for the sake of the just and the unjust." [93]

War is like crucifixion in this respect, Niebuhr asserts, because in its presence we are moved to think more seriously about our responsibilities and about the consequences of our actions. In the sacrifices war entails it reveals the sublimity of human courage, devotion, and selflessness, as well as the depths of our murderousness and depravity. "An almost infinite capacity for goodness is reflected in the dark glass of sinfulness." [94]

Though Niebuhr's argument seems stretched at points, what he wants to convey is clear: God's judgment in the war is more in accordance with the justice revealed through the cross of Jesus Christ than with any other analogy we might apply. And in the face of the manifest facts of massive suffering of the innocents the only accounting that can be given must, looking at the cross, speak of judgment and redemption wrought through vicarious suffering.

Christians know that the justice of God is not only a redemptive justice in which suffering is used in the service of remaking, but it is also vicarious in its method, so that the suffering of innocence is used for the remaking of the guilty. One cannot then speak of God acting in this war as judge of the nations without understanding that it is through the cross of Christ more than through the cross of thieves that he is acting upon mankind.[95]

In his effort to understand war as God's judgment Niebuhr sees three consequences for human action implied by his approach. To

---

[93] *Ibid.*

[94] *Ibid.* Does Niebuhr intend us to see the sacrifice of the innocent in war also as God's sacrifice of loved children, and therefore as a form of his participation in redemptive suffering? The logic of Niebuhr's position calls for it; his words and the parallelism suggest it; but he steps back from any explicit suggestion that God, too, suffers.

[95] "War as the Judgment of God," p. 631.

respond to God's judgment in the war, first, is to stop trying to justify ourselves or damn our enemies by pronouncing ourselves "right" and them "wrong." "Instead of asking whether we are right people or wrong people we shall simply inquire what duty we have to perform in view of what we have done amiss and in view of what God is doing." He continues, "If that duty involves, as I believe it does, resistance to those who are abusing our neighbors, we shall not inquire whether our neighbors are not better people than those who are abusing them." [96] Second, Christians under the judgment of God in war will respond by abandoning "all self-defensiveness, all self-aggrandizement, all thinking in terms of self as central." [97] To be able genuinely to accept responsibility for the neighbor—the kind of responsibility that fights on for the neighbor even when one's own interests are not imperiled, or that contends for justice for the vanquished in the peace settlement—requires overcoming of self-centeredness. Finally, to respond to God's judgment in the war is to respond in hope and trust. Such hope and trust never give up on the one who is our enemy, as though he were too depraved to be redeemed and restored to full membership in the human community. "It does not accept the counsel of despair in the midst of fighting, allowing vindictive measures because by 'fair fighting' our cause might be lost. It trusts that if we do our duty no evil can befall us in life or in death." [98]

In the preceding pages we have watched Niebuhr's theology wrestling to discern meaning and responsibility in the midst of a vast emergency. I chose to begin at that point for two reasons: (1) Niebuhr's ethics of response to the governing (and judging) action of God has been most decisively shaped by emergencies to which he had to attend. And (2) there is a sense in which Niebuhr's *katontological* [99] ethics (ethics of response), as an alternative to classical teleological and deontological approaches, represents his

[96] *Ibid.*, p. 632.
[97] *Ibid.*
[98] *Ibid.*
[99] Niebuhr characterized his approach with this term in his lecture course at least from the early 1950s. In the lectures of 1946–47, however, he speaks of the ethics of response as *apokrinological* ethics.

effort to reflect rationally upon man's life of moral response to continuing emergency or crisis. In his lecture on April 14, 1952, he is quoted as saying:

We were talking of emergency ethics, of our responses to the limitations of life. I think we may say that most of our ethical decisions—both individually and socially—take place on this level. Why is it that devotional books, the classics of Christianity, don't deal with the goals of life, nor with the great rule we should follow? They have rather to do with adversity, poverty, torment, etc., and with what to do in response to these. . . . Ethics is the rational—I'll take the word back if anyone objects, but I think we've too willingly conceded reason to secularism—interpretation of the same problems; it is systematic interpretation, not to be despised.[100]

We turn now to Niebuhr's "systematic interpretation" of God's governing action and man's response, primarily as he offered it in his lecture course.

RESPONSE TO LIMITATION

I have suggested that the synecdochic analogy for man that correlates with the process-structural metaphor for God is that of *man the "patient" and counter-actor*. What the noun "patient" means in this context becomes clearer when we attend to the description of man's experience of limitation with which Niebuhr begins his account of God's governing action. Man is finite being and he is being *conscious* of its finitude. We know that we must die and this leads to anxiety. "The anxiety of which we speak," Niebuhr says, "is not so much the anxiety of those who know they

---

[100] Class lecture, April 14, 1952 (Yetter, pp. 124-25). On April 7, 1952 Niebuhr is quoted as saying: "A great deal of our moral life involves teleological thinking; we set up goals and then find ourselves thwarted. We have ideas about a profession; then our father dies and we must take care of the family. We get ready to build the kingdom of God and along comes a world war. . . . Other moral action we think of deontologically. We have a law: "Thou shalt not kill." But people are killed and we are faced with the problem of what to do with the killer. Most of our conscious moral life has to do with emergency situations about which our ideal ethical systems have nothing to say; yet our real ethics is seen in our responses to these emergency situations. . . . It is this ethics, the ethics we show forth in our life, about which we should talk and study" (Yetter's notes, p. 119).

have boundaries as it is the anxiety of those who know that they are being bound. In our solitude we may, like Nietzsche, contemplate that nothing should bind us, but when we begin to define our situation we find ourselves bound by our definitions of what, who and where we are." [101]

Niebuhr explores a range of the limitations we experience in our finitude. First, there are those limitations that arise from the fact that we are embodied being: the need for space; dependence upon support of various kinds (support can be experienced as limitation); physical vulnerability to attack from disease and other external threats; limitations of energy, endurance, and the like; and there is a temporal limitation by bodies: "at both termini of my temporal existence are bodies—parents and that which [by attacking my body] brings on my death. The group as well as the individual is limited not by non-being, but by other powers which are our terminations, and which define us." [102] Second, there are mental limitations: we are limited in our ability to penetrate the thought of another person because there are things in the experiences of the other that we cannot make our own; our thinking is also limited by the reality of the objects about which we think, and by the language and mental constructs our culture makes available to us for thinking. Third, limitations from within us are operative: "I am a rational being; yet my reason is limited by passions, emotions, drives, instincts. . . . I am confused by forces from within as well as from without." [103] Fourth, there are the limitations that arise from our existence as social selves: "I am a member of a family, a nation, a church. I identify myself with other members of a group; I transcend egoistic boundaries, and again I turn up against boundaries. The nation I am a part of is bounded. My church is not the only church; there are other religions, and there are divisions like those I find in myself also in the body of my own religion." [104]

[101] Class lecture, April 7, 1952 (Yetter, p. 117).
[102] Class lecture, Gustafson's notes, p. 75.
[103] Class lecture, April 7, 1952 (Yetter, p. 118).
[104] *Ibid.*

Limitation is painful. To be man is to suffer[105] the limitations and impingements that come in the extraordinary as well as the routine emergencies of our existence as finite selves.[106] Even as the self suffers the impingements and limitations of others on his existence, he impinges on others. "When I and my society are limited, I press upon the others; I try to keep them finite. But I am always more aware of being killed than I am of killing. I am more aware of being denied than I am of denying." [107]

This centeredness on our suffering, and on the impingement of others upon us, gives rise to that dualism which is typical of most of our operative ethics—the dualism that says, "He that is not with me is against me" (Matthew 12:30); the dualism that says the bad (the bad for our existence) must be eradicated or denied. In this dualistic response we divide our companions in being into camps—the allies and the enemy, the in-group and the out-group, "we" and "they."

There are two great companies, so the dualistic interpretation goes: the Israelites, God's chosen people, and the Gentiles; the believers and the world; humanity and its natural enemies; life and living and the limitations of life and living. This view may be very naive or highly sophisticated; but around it we develop religions of defensiveness. We develop defensive moralities for the maintenance of ourselves and our social groups; we are afraid.[108]

[105] "Language—the history of language—is sometimes very wise. The word suffering originally meant merely being acted on. We act and then suffer action. But when I am acted upon I frequently feel pain. Thus I suffer when acted upon." *Ibid*.

[106] In *Responsible Self*, chap. 4, "Responsibility in Absolute Dependence," Niebuhr suggests that our life in response to "routine emergencies" may be likened to the motorcar driver who must make forty decisions each minute, and for whom "neither obedience to the rules of the road, nor desire to arrive at his goal, offers sufficient basis for his conduct" (pp. 108-9). The entire chapter complements the discussion of the experience of limitation we have looked at here.

[107] Class lecture, April 7, 1952 (Yetter p. 118).

[108] *Ibid*., p. 119. Parenthetically Niebuhr indicates his reliance for this point on Bergson's *Two Sources of Morality and Religion*, which he considers "the greatest work in the field of ethics in the last fifteen years." Among his published writings it is in *Kingdom of God* that Niebuhr shows most extensively the influence of Bergson, but we should not miss the fact that wherever Niebuhr speaks of the ethics of "closed-communities" or of defensiveness the influence of Bergson is present. I am of the opinion that Bergson, with Jona-

TO SEE THE KINGDOM

THE ONENESS AND PERSONHOOD OF GOD RULING

In his lectures Niebuhr turns next to the great philosophical alternative to theoretical and practical dualism in ethics—the ethics of response to oneness, monism. Here, as is typically the case for Niebuhr, it is the moral and existential implications of monistic thinking that absorb him, and not more directly metaphysical concerns. He begins his discussion of monism with Spinoza, "the greatest of the Stoics." [109] In a long discussion of Spinoza he presents that philosopher's counter to individualistic and dualistic interpretations of divine action.

Stop, look and listen before you respond with anger, fear and grief; accept the truth that there is reason in all things, both without and within. It is rational, you are rational. Accept what happens to you as rational, as a rational being. [110]

From Spinoza's perspective of a mathematically ordered, rational structure of the world the perfection of God requires that he be understood as having no purpose. Therefore when misfortune comes —a roof-tile falls on a person or cancer attacks—one does not attribute it to "God's will" for there is no personal intention behind it. Paraphrasing Spinoza, Niebuhr says, "Our emotions are cleansed when we realize we are not intended; bitterness arises from the belief that particular events have will behind them. Further, we cause ourselves unnecessary anxiety when we think that other people are as concerned about us as we are about ourselves." [111] He sums up his discussion of Spinoza thus:

He set forth fundamentals of Christian and Jewish faith in terms of mathematics and logic, stressing truths found throughout the Old and New Testaments: the truth of monotheism, of monism. Reality is one; there is one will behind the multiplicity. We are dealing with one reality in all the experiences of life. We are living in the Kingdom of God. [112]

---

than Edwards, also contributed significantly to Niebuhr's recovery of the biblical concept of *metanoia* and to his emphasis upon revelation as bringing transformation.

[109] Class lecture, April 9, 1952 (Yetter p. 120).

[110] *Ibid.*

[111] *Ibid.*, p. 121.

[112] *Ibid.*, p. 122.

Now Niebuhr begins to unfold his own monistic vision of the governance of God. "God is king. He is something like a ruler. His rule extends over all. But there is something else: the ultimate principle is not logical, not mechanical—though it is these; it is more, it is personal." The rationalism of the Hebrew sees God as the counterpart not so much of the thinking self as of the moral self, the self that makes covenants. "We are told to look for the I-ness and the Thou-ness instead of for thinking." Of the possible symbols for expressing the relation of God as ruler to man, the most compelling, because it has faithful personality at its center, is that of a society—a kingdom or polis. "If you find it imperative to use the symbol of society, you have discovered there the irreducible reality of 'person.' There is something expressed here that can't be abstracted into an idea, that can't be thought of as a thing." [113] For a comprehensive statement of this view of the kingdom I turn to one of Niebuhr's published writings:

This ultimate environment . . . is one, integrated, unified. . . . Its unity is much more like that of human society than like that of human mind or human technique. Hence such phrases as kingdom of God, *Civitas Dei*, Divine Commonwealth are to be employed in referring to it. . . . The will of the members of this society is never sovereign. They neither elect themselves into being, nor can they choose under what ultimate laws they shall live. They are objects of action before they are its subjects. . . . The image of absolute despotism [however] does not fit. There is a tie between monarch and subjects and a relationship among the subjects not compatible with the idea of absolute monarchy. The world is a particular kind of society in which all parts are bound to each other by *promises*. Promise or covenant is the ordering principle. There is nothing arbitrary about the king, for he is above all faithful and has bound himself to govern in accordance with purposes and laws he has promulgated. . . . The fundamental characteristic of the powerful One is that he is faithful, keeping his promise.[114]

How does the faithful One exert his rule and government? Niebuhr answers this question in part by developing a theme we have already discussed above: God is present in *judgment*. Not a judgment that rewards men according to their individual deserts, and

[113] *Ibid.*
[114] "The Idea of Covenant and American Democracy," *Church History*, no. 2 (1954), pp. 131-32.

not a judgment which says that in the long run virtue and faithfulness will be rewarded. But rather a judgment that involves
vicarious suffering. We should recall here our earlier discussion of
God's judgment in and through the cross of Jesus Christ. In his
lectures Niebuhr cited the suffering servant passage in Isaiah 53.

The effects of the judgment (and grace) of vicarious suffering
are not just reconciliation, however. God is working to *reconstruct
the kingdom.* The sacrifices and vicarious suffering are made to
serve the purposes of a God whose governance is continually bringing forth novelty. "Creation did not cease: I am always bringing
forth a new thing, says the Lord." [115] Niebuhr continues:

Here in the midst of destruction, something new is always being brought
forth. Human beings, as we know, must sometimes be placed upon the
anvil and beaten into nobility. Persons come into being in trial and
tribulation (Hebrews 12:6 ff.; Revelation 3:19). Chastening is necessary for creation of being. Why God knows. But we know that suffering
can be creative. [116]

But the suffering of innocence and the principle of vicariousness
are only part of the judging and governing action of God. They
are modes by which another crucial dimension of governance is
exerted. In accordance with the metaphor of kingship this dimension of God's governing activity may be symbolized through the
image of the master statesman. Niebuhr was fond of quoting and
citing Lincoln to illustrate this dimension: "Statesmanship is the
ability to use the meannesses of men for the common good." [117]
God does not directly restrain the willfulness and autonomous striving of men. But his governing action serves his creative and redemptive intention by weaving the deeds of men and their consequences

[115] Niebuhr cites Isaiah 42:9, 43:19, 48:6, 62:2, 65:17, 66:22. Class lecture,
April 9, 1952 (Yetter, p. 124).
[116] *Ibid.*
[117] Quoted in Gustafson's notes, p. 79. Of Lincoln Niebuhr says: "In the
Civil War, few were so genuinely concerned with preservation of the Union as
Lincoln; instead, capitalists in the North were thinking of extending business
southward; position-seekers were rallying to the Republican party to get of-
fices; and abolitionists were concerned only with freeing slaves at all costs,
even the cost of the Union. Yet Lincoln blended them into harmony. And he
did it without the omnipresence and omnipotence we speak of in talking of
God." Class lecture, April 14, 1952 (Yetter, p. 125).

into his good—the cause of his kingdom. Alignment with the kingdom requires us to respond to this statesmanlike activity that works
in and through every action in our action fields. We will not find
God in particular things or events; these are the actions of men,
of groups, or are occurrences in the natural processes. God's doing
is the total context. The Scriptures give the paradigms: Joseph is
sold into slavery. His brothers intended evil in the act but God
thought to do good through it, to save the lives of many (Genesis
45:5-8). In Isaiah 10, a kind of *locus classicus* for Niebuhr, Isaiah
sees through the intention of Assyria to the intention of God in
the Assyrian threat: "Assyria intends your destruction; God intends
your preservation, not your destruction; in not attending to God's
intention you are destroying yourselves." [118] The paradigm of
paradigms, however, is Jesus Christ. He was rejected, despised,
betrayed, misunderstood, and abused. The priests, the nationalists,
Judas, Caiaphas, and Pilate thought to do evil, but God thought
to do good. "God did not do good by Judas's betrayal, but yet he
did not do it without it. God's action was not in any of the events
leading to the crucifixion, but in the context and in the resurrection. . . . Unless there was in some sense resurrection, we would not
say of the crucifixion, God thought to do good." [119]

SELF-DENIAL IN THE ETHICS OF RESPONSE TO GOD AS RULER

Response to the divine intention beyond human situation and
intention requires self-denial.[120] "This does not mean the negation
of the self, but the acceptance of the limitations upon the self,

---

[118] Class lecture, April, 14, 1952 (Yetter, p. 126). See Niebuhr's sermon on
Isaiah 10 in which he applies the Assyria-Israel analogy to the relation of
Russia and the United States. He suggests that in and through their opposition
and threat to each other God intends *metanoia* and reform for each of them.
Each is Assyria to the other. "The Illusions of Power," *Christian Century Pul-
pit*, 33 (1962), pp. 100-3.
[119] Class lecture, April 14, 1952 (Yetter p. 126).
[120] Niebuhr refers to Matthew 14:36, 16:24. On self-denial he says: "John
Calvin gives us this key word to the Christian life in the Institutes: Book III,
Chapter 7. This whole section of our present study hangs on three works:
The last section of Augustine (*City of God*, Book XII; *Confessions*, Book
XIII); Calvin's doctrine of self-denial; and Luther's treatise *On the Freedom
of the Christian Man*." *Ibid*.

whereby others are being affirmed." Niebuhr makes it plain that he is not referring to ascetic self-denial with its dualism and mortification of the flesh. Rather it is an acceptance and affirmation of the limitations that impinge upon us as part of God's governing action. "Limitation may be the beginning of *metanoia*; it may force a man from his egocentricity. Self-denial takes place where one is being limited. If limitations be accepted the revolution of understanding of the self as instrument of God and not as center of existence may take place. God, not the self, is the proper center of all things." [121]

Niebuhr generally concluded his long section on response to divine governing action with a discussion of self-denial in the restraint of others. These are the points he stressed: (1) We have no choice as to whether we shall exert restraint (limitation) upon others; we *do* do so. The moral question is, How shall we be responsible to God, the governor of all, in our impingement upon others? (2) Self-denial is required in our restraint of others. We restrain as those who are under (God's) restraint. (3) We restrain as those who are responsible to God for the neighbor and responsible to the neighbor before God. And (4) restraint in self-denial hopes and aims for the conservation and redemption of the restrained.[122]

Let us try this formulation as a summary of the indicative that Niebuhr's teaching about divine governing action makes visible: Though the intentions in finite actions and events may not be the intentions of God, and the direct consequences of finite action may go against his cause, divine governance and judgment are working so as to redeem and incorporate our action into the divine action of reconstructing and furthering the kingdom of God. The moral and covenantal structure of the kingdom means that self-serving actions of aggression and defense by men inevitably exact great suffering, most often from the innocent. This is made somewhat understandable by the sacrificial suffering of Jesus and by the implied participation of the Father in that and therefore in all

[121] Class lecture, April 14, 1952 (Yetter, pp. 127-28).
[122] Class lecture (Gustafson, pp. 83-86; Yetter, pp. 128-32).

vicarious suffering, which, as the resurrection powerfully shows, can be the occasion for great restoration, reconciliation, and new faithfulness by men to the cause of the kingdom.

The imperative that flows from the indicative may be stated thus: Trust that God is supreme power, that his oneness is the context of all limitations and impingements upon you, and that his governance aims at the restoration and fulfillment of his kingdom. So respond to all actions upon you as to respond to his action and to make the intention of his will your cause.

The triadic structure of the self's life in response to the governing action of God may be represented as shown in figure 6.

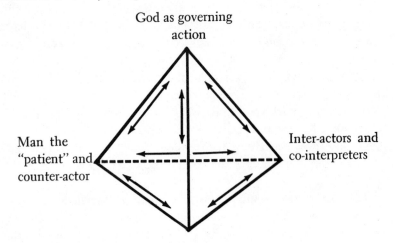

God as governing
action

Man the
"patient" and
counter-actor

Inter-actors and
co-interpreters

Limiting,
intentional structure
in the process

Fig. 6

5. THE PATTERN OF THE SOVEREIGNTY OF GOD

This chapter has attempted to show how Niebuhr, building around his three central metaphors, makes visible the character and action of the God who is sovereign. I have tried to demonstrate that the three metaphors we derived from our study of the development and expression of the conviction of God's sovereignty are the principal poles in his theological-ethical thinking from 1935–37 on. But, more importantly, I have wanted to show by this extensive reportage the interrelatedness and coherence of the principal normative thrusts in Niebuhr's ethics. To see the organism of his thought in its coherence, I believe, is to see more clearly how his published works fit into the total pattern of his thought. It frees us from the temptation or necessity to extrapolate theories of development or to construct patterns of sequential emphasis from his published writings alone and from their order of appearance. This is not to say that there is not development and evolution in Niebuhr's thought. But I am impressed by the way in which that evolution stands in continuity with, and largely represents an elaboration of, the structure and dynamics in his thought (and the problems they raise) that we can identify by 1937.

Perhaps it is worthwhile—and worth the risks of reification it involves—to offer yet one more diagram (figure 7) as a way of helping to focus on the coherence this interpretative effort sees in Niebuhr's thinking. This too has to be understood as an action model—for Niebuhr, as a theologian of the *relation* of God and man, is always more concerned to clarify our understanding of and response to action than he is to communicate and clarify concepts. His *is* a systematic theology. But it is not systematic reflection on the relations between concepts so much as it is sustained reflection on the relations between actors and actions in a very complex but unified system of action.[123]

The geometry of the model has its limitations. A principal one is that the three planes or dimensions of man's life in response can-

[123] Some readers of this passage have taken exception to my claim that Niebuhr's *is* a systematic theology, pointing to the quality of existential involvement in his theological style and to his eschewal of the systematician's task and format. Such objections miss my point, which is really twofold: (1) Niebuhr's theological ethics *is* systematic in its description and analysis of moral decision-making and moral action; and (2) the action system of the kingdom of God is a comprehensive and unified though exceedingly complex whole in Niebuhr's thought; therefore when he develops his ethics of response to divine action it has a systematic quality derived, not from a logic imposed by the theologian's application of conceptual categories, but from his effort to characterize different dimensions of the kingdom viewed as an action system.

not easily be shown in it as inter-living or as being polarities in one existence. I ask you to remember that they really constitute one plane, or better, one action field. Similarly, the vertically rising poles of the triad that pass through each plane also point to unities —the oneness of the God who is experienced as impinging in multiple ways; the oneness of a responsible self whose modes of responding are dimensions of one response; and the companions who are ultimately one community of faithfulness, a common-wealth of being.

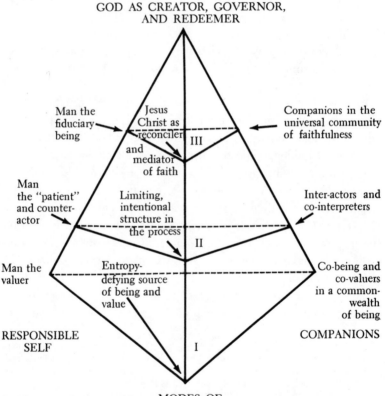

Fig. 7. The triadic structure of our life in response to God's action as I. creator, II. governor, III. redeemer

Chapter V
Faith on Earth

1. BETWEEN BARTH AND SCHLEIERMACHER

Since the time of Kant, Protestant theologians in Europe have generally chosen one of two great alternatives as regards theological methods and starting points. These alternatives, over which much ink and passion have been expended in theological debate, are usually associated with the names of Schleiermacher and Barth. For those who choose to work in the wake left by Schleiermacher, theology has its proper beginning point in the clarification and analysis of human religious consciousness as shaped and nurtured in the community of faith. Theological doctrines, this group hold, are efforts to give rational account of *what* faith knows and *how* faith knows. Theology tries to apprehend that by which the believer is apprehended in religious experience. There is no religiously valid knowledge of God apart from participation in divine reality through experience. Theological reflection, informed by Scripture (the record of Israel's and the church's experience of God), and illumined by present participation in life and history where God is active, has the task of ordering, focusing, and critically evaluating contemporary testimony to apprehension of and by divine power and mystery.

For those who choose to make common cause with Barth, on the other hand, the starting place and purpose of theology are quite different. Suspicious of the alleged subjectivity involved in reflecting on personal and communal experience as the mode of access to knowledge of God, this group want to place radical reliance on an anchor they take to be more objectively established —the self-revelation of God given in Jesus Christ, who through the Scriptures, and by the power of the Holy Spirit, is the Word of God. Given solely from God's initiative, this Word in Jesus Christ is the sole valid point of disclosure of God's nature and will. It comes as both crushing judge and corrective to all our efforts through religion and morality to know and serve and be reconciled to God.

H. Richard Niebuhr had these two great alternatives in mind when he spoke of his indebtedness in *The Meaning of Revelation* to Troeltsch and Barth. "These two leaders in twentieth century religious thought are frequently set in diametrical opposition to each other; I have tried to combine their main interests, for it appears to me that the critical thought of the former [Troeltsch] and the constructive work of the latter [Barth] belong together." [1] Always critical of what he sometimes referred to as Barth's "revelational positivism," Niebuhr was nonetheless deeply committed with Barth to an affirmation of the objective reality, the utterly fundamental priority in being, of God. Precisely because of his conviction of the sovereignty of God, however, Niebuhr found it necessary to reject any limitation of the theater in which God's activity as creator, governor, or redeemer is understood as being exercised.

---

[1] *Meaning of Revelation*, p. x.

This meant that with Schleiermacher, Troeltsch, and the liberals, Niebuhr found it essential to attend with care to personal and communal experience, past and present, in the effort to discern the impingement and activity in it of God. The theologian and the community of faith are to be guided and informed in their effort to discern God's action by the normative interpretative paradigm given in Christ. Niebuhr always affirms the priority and singularity of these eye-glasses for Christians. But he is also ready to grant that there is other experience of God than Christian, and that the Christian witness must live and serve in constant acknowledgment that there may be other valid lenses for discerning and interpreting the character and action of God.

In a fragmentary, handwritten draft for an introduction to the manuscript "Faith on Earth," Niebuhr sought to locate himself and that work in relation to Schleiermacher and Barth:

Between Barth, the great objectivist in theology who proposes to begin and remain with the object of faith and theology, and Schleiermacher, the great subjectivist who undertook to understand the subject with his attitudes and commitments, I cannot judge so as to say that the one is right and the other wrong. Nor do I know of a human court which can make the judgment. Insofar as I am unable to abstract object from subject I can and do take exception to Barth's special dogmatism which requires me to begin with no other object than God as speaking in and proclaimed in the Scriptures. . . . I can only say that Barth's problem is not mine, while Schleiermacher's is, and that I see no reason why I should give up my problem because some folk say it is a pseudo-problem and call my statements nonsense because they cannot translate them into their objectivist language.[2]

2. "FAITH ON EARTH"

Revised and reworked several times, the chapters that make up the manuscript which Niebuhr entitled "Faith on Earth" were given as lectures in the fifties. A projected table of contents shows that at one time Niebuhr planned to publish this material as part of a larger volume that would have included most of the

[2] From handwritten manuscript entitled "Between Barth and Schleiermacher," p. 2.

chapters that he published in 1960 as *Radical Monotheism and Western Culture.*[3] Apparently the entire volume was to have been called *Faith on Earth: Essays on Human Confidence and Loyalty.*[4]

The.e are several reasons why I judge it important to include a chapter on "Faith on Earth" in this book. First, and most obviously, this manuscript represents a major statement by Niebuhr on a theme that lay at the very heart of his concern. It has not been and is not yet available for general use by those interested in Niebuhr's thought. Second, because of the difficulty and complexity of the theme, this work elicited more from Niebuhr in the way of methodological reflection and clarification than any other of his mature works. Careful study of this material promises, therefore, to pay extra dividends in our effort to draw together and comment on Niebuhr's understanding of the task of theology. Third, this material is of special importance for us because its theme and method draw on Niebuhr's interpretation of his own struggle with faith more directly and revealingly than most of his other writings. This is not to say that the work is autobiographical or that Niebuhr writes explicitly about his own experiences. It is clear, however, that in this work Niebuhr's involvement with the subject-object polarity is greater than in other places, and that when he describes the movement in faith—from doubt, hostility, and suspicion, to trust, appreciation, and fidelity—he is surveying terrain he knows existentially as well as intellectually.

In the previous chapter we sought to show, by looking primarily at Niebuhr's lectures on ethics, *what* faith sees as it attends to the kingdom of God. In this chapter we deal with *how* faith sees and knows, and the *process* of its development. Niebuhr's approach is what he calls "The Method of Reflection." The complex phenomenon of faith, he maintains, is an interpersonal structure in which we (and all persons) are involved. It cannot be objectified and

[3] Niebuhr went so far as to submit this manuscript on faith to Harper & Row. Their reader recommended that it be rewritten, shortened, and clarified. Letter from publisher is in the Niebuhr files.

[4] The title comes from Luke 18:8 and its question, "When the Son of Man returns will he find faith on earth?"

made external to us so that we might be able to bring analysis to bear upon it from some other standpoint. Rather, it must be investigated from within, from the vantage point of those who are involved, who are aware of their own fears of deception and their temptations to deceive and defend.

Because reflection on faith is an effort at self-knowledge—faith trying to understand itself—it has to begin, as Niebuhr says, *in medias res*, right in the middle of things.[5] Epistemologically, this means that it begins with neither the subject nor the object of faith, but with the relation of the two. Temporally, this means a beginning with the present, which then tries to move backward and forward to take account of faith's memory and hope. In both respects it means bringing into focus the triadic relationship of person, companions or community, and the Transcendent third who is their common object and ground of faith.

Sooner or later the reader of "Faith on Earth" will recognize that he or she is involved in an unusual communication experience. Implicitly the reader is being asked to follow the progression of conceptual patterns explicating Niebuhr's ideas and perspective. But at the same time direct appeal is being made to the reader's own experience. In this second vein one is invited, challenged, or, perhaps better, enticed, into identification *with*, participation *in*, argumentation for, clarification *of* Niebuhr's discourse. So that while following Niebuhr's *account* of a process the reader is also involved, at least to some extent, in an *experience* of the process. Hans Frei has a helpful analysis of this double quality or dynamic of Niebuhr's writing:

Niebuhr has related himself to his hearers and readers in such a way as to convey in conceptual terms the actual movement of his concrete thought as it reflects, in turn, the decisions, acts and interpretations by which one responds to the prior action of God in creation, judgment and adoption. This is of course far more than an author's customary indication that he is proceeding from one idea to the next. *The Meaning of Revelation*, for example, keeps the reader in an actual intellectual motion reduplicating that of the book, and just as real. Such a double process is existential communication. In achieving this quality, Niebuhr's

[5] "Faith on Earth" chap. 2, "The Method of Reflection," p. 28a.

writings, together with Barth's earlier works, seem to me to be unique in modern theology.[6]

Niebuhr's success in involving the reader results from the dialogical strategy of his argument. With the sure sense of the experienced teacher Niebuhr's text anticipates and expresses protests, objections, or questions that occur to the reader, and then incorporates them or answers them as he proceeds. This is what I had in mind when I said earlier that Niebuhr "entices" the reader into involvement with the text. In this case, as in the case of Plato's dialogues, the mild risk of letting someone else do your thinking for you is amply offset by the richness of the dialectic, the gains of involvement, and the urges to independent thought that result. A second factor contributing to the involving quality of "Faith on Earth" results from the depth and acuity of Niebuhr's insight into the psychology of believing and faith. More than any other this work shows Niebuhr to be profoundly acquainted with the topography of the soul—the soul in fealty and rebellion, in faith and despair.

THE BOUNDS OF THE INQUIRY

The boundaries of Niebuhr's inquiry are quite wide and inclusive. At the most basic level he is interested in *human faith*—in fidelity, trust, loyalty, and belief as they are variously present in law, politics, science, and economics as well as in interpersonal relations, the family, and religion. Under the influence of G. H. Mead, Josiah Royce, and especially Martin Buber, Niebuhr wants us to understand that there is a *tacit* covenantal structure that makes human community and human selfhood possible. There is no community at any level without a modicum of interpersonal trustworthiness and "good faith." Similarly, without the consistent caring and interaction of trusted others the development of selfhood would be severely crippled or impossible. This tacit covenantal structure, which must always be renewed and regenerated, seemed to Niebuhr to be particularly threatened in our time. In one passage it is as if he anticipated the kind of pervasive and banal corruption that

---

[6] Frei, "Niebuhr's Theological Background," in Ramsey, ed., *Faith and Ethics*, p. 16.

surfaced in the 1972–73 Watergate affair in the United States:

The experiences of the twentieth century have brought into view the abyss of faithlessness into which men can fall. We see this possibility —that human history could come to its end neither in a brotherhood of man nor in universal death under the blows of natural or man-made catastrophe, but in the gangrenous corruption of a social life in which every promise, contract, treaty and word of dishonor is given and accepted in deception and distrust. If men no longer have faith in each other, can they exist as men? [7]

For Niebuhr this tacit covenantal structure is not merely *diadic*. That is to say, it is not simply a matter of interpersonal and interinstitutional honesty, dependability, and regard. Manifesting again the deep influence of Royce on his thought, Niebuhr wants us to see the *triadic* structure of the tacit covenant that makes possible and sustains community and selfhood. In a faithful marriage the partners are not only loyal to each other; they are also loyal to a third entity—the cause or ideal of marriage. Similarly with citizenship in a national community. Citizens are not only bound to each other on the basis of neighborliness or mutal regard; they also share in common a loyalty to the nation and to the ideals for which it stands. In each of these cases interpersonal loyalty is deepened and reinforced by mutual commitments to superordinate centers of value. Persons are covenantally bound not only to each other and to a loyalty held in common, but also in loyalty to the loyalty of the other. Following Royce, Niebuhr refers to the third entity in the triad of loyalty as the "cause."

Our analysis, in the previous chapter, of the hierarchy of triads in the ethics of response prepares us somewhat to see that as regards faith Niebuhr is also working with a model of triads related in a hierarchic fashion. Faith, as we shall shortly see more fully, is not only a matter of loyalty to companions and to shared causes. It also involves *trust*—trust in the faithfulness of the other to oneself and to the common cause, but also trust in the worthiness, the reliability, the faithfulness of the cause itself. The thirds or

[7] "Faith on Earth" (hereafter cited as *FE*), chap. 1, "Faith in Question," p. 1.

common causes that elicit our trust and loyalty vary both in their range of inclusiveness and in their ability to bear ultimacy. Similarly, the communities of companions with whom we share commitments and loyalties vary in scope and in degree of universality. For Niebuhr, our allegiances to less than ultimate causes, and our membership in less than universalizing communities, are organized under the framework of larger faith triads. The loyalty and trust invested in these larger triads center in values or causes that must bear the weight of ultimacy and that must sustain as much inclusiveness and universality of scope or we and our communities can stand.

In *Radical Monotheism and Western Culture* (which was to have been the other half of "Faith on Earth") Niebuhr describes three types of faith, distinguishable by the different center or centers of loyalty and trust that provide the focus for the person's or community's most comprehensive faith triad. "Polytheism" characterizes a diffuse hierarchy of trust and loyalties. Multiple centers of value compete and coexist for the person or community, with none of them having the power to provide a real organizing framework for the others. For the polytheist, in Niebuhr's terms, there is no one hierarchy of triads, but many. And they are likely to be competing and conflicting within the person or the community. "Henotheism," on the other hand, typifies a structure of faith in a person or community where there *is* a true center of trust and loyalty, and therefore a unified hierarchy of lesser triads of trust and loyalty. Henotheism, however, involves claiming more universality for the central value and its community than in fact it can sustain. It involves placing a heavier burden of ultimacy on the central object of trust and loyalty than it can bear. Though henotheism solves the problem of internal value competition and conflict for the person or community, it is likely to involve its faithful in excesses of confidence in their own righteousness and the righteousness of their cause, with potentially violent consequences for their neighbors.

Niebuhr's name for a faith hierarchy in which lesser triads of trust and loyalty are properly and proportionately organized under the only worthy central allegiance is "radical monotheism." In radically monotheistic faith, trust and loyalty are enlarged, imagination and ethical sensitivity are quickened, and the ideal of community is universalized in response to the vision of a God who is infinite in value, power, and love. God is seen as faithful to all that issues from him. All that *is* participates in a commonwealth of being where each one has value in relation to the source and center of value.

This short excursus through the central argument of *Radical Monotheism and Western Culture* was necessary in order to show how, for Niebuhr, the tacit covenantal structure underlying the institutions and patterns of social life is inseparably linked up with faith as understood in more explicitly religious terms. The task of religion in society and culture is to criticize, to renew, and continually to transform the larger, organizing, and meaning-giving triads of trust and loyalty which provide the validation and sanctioning rationale for structures of faithfulness at more mundane levels. In *"Faith on Earth"* Niebuhr's discussion wants to include this entire range of relations, bringing it into engagement with his understanding of Christian faith and its radical monotheism.

I have tried to suggest the breadth and scope of Niebuhr's inquiry, showing how, for him, faith and faithfulness are dynamics in the life of human society and culture in all their dimensions. Theological inquiry into faith, he maintained, must view it in relation to all these dimensions and help us to grasp faith's interdimensional linkages in a complex whole. This brings us to the point where it will be helpful to distinguish three different levels on which Niebuhr's analysis of faith is simultaneously being carried on. Until these levels are sorted out, the reader of "Faith on Earth" is likely to find the path of Niebuhr's discourse filled with seeming ambiguities.

FAITH AS INTERPERSONAL STRUCTURE

To describe "Faith on Earth" as a "structural and dynamic" analysis of faith as a phenomenon would be correct as far as it goes. But it does not go far enough. Careful consideration of this work leads one to see that Niebuhr's structural analysis has in view two different kinds of structures related to faith. These two different foci constitute two of the three levels on which Niebuhr's inquiry proceeds. The first structural aspect of faith he has in mind is one to which we have already given attention—faith as an *interpersonal* (triadic) *structure*. In addition to the dynamics of trust and loyalty related to valuing, which we have already discussed, Niebuhr devotes considerable attention to demonstrating that *all our knowing and communication occur in the context of triadic interpersonal structures.* Influenced by B. L. Whorf and others, Niebuhr was deeply aware of how language, a socially constructed and socially transmitted medium, shapes not only our conceptualizing and communicating, but also our perceptions and our preconscious interpretations of events, relations, and objects in our worlds.

All the words we use and the concepts associated with the words indicate the acceptance on trust of the statements of our fellow-knowers. Language and knowledge are inseparably interwoven and language is received in trust and belief. "The language of our mother tongue," as a philosophically minded linguist points out, "determines not only the way we build sentences but also the way we view nature and break up the kaleidoscope of experience into objects and entities about which to make sentences. We cut up and organize the spread and flow of events as we do largely because, through our mother tongue, we are parties to an agreement to do so, not because nature itself is segmented in exactly that way . . ." We usually remain unaware of the effect of language on our knowledge, whether of natural or other events, and of the partial dependence of direct knowledge on society, and of our personal knowledge on our believing our companions.[8]

In Niebuhr's view we, as knowers, never relate im-mediately to an object of our knowing. To be sure, we usually do have direct relation to, and therefore personal experience of, any such object, but his point would be that we don't come to such a situation of perception and interpretation without the aid of language and concepts accepted from others. Nor do we engage in such knowing

---

[8] FE, chap. 3, "Believing and Knowing in Community," p. 47. The quote within the quote is from Benjamin Lee Whorf, "Language and Logic," *Technology Review*, 43, no. 6 (April, 1941).

without being aware of, *ac-knowledging*, the presence of others—
of co-knowers whose perceptions and interpretations must be put
alongside our own, and about whose trustworthiness and faithfulness, to us and to truth, judgments have to be made. Much of our
so-called knowledge is based solely on the reports of others in whose
observations and judgments we place trust. I think Niebuhr goes
too far in a Buberian direction when he suggests that we accept
the claims and statements of others—for example, scientists of
various kinds—solely on the basis of our trust in their loyalty to
us and to truth in some personal sense. Surely it puts excessive
strain on I–Thou analysis to try to subsume under it, as Niebuhr
seems to suggest, every circumstance in which I take the word of
another, as though in accepting his word I were placing *personal*
trust in *his personal* faithfulness to me and to truth. Account
must be taken of professional ethics, general legal sanctions against
deception, and the pressure of social role-expectations. But we can
all agree that Niebuhr has his hand on something important when
he claims, "What we acknowledge in all those acts of believing
which are ingredient in our acts of knowing is the presence of moral
subjects, that is of persons, that is of beings who live as self-
building, as promise-making, promise-keeping, promise-breaking,
covenanting selves and never merely as knowers." [9]

FAITH AS ORGANIC STRUCTURE

Now I want to turn to the second level in Niebuhr's structural
analysis of faith. Here we are concerned with the phenomenon
named faith *as itself a complex organic structure*. In the first
chapter of "Faith on Earth" Niebuhr generates, in a somewhat
confusing way, a great number of questions that arise in connection
with the word and idea of faith. Mention has already been made
of his desire to take account of faith as it comes to expression in
such seemingly disparate realms of discourse as law, politics,
economics, and international relations, as well as in the sphere
relating to God, church, and creed. When he examines the many

[9] *FE*, chap. 3, "Believing and Knowing in Community," p. 53.

uses and contexts of the idea of faith he sees good reason to
question whether it is a useful term at all:

Is not the word *faith* so highly equivocal or even indeterminate in
meaning that it cannot be significantly used in such various connections
in the course of one conversation? Now it means belief in a doctrine;
now the acceptance of intuited or self-evident truths; now fidelity or
loyalty to a person or a cause; now confidence or trust; now piety in
general or a historic religion. In some cases the word applies to man's
relations to the supernatural but again it refers to human inter-personal
relations. Do not these meanings vary so greatly that it is an illusion
to think of all these *faiths* as having anything in common that can
be a fit subject for inquiry? It may be so. It may be that the visual
or auditory sign, *faith*, represents not one word but several, pointing to
various unrelated things or concepts, as the sign *organ* means in one
context a musical instrument, in another, a part of a body, and in still
another, a newspaper. But it may also be that *faith* points to a complex
structure of which now this, now that element is focussed in the attention while the remainder of the structure is implied. It may be a word
like *reason*, which, equally various in its uses, yet seems to indicate a
single complex process of perception and conception, distinction and
relation, experience and abstraction, intuition and inference, contempla-
tion and measurement.[10]

As he continues in this passage Niebuhr begins to suggest how, in
his mind, the two levels of structural analysis we have distinguished
are interrelated:

Should it appear that believing a proposition is intimately connected
with trusting a person, that trust and fidelity are inseparable, that trust
in God and interpersonal faithfulness are closely associated, then it
might also be indicated that there is a structure of faith, while the
stresses and strains in that structure might also be brought into view.
On such an inquiry we embark, not in the hope of being able to map
the world of faith but with the desire to understand, albeit roughly
and in outline, the relations of some of its continents and seas.[11]

To illustrate the fact that different observers see both some of the
same and some different dimensions of the organic structure of
faith when they undertake to define it, Niebuhr takes his reader
through a sprightly and insightful survey of several classical inter-

[10] *FE*, chap. 1 "Faith in Question," p. 4.
[11] *Ibid.*, pp. 4-5.

pretations of faith. His focus—as might be expected of an ethicist —is on the relation between faith and action. He notes that from the beginning in the Christian community the question whether faith is irrelevant to action has been the subject "of exhortation, confession and soul-searching."

The question so raised in the Christian community has been endlessly but not unprofitably debated by churchmen and others. There seems to be general agreement among them that while there is a faith that is not relevant to action, there is also something in the human mind, also called faith, that is so relevant and that there is some connection between the two kinds of faith. They have been distinguished, following the suggestion of the *Letter of James*, as dead and living faith. The former does nothing; the latter issues in action. Dead faith is belief in propositions, such as that God is one; living faith includes love.[12]

In Thomas Aquinas, Niebuhr finds the distinction being made between a faith purely intellectual, and thus lifeless, and one that is both intellectual and voluntary, directed toward the divine good. Cardinal Newman made a distinction between "notional assent and inference" and "belief or real assent." Only the latter involves the whole person in such a way that the object of faith is related to as a reality vividly imagined, felt, and loved. For Luther there was a distinction between faith *concerning* God (which, he said, "is on the same level with the assent I give to statements concerning the Turk, the devil and hell"), and faith *in* God. "Such a faith [as this latter] is mine," he said, "when I not only hold to be true what is said concerning God, but when I put my trust in him in such a way as to enter into personal relations with him, believing firmly that I shall find him to be and to do as I have been taught. . . . Such faith which ventures everything on what it has heard concerning God, be it life or death, constitutes a Christian man." [13] In Calvin, Niebuhr finds the same distinctions being made that were found in Aquinas and Luther. But Calvin's special contribution lies in his concern "to define *saving* faith in opposition to a common or general believing of doctrines." Niebuhr notes the

---

[12] *Ibid.*, p. 7.
[13] *Ibid.*, p. 9. Quote from Luther is from *Luther's Catechetical Writings*; trans. John Nicholas Lenker (Minneapolis: The Luther Press, 1907), vol. 1, p. 203.

significance of first-person pronouns—*our, we, us*—for Calvin. What distinguishes living from dead faith is the fact that in the former every statement of doctrine means me." Quoting Calvin: "The principal hinge on which faith turns, is this—that we must not consider the promises of mercy, which the Lord offers, as true only to others and not to ourselves; but rather make them our own by embracing them in our hearts. . . . In short, no man is truly a believer, unless he be firmly persuaded that God is a propitious and benevolent Father to him." [14] When he looks at Kierkegaard and Rudolf Bultmann, Niebuhr finds in both cases a distinction being made between these two kinds of faith. But he also finds in both writers a need to affirm the interrelatedness of the two types, and the partial dependence of the second—subjective or existential trust and obedience—upon the first.

In his summary of the results of this brief inquiry into the history of the Christian discussion of faith and action, Niebuhr points again to the character of faith as a complex organismic structure:

Even so fragmentary a review of phases of the long discussion about faith and action or faith and ethics has made evident that men have used the term faith to refer to a rather complex experience or attitude of the human self. There seems to be general agreement that belief as assent to propositions is a part of faith but it is also agreed that belief of this sort does not by itself modify conduct, while there is a "faith" that radically affects attitudes and behavior. . . . It is as though each participant in the discussion affirmed, "Of course there is such a thing as believing statements; and in religion such a thing as believing statements about God, Christ and man; but there's more to faith than that." However, when he defined the *more* each speaker directed attention to a different feature. In the one case the faith that went beyond belief was voluntary devotion to the good; again it was a kind of perceptive and imaginative immediacy of reality; for a third it was trust in a person; for still others it was the personal appropriation of truth or radical obedience in the presence of the Unconditioned. [15]

He concludes:

[14] FE, chap. 1, "Faith in Question," p. 10. Quote from Calvin is from *Institutes of the Christian Religion*, bk. 3, chap. 2, sections 13 and 16.
[15] FE, chap. 1, "Faith in Question," p. 12.

As in so many other cases, a discussion which began with the reflection that there are two sides to any problem issues in the recognition that this bit of experience or reality is multidimensional. "The other side of faith" is not one side. Faith, if indeed it be a whole of some sort, seems to be something like a cube; one of its sides, the top, appears to be visible from every point of view; the other sides present themselves variously to various viewers; perhaps the bottom and the insides remain unseen by all.[16]

Let us recapitulate for a moment. We have seen that Niebuhr's structural analysis of faith is carried out on two distinguishable though interrelated levels—the first being that of faith as an inter-personal structure, triadic in form. The second attends to faith as an idea and phenomenon, calling attention to its character as a complex, multidimensional, organic structure. We come now to the third level at which he is working—one that presumes and incorporates the other two levels as context, but which has its own distinct focus. At this third level Niebuhr's concern is with the *person* in faith, or with *personal faith*. We may call this the level of *existential analysis*.

FAITH: AN EXISTENTIAL ANALYSIS

It is in his inquiry into faith on the level of existential analysis that Niebuhr reveals himself most clearly as a true descendant of Schleiermacher. He chooses as his starting place for the existential analysis of faith not some pristine, pre-Fall state of man, or man up against the abyss of nothingness, struggling with the question of suicide. Rather, consistent with the method of reflection—faith trying to understand itself—he begins from the standpoint of one who, by the grace of God, finds himself standing in the community of faith. The question becomes then (though Niebuhr would not have used this language) How did this miracle occur? To put it his way, "How is faith possible?"

In a sense it is at this point, when Niebuhr takes on the existen-tial analysis of faith, that he "blows his cover" and reveals the *confessional* grounding of his phenomenological analysis of faith.

---

[16] *Ibid.*

To be sure, he gives signs all along that he is writing about faith as a man of Christian faith. But until chapter 5, "Broken Faith," he doesn't make it clear that he understands himself to be writing "from faith to faith"—that he presumes his audience to be members of the community of faith interested, with him, in understanding the faith that is in them. In his phenomenological analysis of the structure of faith in the double sense we have examined, Niebuhr addresses his audience primarily as thoughtful men and women, interested in reflecting on and understanding their lives and actions as members of a community and as makers and bearers of commitments. There is no explicit presumption that they understand their lives of faith in terms of Christian faith. At the end of chapter 4, however, he begins to suggest that the tacit covenantal structure requisite for human community implies that there is an ultimate covenantal structure to reality, and that the ubiquitous presence of the triadic structure of trust and loyalty implies the idea of an ultimate, transcendent loyalty and cause. At that point he seems to feel the need to deny that he is offering a new "pistological" argument for the existence of God.[17] He does not want to be involved in cheap apologetic; nor does he want to seem to have taken on the role of the philosopher and to try "so to abstract from our actual faith as to pretend that in moving from the familiar ground of ordinary personal loyalties to the faith in God we are moving from the known to the unknown." [18] Niebuhr's eschewal of the apologist's role, however, is somewhat ambivalent. He clearly believes that reality has a fiduciary or covenantal structure, and that "the familiar ground of ordinary personal loyalties" is continuous with a larger network of trust and loyalty centering ultimately in One who is supremely faithful. In opting for the method he calls "confession and demonstration," Niebuhr does so not only because it is more honest, but also because it is ultimately the more effective apologetic. Echoes of both Anselm and Schleiermacher can be heard in this description of his task and method:

[17] FE, chap. 5, "Broken Faith," p. 2.
[18] Ibid.

If the theologian undertakes to do what the philosopher does he is not keeping faith with those to whom he is speaking, for he counts himself a member of the community of faith in God. In his own thinking he is not moving from known to unknown when he moves from man's faith in man to man's faith in God; he is rather seeking to understand one known by means of another known. Moreover he is aware of the fact that faith in God is not for him an inference, nor has it been established by inference. Hence, however much he may feel that others ought to recognize that the reality of human faith implies the existence of the God of faith, he also recognizes that the implication is probably clear to him because he knows this faith in God to begin with; he sees how it is involved in everything else in human existence. His method therefore must always be the method of confession and demonstration. Theology is an effort to understand a faith that has been given, not an effort to understand in order that we may believe.[19]

He continues, "Our procedure therefore must be this, that we now use the understanding we have gained of the general structure of faith in interpersonal life for the sake of analyzing, as best we may, that faith in God of which we are conscious in ourselves in the company of the faithful.[20]

Paradoxically, it is when Niebuhr turns to a consideration of the "faith in God of which we are conscious in ourselves in the company of the faithful" that he discloses the deepest insights into the psychology of rebellion and unbelief. When we direct our attention to our faith in God, and to how we came to it, Niebuhr says, "we become aware . . . that it has always been present to us in a negative form and is now so present to us. Faith in God is the accompaniment of our existence as selves but first of all it is a dark background; it is present negatively as distrust and fear and hostility." [21] When we as selves come to a position of some trust in the God to whom Jesus points as Father, we become aware, Niebuhr suggests, that all along, without consciously acknowledging it, we had some recognition of relatedness to and dependence upon such a One:

We are accompanied in all our personal existence by the existence of other selves. Each I has its Thous which it acknowledges immediately.

[19] *Ibid.*
[20] *Ibid.*
[21] *Ibid.*

But each self facing its companions in relations of trust and distrust, of loyalty and faithlessness, is also aware of that last reality on which both it and the other are dependent. It is aware, as Schleiermacher pointed out, of its absolute dependence; but it would be better to say, that it is aware of the Absolute on which it and its companions are dependent.[22]

There follows in Niebuhr's text a flurry of metaphorical efforts to strike a chord of recognition of this awareness in the experience and memory of the reader. "This transcendent reality, this last fact, this Unconditioned, is no thing among things; it is no visible or conceptual reality. It is the inescapable, the radical source of self-existence, of the being of selves in time and place among other selves."[23] We have no explanation for the fact that we are here, now, among these companions. We did not choose to be; and, Niebuhr asserts in an interesting passage, "we recognize also, that we do not have the freedom not to be, though we have the dreadful freedom of killing our bodies. If it is so that our selves continue after physical death then we can do nothing about it."[24] "In our existence as selves, in our unfree freedom, we are in the presence of that which determines us."[25]

The relation of the self to this mysterious, transcendent, determining power, Niebuhr argues, is *personal* relation. It is personal because we become selves in the presence of companions—as I's related to Thous. But it is also personal because it is a relation of faith. That is to say, it is a relation in which the self takes up a disposition toward the Transcendent, and bases that disposition on assumptions or interpretations concerning the Transcendent's disposition toward the self. But this relation is faith in its negative form. It is distrust, disappointment, suspicion, and hostility. "Our natural faith, our ordinary human attitude toward the transcendent source of our existence is one of disappointment, or distrust, and of disbelief. In this very distrust it is an acknowledgment of

[22] *Ibid.*, p. 3.
[23] *Ibid.*
[24] *Ibid.*
[25] *Ibid.*, p. 4. Cf. *The Responsible Self*, Chap. 4.

someone there; it is a personal attitude and it is directed toward something personal or it personalizes that toward which it is directed." [26]

As he continues this existential analysis of faith Niebuhr makes a remarkable contribution to the psychology of religion in his discussion of three great patterns in which man's natural religion of distrust and suspicion of being comes to expression. Though he illustrates each type with allusions to classical myths and modern literature, it is plain that he intends these three patterns to be understood as moments in the faith disposition of each of us toward the inscrutable source of our being.

"The mind of the flesh," says Paul, "is enmity to God." We may state the thought more abstractly for the moment saying that our natural, though not our fundamental, human relation to the Tanscendent is one of distrust toward what is conceived to be deceptive, a distrust which appears in hostility, fear, and isolation. . . . Sometimes defiance marks the human attitude in man's encounter with the ultimate antagonist; more frequently the sense of antagonism appears in the form of human fear before the powerful enemy; and perhaps still more frequently the effort is made to put all thought of that Other out of the mind while the self devotes itself to the little struggles and little victories of life.[27]

Behind the stance of *defiance* to the powers that be, there lies a deep sense of disillusionment. The defiant person sees the great vistas open to human imagination and hope, but is oppressed and crushed by the truncations and wastage with which life seems so replete. In the hardy soul, with courage to overcome the fearsomeness involved in rebellion against the gods, disillusionment becomes defiance and rebellion—sometimes in the adolescent, boastful form of mocking God for having created such a world, sometimes in the more wise and tragic form in which a self, bound to other human selves, protests against Omnipotence on their behalf.[28] Niebuhr's

---

[26] *Ibid.*, pp. 5-6.

[27] *Ibid.*, p. 7. Note the continuity of this analysis with our earlier discussions of Niebuhr's appropriation of Whitehead's formula about God as *void, enemy,* and, finally, *companion.* Here the focus is on "God the enemy." One way of understanding "Faith on Earth" is to see it as the working out *in extenso* of that paradigmatic formula and its theme.

[28] *Ibid.*, pp. 8-9.

treatment of Bertrand Russell as an example of this latter genre is as sensitive an appreciation as one could hope for. At its conclusion he writes:

We may summarize Russell's attitude toward that which is, toward the structure of things, . . . by the statement that if the nature of things is the creation of a transcendent God, then that God is our enemy, and if it is not then the world itself is our enemy, and must be resisted though the fight may be carried on without personal hatred. What man is up against is not something neutral but something that is against him. Hence the proper attitude of man toward the Transcendent is defiance in the name of humane feeling or of spiritual values.[29]

There is a natural religion of *fear* that is the counterpart of the natural religion of defiance. They both arise out of the same sense of enmity and hostility toward the Transcendent. "The natural religion of anxiety and fear . . . is either more aware of the all-powerful character of what man confronts than Promethean defiance is, or it is less confident of human power to contend with the Omnificent, or it is less loyal to fellowmen and simply more self-centered. In any case it seeks to deal with the same situation of enmity between the Ultimate and man . . . only its approach is one of appeasement."[30] In studies of Greek religion Niebuhr found an account of the *Diasa* of Athens, described by Gilbert Murray as "a ritual of placation, that is of casting away various elements of pollution or danger and appeasing the unknown wraiths of the surrounding darkness. The nearest approach to a god contained in this festival is Meilichios. . . . His name means 'he of appeasement' and he is nothing else." After quoting Murray, Niebuhr adds a penetrating aside:

The subjectivist prejudice of social psychology leads [Jane] Harrison and Murray to interpret such a figure [as Meilichios] as the projection of the emotion of the ritual. We shall do better, I believe, to think of these shadowy figures, the wraithlike, insubstantial gods of appeasement, as symbols of that transcendent, that nature of things before which man is afraid.[31]

[29] *Ibid.*, p. 10.
[30] *Ibid.*, p. 11.
[31] *Ibid.*, p. 12. Quote from Murray is from *The Five Stages of Greek Religion*, pp. 28 ff.

A large part of the religious action and concern of human beings, Niebuhr points out, focuses on the appeasement and placation of the unknown gods whose threats and potential harm hover about us like ethereal shades. We invoke them to explain misfortune and tragedy and to assuage the guilt of irresponsibility. We name them in prayer and ritual, and through the naming derive some sense of control in face of them. These fears and anxieties are by no means groundless, Niebuhr contends.

The Unknown which is feared is not the realm of the as yet undiscovered finite enemies of the body and mind of man, but rather that unknown Fate or Law or nature of things which ordained and will destroy the self. Therefore the ghosts and deities and symbols which to psychologism seem to be projections of an irrational inner fear, may be regarded also as symbols of that Transcendent reality which man confronts but from which he flees in his distrust. There is an object of this religious fear; what the fearsome man regards as the object is indeed a fiction of his imagination; but the object is nevertheless present. There is something of which he is afraid. It is life itself; it is the principle of life; it is the ultimate reality that he is up against, the counter-part of his existence as a self.[32]

The third great strategy for dealing with the presence of a threatening Transcendent takes the form of the natural religion of *isolation* and *forgetfulness*. This is the strategy of evasion and denial. It covers both disillusionment and fear with fantasy and illusion. Its happiness is shallow because it must serve to mask and defend against unacknowledged but nonetheless felt fears. Its rage and despair are mere shadow facsimiles because to punch through to real emotion would be to open up to the abyss. The strategy of evasion "appears in the frequently lauded bright worship of Greece, but no less in Christendom, perhaps particularly in spiritualism and in Jesus-pietism, or in a worship of the Virgin and saints, and of a kind, heavenly Father (insofar as he is one God among many) which peoples the world the self inhabits with kindly, beneficent powers, which regards death as an illusion, evil as mere appearance." [33]

[32] *FE*, chap. 5, "Broken Faith," p. 14.
[33] *Ibid.*, pp. 15-16.

To Niebuhr it seems unlikely that the religion of evasion ever really succeeds: "Behind the Olympian deities there always lurked the darker shadows of a Transcendence that needed to be appeased. . . . Of this form of natural religion as of the others it is true, as Kierkegaard points out, that it is an expression of despair, though this despair is the sadder because it is not aware of itself as despair." [34]

Whence comes this enmity against the One from whom we issue? What can explain the deep disillusionment, the lowering hostility that colors our natural relation to the Transcendent? From the standpoint of a reconciled faith, Niebuhr says, two things may be said. First, this fall is a genuine *fall*. It is not representative of our original or fundamental relation to the Other. The Genesis myth of Adam and Eve's becoming crossed with God conveys a profound point: enmity is not our proper, or fundamental, relation to the Creator. And more important, it suggests that the fall is not the destruction of the order of faithfulness but rather its perversion. "Faithlessness does not eliminate the order of faith but perverts it. The order still exists; if it did not, not even distrust would be possible. If fall means distrust of God and disloyalty to Him, it cannot mean the total destruction of our relation to God; it must rather mean that an ambivalence has entered into our personal relations which poisons and corrupts them." [35] And second, the fall is a complex interpersonal event in which the whole structure of faith is involved. This means that no mechanistic account of cause and effect, and no individualistic interpretation which tries to bring some*one* before the bar of justice as responsible for the fall will do. In a poignant passage Niebuhr evokes the universal human experience of awakening, from naïve joy in the seemingly infinite promise of life, to the harsh realization that the promise cannot be fulfilled. "There is in the background of existence," he writes,

whether as memory of childhood, or as Platonic recollection of something heard in another existence, or as the echo of an inner voice, the

[34] *Ibid.*, pp. 16-17.
[35] *Ibid.*, p. 18.

sense of something glorious, splendid, clean and joyous for which this being and all being is intended. It is not a selfish or individualistic sense of promise; as though one felt oneself preferred to others or as though the promise would not be kept unless others were granted a smaller share of everlasting vitality. That mean and narrow mode of thinking comes later. The promise of life is the promise of glory and splendor, not for me, but for existence and for me as part of this world of being. But to our personal life which begins with such a sense of promised brightness there comes, whether in childhood or adolescence or later, the great disillusionment.[36]

Because of this primal deception, this inevitable disillusionment, we learn to live as those who expect betrayal and disloyalty. We develop what we have elsewhere called a "wisdom of survival," ready to take before we are taken, to do before we are done, and never to trust anyone or anything too much, lest we be deceived.

Treason begets distrust, distrust treason. In the great fear that all life is a deception these selves who cannot live except by faith seek to gain a little satisfaction by new faithlessness. In the knowledge that they must die, that the promise of life is a deception, they seek to maintain themselves a little while by making promises they do not intend to keep and by pretending to trust where they are deeply suspicious. . . . We are fated to be loyal and to live by trust, but all our loyalty appears only in the corrupted form of broken promises, and our trust in the perverse form of the great suspicion that we are being deceived.[37]

In these latter pages our following through the level of the existential analysis of faith has brought us to the point where all three levels of analysis seem to converge. The interpersonal structure of faith is seen as warped, twisted, and threatened by overwhelming corruption; the organic structure of faith appears fragmented and is present more in its negative than in its positive forms; and existentially, human selves—requiring a modicum of mutual trust and loyalty to maintain themselves, and needing common commitments to superordinate centers of value for the continual renewal of personal and social life—are seen as caught in their alienation from themselves as faithful beings, from trusting relations with their companions, and from the Other who is the ground and source

[36] *Ibid.*, p. 20.
[37] *Ibid.*, pp. 22-23.

of being. The analysis of faith on these three levels, carried out from the standpoint of restored and reconciled faith, has brought the order of faith into view. But it has brought it into view in a fashion more like showing the bombed-out ruins of a splendid city than revealing the city itself.[38] In this convergence, where both the bleakness and the promise of the human situation come into sharp focus, we have a striking instance of the kind of drama which gives Niebuhr's theology its multileveled impact. For the reader who has followed the sometimes rambling pursuit of each of these levels of analysis, and who has engaged in the exercise of reconstructing in his own mind the interrelatedness of the three levels as Niebuhr's mind grasped them—for the involved reader, to come to this present point of convergence is to be conscious of a deep hunger, a deep longing, a poignant desire that things should be different. To be asked, "Do you believe the analysis? Do you accept it as valid?" while one is under that spell would be almost beside the point. No purely intellectual response is possible to this kind of theology. One has either dropped the work hours ago and wondered why anyone would write and expect others to read such a convoluted discourse, or he has come to this point in the text with hope and expectation that the renewal of faith is possible, that there will be the promise of a new covenant.

A reader such as this latter one is not disappointed by what follows in Niebuhr's text. In the last two chapters, "The Reconstruction of Faith" and "The Community of Faith," Niebuhr portrays with subtle and powerful artistry the redemptive encounter of broken faith with the healing, reconciling power of the faithful Jesus Christ.

JESUS CHRIST AND THE RECONSTRUCTION OF FAITH

In considering Niebuhr's account of the work of Christ in the reconstruction of faith, we do well to recall his statement, cited

---

[38] The figure is not mine but Niebuhr's. In one of the draft introductions to this manuscript he likened the effort to portray the order of faith to the task of reconstructing the image of a bombed-out city using old maps, memory, and the surviving fragments of buildings and streets.

earlier, that "theology is an effort to understand a faith that has been given, not an effort to understand in order that we may believe." The reader of this christological section of "Faith on Earth" will see how little weight Niebuhr's claims about the restoration of faith in Christ place on the flesh-and-blood historicity of the man Jesus. Instead, the weight is placed on what Niebuhr will call the *facticity* of the risen Jesus Christ, present, active, and powerfully redemptive in the faith of the community formed around him. It is the Jesus Christ accessible in the present and historic faith of the Christian community with whom we have to deal, and whose resurrection is forever recurring as he encounters persons in such wise as to make them suspicious of their suspicion of being, and to initiate in them a restored ability to trust.

In the midst of our warped and twisted life of faith there is a prospect of healing. "More than that," Niebuhr says, "there is the assurance that a new promise, namely the promise of healing, will be kept. This is the prospect and this is the promise of which Christians speak. This is the New Covenant, which is not a substitute for the old promise given with life but is based upon it, yet so that it is not only the reinforcement of what we once believed but the answer to our disbelief of the first promise." [39] Niebuhr then differentiates two ways of reflecting and communicating as Christians: "We may do so as members of the rather amorphous society which is called the Christian religion, or we may do so as those for whom the primary companion in all thinking and interpretation is Jesus Christ." [40] In identifying these two alternatives, of course, Niebuhr is simply operationalizing his earlier distinction between "living" and "dead" faith for service in this present context. In a picturesque passage he suggests how the church, "the rather amorphous society which is called the Christian religion," is shot through with the same distrust and betrayals and "bad faith" that infect the larger community of humankind. "Nothing is more evident in human history," he writes, "than the fact that the church as the historic society of Christians had its origin in

[39] *FE*, chap. 6, "The Reconstruction of Faith," p. 3.
[40] *Ibid.*, pp. 3-4.

Judas' betrayal and Peter's denial quite as much as in Jesus' faith, and that it tries to continue in existence by means of repeated acts of faithlessness to its cause and to its companions." [41]

Yet, within the church as institution, and beyond its borders, there is another Christianity. Not definable in terms of organization, beliefs, rites, or doctrines, neither is it an ethics or individual piety. "It is rather the interpersonal movement of faith that centers in the person of Jesus Christ; yet it does so in such a way that he directs all trust and loyalty away from himself to the Transcendent and circumambient. This is the hidden movement in the churches." [42] It is to this "movement," this hidden life and community of faith within and beyond the visible church, that Niebuhr points when he wants to document the facticity of Jesus Christ and his resurrection from the dead. "In this interpersonal life Jesus Christ is not the founder of a religion; he is not an object about whom believed and disbelieved doctrines are taught, as when his two natures are defined, or his place in the Trinity is examined. He is personally present as Master and Lord. He is the personal companion who by his loyalty to the self and by his trust in the Transcendent One reconstructs the broken interpersonal life of faith." [43]

It is the personal quality of the relation to Jesus Christ in faith that Niebuhr wants to underscore. As in *The Meaning of Revelation*, the relation to Jesus that is saving or redemptive is one that occurs in the *internal*, the *personal* history of the self and the community of faith. "At the level of our existence where we are personal Jesus Christ is not an object, but a person. He is trusted and receives loyalty; he is not an object of our reasoning, not the object of a common knowledge, but the acknowledged companion." [44]

The Jesus of *our* history, Niebuhr asserts, is the Christ of faith.

[41] *Ibid.*, p. 5.
[42] *Ibid.*
[43] *Ibid.*
[44] *Ibid.*, p. 6.

We have no other access to the person known in history as Jesus the Christ than through the testimonies, witnesses, and accounts of those who knew him as Lord, or knew others who so knew him. The Jesus Christ we know as our contemporary is the risen Christ. "The Jesus Christ we acknowledge in personal trust and loyalty— slight as it is—is Jesus Christ risen from the dead, Jesus Christ among us." [45] If we move backward from this present givenness of Jesus Christ in whom we have faith, we remember him as having been introduced into our interpersonal lives by persons who were both committed to him in trust and loyalty, and with him were loyal to us and our companions. If we know Jesus through the work of objective historical scholars, that knowledge concerns the life of a human subject "who made certain interesting statements about God and man and the times in which he lived." But if we were introduced to him as a *person* by such scholars, Niebuhr says, "it was not by their scholarship but by their faith-relation to him and to us. . . . There is no possibility," he concludes, "of gaining access to Jesus Christ except as he is presented to men by those who have faith in him." [46]

As he proceeds in his argument Niebuhr demonstrates that he can be as skeptical as anyone regarding the historical reliability of the New Testament sources as documentation for details of the life and actual sayings of Jesus. Confidence in Jesus as savior, Niebuhr remarks, cannot be based on claims of the reliability of our historical information about him. But it doesn't need to be. For Niebuhr it is the presence of Jesus in our history as a massive, inconquerable fact that constitutes the basis of faith.

This Christ of faith does not wait for us to discover him as we must try to discover those historical beings who have left the traces of their erstwhile biological existence on the landscape and the institutions. We encounter him. He meets us. And he meets us in the persons we encounter. He does not meet us as he met Paul on the road—a flash of light and a disembodied voice, and yet there is something like this

[45] *Ibid.*, p. 7.
[46] *Ibid.*, p. 8.

227

in our meeting. For we do not meet him incarnate but as risen. He meets us as the unseen head of a company of believers in him, that is of men and women who seek to be loyal to him, for whom he is the cause, who trust him.[47]

The question about such a Christ as this is not "Did he arise from the dead?" but "Did he ever die?" [48]

There is no way in short compass to convey the richness of what comes next in Niebuhr's text. Niebuhr points to the steadfast faith of Jesus Christ as his most striking feature. He is present to us as person among persons, encircled as we all are by walls of distrust, hostility, and doubt. In his existence, as in ours, the "facts of life" underline the operational premise: we are being slain; there is that against us which means our destruction; the promise of life is a great deception. Yet despite all this the Jesus Christ known to us in faith manifests the most complete and sure confidence toward that One who is over against us, calling him Father. Jesus' sonship to the Father is visible in two dimensions of his faith. He is unshakably loyal, on the one hand, to God and his kingdom. He trusts that God is the creator, and that the creator is faithful to that which issues from him. He trusts also that God is lord of history—that he is ruling, and that his rule is righteous. On the other hand, Jesus' sonship is expressed in his loyalty to his fellow-man. Though he does not trust his fellow humans—or trusts us to be untrustworthy—he is totally committed to the liberation and restoration of his companions as children of the Father. In these respects Jesus is both Son of God and exemplary human being. "To try to explain this miraculous personal sonship to God physically, as some early disciples did in stories of the virgin birth, seems to add nothing to its remarkable character. It is the personal relation of a faithful, trusting, loyal soul to the source of its being which is the astonishing thing. This is a superhuman thing according to all our experience of humanity. Yet it is humanity in idea, in essence. This, we say, as we regard him, is what we might be if

[47] *Ibid.*, p. 9.
[48] *Ibid.*, p. 11.

we were not the victims and the perpetrators of treason and distrust." [49]

That this one who was so consistently faithful to God and humanity should be the subject of betrayal and hostility among us is only consistent in light of our relations of negative, twisted faith to each other and to the Transcendent. It could not have been otherwise. Had his faithfulness escaped violent encounter with the structures of treason and suspicion, it would not have touched us. On the other hand, had he been spared suffering and death, then his witness of faith would have had no credibility among us—who question at the deepest level whether goodness is powerful, or whether the power over against us can be trusted as good. He was steadfast in faith—to God and man—even unto death on the cross. No stay of execution, no miraculous intervention by the One in whom he trusted, spared him the taste of inscrutable darkness that awaits us all. He died.

"It seems most strange," writes Niebuhr, "that by that recollection which we have of the betrayal and the disastrous end of the one who trusted in the Power of Being as utterly faithful to him, we should have had introduced into our lives a little ability to trust. It seems most strange that when the one who had heard and believed the promise of life given to him—'Thou art my beloved Son'—that when this one had the promise of life cancelled—that then we should in the recollection of this one believe that his God is indeed our Father, that his Father is the Determiner of Our Destiny. This is the resurrection of Christ which we experience." [50] No missing body, no encounter in the garden or on the road to Emmaus, no blinding light or hand in the riven side. "Our evidence for [the resurrection] is not in beliefs about empty tombs or about appearances to others, but in our acknowledgment of his power." Niebuhr confesses:

What has happened is that this forsaken and rejected Servant of God has been given a name above every name among us. . . . He is built into

[49] *Ibid.*, pp. 14-15.
[50] *Ibid.*, p. 17.

the structure of our conscience, not so that we cannot offend against him, but so that it is he who is offended in our offenses. He is present with his wounds and in his rejection in all the companions whom in our great disloyalty we make the victims of our distrust of God and our diseased loyalties. That Jesus Christ is risen from the dead and that he sits at the right hand of God exercising power over us, that is one of the most patent facts in interpersonal history.[51]

In a way reminiscent of *The Meaning of Revelation* Niebuhr addresses the question of what it means to claim that in Jesus Christ we are reconciled to the Father. It means, he says, that *Jesus Christ reveals God.* In his explication of this claim, however, he draws a clear contrast between his christological approach and that of Barth, or any of the long line of theologians whom Pannenberg characterizes as doing "Christology from above":[52]

What we can mean by that does not seem to be what certain theologians seem to think, that apart from Jesus Christ we do not acknowledge God at all, for we do acknowledge him with perhaps all of our human companions in fear, hostility, and evasion; yet we do not acknowledge him as God, as the supreme object of our devotion, as the faithful one in whom we trust, as the one in whose kingdom we are bound to all our fellow citizens in creation.[53]

In the fellowship of Jesus Christ our operational premises of self-centeredness and defensiveness are interrupted. Our conscious and unconscious interpretations of life from the standpoint of our obsession with our own survival, security, and significance are jarred loose. Our pervasive distrust of being is qualified, and our narrow loyalties begin to be enlarged. "A great *metanoia,* a revolution of the personal life begins in us and in human interpersonal history." [54]

Echoing the influence of John's Gospel, with its theme of the Son glorifying the Father, and of the Father glorifying the Son,

---

[51] *Ibid.,* p. 19.

[52] Wolfhart Pannenberg, *Jesus—God and Man* (Philadelphia: The Westminster Press, 1968), pp. 33-37.

[53] FE, chap. 6, "The Reconstruction of Faith," p. 20.

[54] *Ibid.*

Niebuhr comes to the double affirmation that lies at the heart of his Christology:

We explain what has happened in the life of faith, in which just and unjust live, by saying that in this coming of Jesus Christ to us the Son reveals the Father and the Father reveals the Son. The Son reveals himself indeed as Son in his moral, personal character. By his trust in the Transcendent Source of Being, by his loyalty to all to whom he trusts the Father to be loyal, by his faithfulness to God he makes himself known to us as one who has the character of a Son.[55]

But the moral account is not enough. It is not sufficient to affirm Jesus' sonship solely on the basis of his remarkable faith. There has to be a corresponding affirmation of him by the One to whom he is faithful:

He is not made known as Son of God in reality until he is established in power, until it becomes clear that such a character of trust and loyalty is indeed in complete harmony with the nature of things. By his resurrection from the dead his establishment as the ruler of life, by the power of his resurrection as Paul has it, it is established that the Transcendent One is indeed what Jesus Christ in his faithfulness and trust acknowledged him to be, and it is equally established that the faithful servant is acknowledged by Reality itself. . . . What happens in the establishment of Jesus Christ in power over the personal life is that the double hypothesis of his historical existence is validated: The Lord of heaven and earth is indeed the faithful loyal Father, and Jesus Christ is indeed of one nature with that Father.[56]

From faith to faith. Jesus' establishment as sovereign companion, and as mediator of faith in God in the lives of the faithful, is the present, vital evidence of his resurrection. His resurrection and power, on the other hand, are the vindication of his complete trust in the Father, and reveal the Absolute One—first known to us as enemy—as being faithful with redemptive intent to us and to all creation.

In the companionship of Jesus Christ, and in the faith mediated

[55] *Ibid.*
[56] *Ibid.*, pp. 20-21.

by him, two great questions, which lie at the heart of our deep
suspicion of the Power whence all things come, find solution:

> The great anxiety of life, the great distrust, appears in the doubt that
> the Power whence all things come, the Power which has thrown the
> self and its companions into existence, is good. The question is always
> before us, Is Power good? Is it good to and for what it has brought into
> Being? . . . We recognize goodness in that which maintains and serves
> being. But our great question is whether goodness is powerful, whether
> it is not forever defeated in actual existence by loveless, thoughtless
> power. The resurrection of Jesus Christ from the dead, the establish-
> ment of Jesus Christ in power, is at one and the same time the demon-
> stration of the power of goodness and the goodness of power. . . .
> When Jesus Christ is made known as Lord it is to the glory of God
> the Father. And the Absolute is made known as Father in glorification
> of the Son.[57]

THE QUESTION OF THE HOLY SPIRIT

There is a change of key as Niebuhr comes to the last chapter
on "Faith on Earth." Here we find him stepping back from the
passion and involvement of the effort to bring the resurrected
Jesus Christ into transforming encounter with the trilevel, broken
structure of human faith. Niebuhr recognizes that faith is only
one of the virtues of Jesus Christ.[58] He affirms that neither faith,
nor hope, nor love—nor dependence, nor wisdom—can be taken
as the prime foundation on which the Christian life rests. Entirely
consistent with what has been the principal claim and focus of
our study—Niebuhr's grounding of his theology in the conviction
of the sovereignty of God—he asserts:

> The foundation is God, Father, Son and Holy Spirit, and . . . the
> unity which is present in life with God and Christ and neighbor comes
> from Him and from Him alone. To seek to base the life with God and
> one's companions on anything less than Him—even though this be
> faith, or love, or hope, is to fall into the temptation of idolatry.[59]

Following this expression of trinitarian faith Niebuhr turns to

[57] *Ibid.*, pp. 21-22.
[58] Cf. *Christ and Culture*, pp. 11-29.
[59] *FE*, chap. 7, "The Community of Faith," pp. 1-2 n. "Perhaps Schleiermacher ran into his greatest difficulties and errors in trying to build a system
of theology on the basis of the idea of absolute dependence."

consider some of the questions his analysis of faith raises for the traditional Christian doctrine of the Holy Spirit as a co-equal person in the Godhead with the Father and the Son. We have seen how his analysis of faith portrays the process of movement from negative confidence in the mysterious, impersonal source of life, to a more personal sense of relatedness in enmity and distrust, to, finally, a reconciliation to Being in which the personal relatedness is apprehended as trust and mutual loyalty. Such an analysis of faith, Niebuhr asserts, "leads . . . directly to this conclusion, that the Creator is Spirit, in this sense of Spirit, that he is Being with the inner reality of self-hood, covenanting and keeping faith." [60] In this same, essentially moral sense, the analysis of faith makes it clear that there is in man a similar quality of spirit. "Man is a living soul, not only as one in whom there is breath, or in whom there is experience and thought, but as one who cannot live except as he lives by faith. . . . There is a spirit in man, which not only proceeds from the Father in the sense that man was and is being created so as to be and to become a covenanting self, but also in the sense that this inner selfhood is in every moment dependent upon the presence of the Other Spirit, a Universal Thou." [61] Moreover, this analysis of faith has made it clear that Jesus Christ as Lord is also spirit in this same sense. "The Christ of our life in faith is not simply the historic individual Jesus, though he is that too, but he is the inner personal companion who as person is present in the memory and expectation of the believer." [62] Father and Son, Son and believer, believer and the Father—all are bound together in a unity of Spirit. This unity is not *identity*, Niebuhr affirms, though the inner life of spiritual selfhood in community is a unified life. "Personality," he claims, "precludes identity." [63]

In this perspective, Niebuhr points out, the Spirit is not understood as a *person* in the same sense as are the Father, the Son, or the believer. Rather, Spirit "is an attribute of the two persons in the

[60] *Ibid.*, p. 3.
[61] *Ibid.*
[62] *Ibid.*
[63] *Ibid.*, p. 4.

233

Godhead and that which makes it possible for us to be selves with them." Noting that this suggests a kind of binitarian formula— God is Father and Son in two persons—Niebuhr seems to want to link Spirit with that in man which is distorted and perverted in the condition of broken faith, and which in restored faith makes right relation possible with the now trusted ground of being. "The Spirit is that which, being of the very nature of God, is given and matured and restored to human persons. It is the principle of community among selves who are united in trust and loyalty to Father and Son." [64]

Having shown the binitarian logic of his position, Niebuhr backs away from asserting it positively as an alternative to classical trinitarianism. His reasons for this reticence really seem to boil down to one: even though his own experience and judgment do not allow him to recognize the Spirit as person in the same sense as the Father and the Son, it would be a breach of faith—a lack of loyalty to and trust in the historic community of faith—to deny an affirmation which has been so central and remains so central in its witness to its experiences of the ground of faith. Niebuhr's way of reasoning about this difference in position is a revealing expression of his understanding of the task and accountability (and proper humility) of the theologian:

We may refrain from making either our existential experience and our understanding of it or the records of the experiences of the founders of our community normative. We shall consider only one reality as normative, God in Christ, Christ in God, to whom the faith of the past and ours is directed and from whom it proceeds. . . . We shall not repeat the beliefs of the past as statements reflecting of our own faith; this we cannot do and still keep faith with our fellowmen; yet we shall trust these men of our community who so reported what they

[64] *Ibid.* Readers who are familiar with the idea of the *religious a priori* in the work of Troeltsch may find a certain similarity between it and the interpretation of Spirit that Niebuhr is offering here. An important difference is that for Niebuhr the restoration of the Spirit—restoration of the capacity for discerning and rightly responding to the Father through companionship with the Son—is a gift given by grace. As he puts it, Jesus Christ comes to meet us; and in the meeting our seeing, our discerning, and our capacity to respond are transformed.

understood of their life with God and we shall think of these beliefs, as reports and prophecies. Sometimes, perhaps, we shall understand the reality to which they refer.[65]

Then he states with as much precision as possible how he stands in relation to the church's historic witness to the Spirit as a person in the Godhead:

We . . . say that in our life in faith we know that God is Spirit, that the Lord is the Spirit, that the spirit in the human being proceeds from the Father and the Son. That the Spirit which proceeds from the Father and the Son is interpersonal reality. We can attach great significance to the statement that the Spirit is consubstantial with Father and Son. What we cannot say for ourselves is that the Spirit is not the Father, that he is not the Son, and that he is equal to Father and Son—as a power or a person like them but distinct from them. But those of us who speak in this fashion are not in a position to deny that the classic formulation is true. We can believe it; it is not an expression of our trust in God, however, and not an oath of loyalty to him but only an expression of our lower trust, our secondary but real loyalty to the community of faith which has so expressed its trust in God and so made its vow of fidelity. I believe that there is a Holy Spirit.[66]

The foregoing is representative of the kind of integrity Niebuhr sought to maintain as he lived faithfully in the triadic relation between the records and tradition of faith, his conclusions about his own experiences and those of his contemporary companions in community, and the mysterious One whom we try to apprehend in faith and by whom we are apprehended.

THE COMMUNITY OF FAITH

In the last part of "Faith on Earth" Niebuhr offers his vision of the future opened up by the restoration of faith brought about in our communal and personal history by Jesus Christ. It is a broad vision—as broad and inclusive in its depiction of restored trust and fidelity as was Niebuhr's earlier characterization of the broken structures of faith.

[65] *Ibid.*, pp. 6-7.
[66] *Ibid.*, p. 7.

The community of faith which rises into view as the great possibility with the restoration of faith in the Creator by Jesus Christ is the community of every self with God in his loyalty to all that he has made, to all the companions of the self; it is the community of fidelity in which all selves bind themselves and are faithful to all their companions as those to whom God is faithful.[67]

This vision of the community of faith comes into view both as present reality, already established and being fulfilled by the faithfulness of God, and as future possibility demanding the most strenuous investment of human trust, loyalty, and work. It is not enough to suppose, as Luther sometimes did, that the same grace which restores and makes faith possible also somehow insures its active engagement in rebuilding the broken connectives of the warped and twisted life of faith. There is a *will to believe* involved in the human response to God's redemptive loyalty. The future of faith—the completion of the community of faith—represents a challenge to a life of continuing responsibility for those whose faith has been reestablished through Jesus Christ. Commitment and action-on-commitment are required of us.

The restoration of faith is the challenge to a life of continuing responsibility. By faith we are called to the work of faith; through trust we are challenged to will to believe, to will to be faithful, to will that every treacherous flaw in us be made right. Trust is gift; God's loyalty to us and to our companions is sheer grace. The response of loyalty to Him and them in Him is our task and our responsibility.[68]

Because of our human responsibility in the rebuilding of the covenantal structure of collective life, our hopes for its coming are ambivalent. We will not even begin to rebuild the fiduciary structure of human community without undergoing painful *metanoia*, self-denial, and radical, costly change. "The prayer, 'Forgive us our sins' is something like the petition which we address to a surgeon: 'Cut out my cancer.' The prayer, 'Thy Kingdom come' is something like the petition addressed to a powerful empire: 'Put down our rebellion.' " [69] Furthermore, such progress as

[67] *Ibid.*, p. 8.
[68] *Ibid.*, p. 10.
[69] *Ibid.*, pp. 10-11.

is made toward reestablishing interpersonal trust and fidelity increases the possibility of and temptation to deception. "The more men trust in one another's loyalty, the greater the temptation to the abuse of that loyalty, the greater also the temptation to deceit or hypocrisy." [70]

Niebuhr's narrative goes on to stress that, while the restoration of faith in the human commonwealth is an eschatological reality, we must nonetheless remember that it is also "historic and archaic, as having been with us from our beginnings." [71] Here, following Augustine,[72] Niebuhr points out that we live our lives in the present suspended between memory and hope. To say, "I believe in the Holy Catholic Church," is to express faith in the future faithfulness of God. But it is also to look backward in "an acknowledgement of the presence to us of the community of faith which stretches backward as the long procession of those who trusted and were not put to shame, who were loyal to their companions in their loyalty to the God who kept covenant with them all and hallowed as he required their covenant-keeping with each other." [73]

It quickly becomes evident that Niebuhr has in mind a *very* catholic church. The community of faith is not divided between the living and the dead. Members in every generation and every century are equidistant in time for us:

Our relations to men of faith who lived in the sixteenth century are not mediated by all the men who have lived between these times biologically. There is a kind of foretaste of the resurrection of the dead in the community of faith. We find ourselves standing alongside Luther and Calvin and Pascal as they and we confront the same Transcendent, mysterious Creator and are reconciled by the same Lord Jesus Christ.[74]

[70] *Ibid.*, p. 11.

[71] *Ibid.*, p. 12.

[72] *Ibid.* See *Confessions*, bk. 11. In this and what follows one can also see signs of the influence of Royce's notion of the "Beloved Community," Troeltsch's idea of the *latent* church, and Bergson's concept of *duration*.

[73] FE, chap. 7, "The Community of Faith," p. 12.

[74] *Ibid.*, p. 13.

Furthermore, this is an inclusive community. There are no distinctions in it; no Jew or Greek, no B.C. or A.D. companies.

The faith of Abraham is as great as the faith of Paul, the trust of the prophets is as great a gift, their loyalty as much to be relied upon as the faith of the apostles. Faithfulness is present in the integrity and confidence of a Socrates as well as of an Amos. It is a very catholic church.[75]

Here, as so often in this manuscript, Niebuhr is unclear about how the community, whose faith finds expression and basis in the biblical word of God, is related to the universal community of all persons bound in tacit covenant under the sovereignty of God. He devotes considerable attention to discussing the Bible both as the tested, valid record of God's faithfulness in the covenant, and as the locus of reference for the disclosure that the faithfulness of God is a fundamental quality of reality. "The Scriptures are the indispensable handbook, the indispensable companion, the interpreting community of faith at my side in all my encounters with God, with Christ, with my neighbor." [76] Yet when he comes to discuss the relationship between the institutional church and the universal community of faith, it is clear that the latter not only extends beyond the former temporally but that *universal* seems to mean what it implies:

Every person, so far as he is a self, participates in the life of faith and is a subject of redemption, thus belonging to the Catholic church more or less actively. Every person, so far as he participates in the anxiety, distrust and disloyalty of the world—that is to say every person—is outside the community of faith. The line between church and world runs through every soul, not between souls.[77]

The visible church distinguishes itself from the universal community of restored faith by "the anxiety of its life, by its fear of death, by its compromises with lies, by its effort to induce men to

[75] *Ibid.*, pp. 13-14.
[76] *Ibid.*, p. 16.
[77] *Ibid.* p. 17.

put their confidence in it or in its rites or in its Bible." [78] It is not the universal community of faith. Yet, asserts Niebuhr, the community of faith does not exist without it. The visible church, it seems, is the community which knows the promise of the restoration of faith. It is the community partly transformed and under transformation by the faith of Jesus Christ.

One may carry forward the hypothesis that the visible church consists of our religious life in society, partly transformed by the faith of Jesus Christ, just as the family, partly transformed by that faith is a Christian family, and the nation, insofar as it is transformed by Christ is a Christian nation. It is then the natural religious life of man becoming Christian religion, and [it] takes its place in the total history of mankind alongside Christian philosophy and science, Christian economy, Christian politics.[79]

To the extent that religion is the central element in our cultural life, its reconstruction and reform are of central importance, just as its fall or failure has the most serious consequences. "But," concludes Niebuhr,

the reconstruction of faith is not something confined to worship, the numinous feelings, the relations to the unseen world. It is something that extends into the whole of life. And so we see how the community of faith not only comes into appearance in our religious life where it modifies, transforms, corrects our constant tendencies to fear, but in our domestic and our total cultural life.[80]

3. SOME CRITICAL REFLECTIONS

THE INTERACTIONIST DYNAMIC IN NIEBUHR'S
THEOLOGICAL COMMUNICATION

Niebuhr called his method in "Faith on Earth" the "method of confession and demonstration." More than any other theology I

[78] *Ibid.*, p. 18.
[79] *Ibid.*, pp. 18-19.
[80] *Ibid.*, p. 19.

have read in recent years, this piece of work draws the reader into that intense space where the hungry and despairing soul encounters that which can really help and change. This is serious theology. This is theology that knows that it is not worthy of that name unless it brings the reader into vulnerable proximity with a transaction which can transform and save. Here, in personal and interpersonal terms, Niebuhr patiently leads the reader in the construction of an understanding of our situation of malaise.[81] Then in a true drama of sin and salvation, he confesses the power of Jesus Christ—faithful man and risen Son of God—to restore faith between persons and God. Like the malaise of broken faith, an apprehension of which the reader has to construct for himself, the encounter with Jesus Christ must also be constructed. The reader has Niebuhr's guidance; he has the Scripture, the record of faith; he has—Niebuhr presumes—some chance of encountering the risen Jesus Christ in the witness and lives of companions in the church. But in the convergence of these, juxtaposed with the emptiness and distrust of his life, the reader must respond to the confession of Jesus Christ with his own soul's construction and reception of the risen Lord. This is an interactionist theology, based on a profound understanding of human knowing, development and change.[82]

When one begins to get a grasp on this interactionist quality of Niebuhr's theological communication, it becomes clear that, in the disagreement between Barth and the followers of Schleiermacher in theology, Niebuhr may have opted for the Schleiermacherian path as much on educational and communicational grounds as because of differences with Barth about the content of faith. The

---

[81] *This is the key*: he leads the reader in the construction; *but the job of construction is the reader's*. Niebuhr makes of the reader a companion, standing alongside, who can see for himself as Niebuhr points. As they both attend, and Niebuhr guides, the reader constructs his own interpretation of what he sees and hears.

[82] Knowing is something we *do to* and *with* that which is known; it is an *acting on*, a *constitution* of what is known from elements or data that were previously present, but not unified or put together in the mind of the knower in such a way before. For Niebuhr faith is a kind of knowing that involves this dynamic. "Faith on Earth" is, in this interactionist sense, an educational aid—a workbook, if you will—unto faith.

content of faith, Niebuhr saw, is a construction in the mind of each believer. Of course, beliefs and dogmas can be transmitted from one person to another, and beliefs, dogmas, and their contents are important elements in a person's construction of the contents of his or her faith. But prior to content *faith originates in relation.* Beliefs, dogmas, and concepts become important because we employ them in constructing and interpreting our understandings of relationship.

Niebuhr's theology begins with relation—the relation of person to person, of person to community, of person and community to the mysterious One who is over against us. It involves the reader in the bringing to awareness of the implicit faith that is being expressed or denied in such relations. When it presents Jesus Christ it presents him as *person inviting relation,* as *companion mediating relation* with the Father. In the interaction with Jesus as companion, with the God of Jesus' faith, to whom he relates us, and with companions in community, our faith is constructed and reconstructed within us. In "Faith on Earth" Niebuhr attempts both to describe this interactional process and to lead the reader in experiencing it.

SOME CRITICAL PERSPECTIVES ON "FAITH ON EARTH"

Writing a critique of a theological piece like "Faith on Earth" is a tricky business. If the interactionist approach works—if the reader enters actively and constructively into the task—then the results of the reading are almost as much his as they are Niebuhr's. Such a success makes achieving a critical perspective somewhat difficult. If the strategy fails—if the reader, expecting the transmission of beliefs, concepts, and information, evades the constructive process—then the critique could be, "It is not what I expected." But would we take the evaluative judgment of such a reader as being in any sense reliable?

The helpful criticism of a work like this requires a two-phase involvement. One must enter as fully and energetically as possible into the interactionist spirit of the narrative, investing in the process of inner construction and reorganization toward which the writing is directed. Only after this kind of full participation in the dialogue will the critic be in a position to step back from the interactional relation and try to assess what has happened, what has been constructed.

It seems useful to make our critical approach to "Faith on Earth" from two levels. Having devoted considerable attention to explicating the work's intention and strategy of providing an experience as well as the description of a process, we are entitled to ask ourselves how well the strategy succeeded. At the first level our question will be: How adequate was Niebuhr's artistry and skill to the task he undertook? Does he achieve his aims for the work? At the second level we will focus on the interpretation of the Christian gospel—the normative account of the content of Christian faith—which comes to expression in this work. How well and to what degree does Niebuhr "keep faith" with the community of Christian faith? How far should we understand his theological position, as expressed in "Faith on Earth," to be representative of biblical faith?

First, how well does Niebuhr's big manuscript on faith succeed in its interactionist intent of involving the reader in the construction of a personal apprehension of the drama of the reconstruction of faith? Without benefit of testimony from other readers I can only rely on an analysis of my own experiences with this text through several readings. Others' experiences will undoubtedly be different.

On the whole the three-phase form of the work, paralleling the three parts of many sermons, serves Niebuhr's intention quite well. In the first phase he aims at bringing the structure of faith, twisted and broken, into view. In this first phase, through the structural and existential analysis of faith described earlier, he invites participation in and identification with the experiences of betraying and betrayal, broken promises and disillusionment, that mark our lives in unreconstructed faith. The second phase answers the dilemma epitomized in the first by its presentation of Jesus Christ as the victim of broken faith and as the mediator of the New

Covenant. We are invited to trust him and join ourselves to him in faithfulness. Phase three stresses the eschatological vision of a universal community of faith and depicts how human will and work are required to assist in its fulfillment. There is true drama in this presentation; and the language, though often impersonal and abstract, still finds ways to stir resonance in one's own memory and experience with the movement which Niebuhr describes.

Several ambiguities in Niebuhr's thinking somewhat mar and dilute the impact of this work in relation to its intent. The first grows out of Niebuhr's unclarity about the character of his assumed audience. Through the first four chapters Niebuhr writes, in the main, as though he were addressing people whose only qualification would need to be reflective interest in understanding the pattern of their moral lives. He presumes they are persons of faith— at least within the tacit covenant that is requisite for human selfhood and community. But it is not clear that he assumes them to be men and women who already understand their life of faith through fellowship with Jesus Christ. Therefore, it comes as something of a jar when, in chapter 5, he denies all apologetic intent and begins to speak of the experience of the risen Jesus Christ as an indisputable fact of our lives in the community of faith formed around him. A similar hiatus appears at the end of chapter 4, when Niebuhr extrapolates from the analysis of the triadic structure of trust and loyalty the presumption of a universal awareness of an ultimate object of loyalty, "which obligates and demands trust and which unites us in a universal community." [83] Later it becomes clear that Niebuhr, in his method of "confession and demonstration," is writing from faith to faith. One wonders whether, if that had been made clear at the outset, the book would have lost some of its intrigue and excitement; and further, whether Niebuhr, had he been less scrupulous about avoiding any semblance of apologetic, might not have made a much stronger case by openly trying to work from man's faith in man to man's faith in God, demonstrating that the tacit covenantal structure of our common life implies a universal covenantal structure in reality.

[83] FE, chap. 4, "The Structure of Faith," p. 22.

A second set of ambiguities centers on Niebuhr's double usage of the metaphor of *structure* in relation to faith. We have seen how at one level he means faith as a structure of interpersonal relations, and at another, faith as a complex, inner-differentiated structure of attitudes, values, and commitments within the person or community. Though a careful reader can sort out these two levels, Niebuhr would have strengthened the work if he had made that differentiation himself. Also it would have helped clear up the larger ambiguity surrounding the term "faith" had he coined language to differentiate between "common" or "tacit" faith (faith before its conversion and explication in Jesus Christ), and "restored" or "explicit" faith (faith after its enlargement and transformation through revelation).

Finally, the impact of Niebuhr's "phenomenology of faith" is clouded by a set of operative assumptions that he does not adequately address and defend. These all seem to center in a bifurcation between relations that are *personal* (those involving what one understands oneself essentially and totally to be), and those that are *impersonal* (merely functional, involving only part of oneself, and not contributive to altering or maintaining one's essential sense of identity). Because for Niebuhr faith involves one's *personal* life—one's personal relatedness to other persons, to causes, to God—the relation of faith to other dimensions of life, knowledge, and interpersonal interaction becomes problematic. One may say that as regards faith everything is subsumed under the category "personal." Or, conversely, we can say that Niebuhr extends the category "personal" as far as is necessary to include all dimensions of experience pertinent to faith. In either case it involves him in the distinction between *inner* and *outer* history (as in *The Meaning of Revelation*, chapter 2) and in the implicit bifurcation of *nature* (the world of objects and events not filled with personal impact) and *history* (the sphere in which things occur in such a way as to affect my personal self-understanding and faith). We will come back to this cluster of ambiguities at a later point.

Let us shift now to the second level of critical engagement, that having to do with the adequacy of "Faith on Earth" as the presentation of a normative understanding of the content of Christian faith. One is impressed in the reading of this text (as with all Niebuhr's work) by his firm grounding in Scripture, his familiarity with the church fathers, and his competence in the broad catholic tradition that spans the Christian centuries. He is never naïve in taking a theological position or in offering an interpretation. He knows where the position he represents stands in the historical debates, and in almost every instance he is able to achieve a formulation that will hold in polar tension the elements of truth in both (or the many) sides of any issue. One may say, further, that Niebuhr takes the theologian's accountability to the tradition very seriously. Yet, as the discussion of the doctrine of the Holy Spirit earlier in this chapter indicated, he was not inclined to capitulate to tradition in matters where his own spiritual and intellectual integrity would be violated.

Niebuhr's primary contribution to the interpretation of the gospel in "Faith on Earth" comes in relation to Christology. The other doctrines—of God the Father, of the Holy Spirit, of sin, of the church—are formulated primarily in relation to the reconciling, redemptive work of Jesus Christ. The principal criticism I have of this christological statement concerns its already noted lack of interest in the Jesus of history. It is true that in none of his other treatments of christological themes does Niebuhr engage the question of the historical Jesus frontally. As in "Faith on Earth," he is always clear about the fact that we have no access to the man Jesus save by way of the testimony of those who know him in faith. But in others of his works Niebuhr does place a great deal more weight on the *Jesus of the New Testament*, his teachings, attitudes, and actions, than he does in "Faith on Earth." In "The Mind of Jesus and the Social Gospel" Niebuhr focused radically on the faith and teachings of Jesus. There it is the man Jesus, a Jew described in the New Testament, whom Niebuhr writes about. No less in *Christ and Culture*:

The Jesus Christ of the New Testament is in our actual history, in history as we remember and live it, as it shapes our present faith and

245

action. And this Jesus Christ is a definite person, one and the same whether he appears as man of flesh and blood or as risen Lord.[84]

The same reliance and emphasis upon the portraits of Jesus given in Scripture comes to expression in Niebuhr's section on the Sermon on the Mount in *Christian Ethics*.[85]

My point is that Niebuhr's christological position in "Faith on Earth," while deepening our understanding of his teaching about the reconciling, mediating work of Jesus Christ, does not fully live up to his own more adequate formulations elsewhere which demonstrate the necessity of substantiating the Christ of faith by reference to the New Testament depictions of Jesus of Nazareth. By Niebuhr's own standard the Jesus Christ of "Faith on Earth" is more *docetic*, more a product of the faith projections of those who know him and trust him as contemporary Lord, than he is a concrete figure testified to in the recorded memory of contemporaries and near-contemporaries. This makes "Faith on Earth" more liable than it need have been to the criticism that it opens the way for subjectivistic understandings and distortions of Jesus Christ. And the loss of concreteness and the neglect of the struggle toward the right apprehension of the Jesus of the New Testament makes Niebuhr's talk of Jesus as person here more abstract—and less personal—than it would have been had he brought into this writing "Jesus the revolutionary strategist" or the Jesus of the many virtues from *Christ and Culture*.

Especially troubling is Niebuhr's avoidance of any direct statement on the relation of the gospel's witness to the resurrection of Jesus and the contemporary experience of the risen Jesus Christ in the community of faith. Niebuhr makes the cryptic suggestion, following C. H. Dodd, that "among early Christians there were evidently men who, like the writer of I John, did not move forward from an experience of Christ rising from the death to the Christ seated at the right hand of power, but backward from the acknowledgement of the latter to the conclusion that therefore he had risen

---

[84] *Christ and Culture*, p. 13.
[85] *Christian Ethics*, pp. 31-36.

from the dead. This," he continues, "doubtless is the manner of much personal conviction in our time, for we live in the time of Paul and not in that of Peter and the twelve." [86]

The vindication of the authenticity of Jesus Christ as Son of God comes, for Niebuhr, in the resurrection. The resurrection, in turn, is vindicated by our awareness of the contemporary facticity, the reality of Jesus in our midst in the community formed around him. Both of these are important and essential christological claims. This circle of faith, as Niebuhr draws it, is saved from being fatally too small and subjective, however, only by Niebuhr's clear insistence that in the faith of the community the biblical account of Jesus' life, death, and resurrection is the starting point and the normative point of reference. The objection I raise here is that, having made this acknowledgment, Niebuhr tends, in this work, to evade the crucial issue which the community of faith in Jesus Christ cannot afford to evade as it approaches the gospel accounts of Jesus: namely, what is the relation between the event-quality of the Gospels' witness to Jesus as risen Lord, and the confession of the community of faith that the risen Christ is present and vindicated as the Son of God in his contemporary power and faithfulness? While it is impossible to press behind the statements of faith in the resurrection given in the New Testament to the nature of the event itself, Christian proclamation must anchor its confession of faith in Jesus' resurrection and sonship in the event-quality of the resurrection. We cannot evade this stumbling block, which only by being accepted, acknowledged, and worked with, becomes the cornerstone of faith.

[86] *FE*, chap. 6, "The Reconstruction of Faith," p. 19.

Chapter VI
Niebuhr's Legacy

From the conception and through the writing of this book my purpose has been to try to take the reader "inside" the thought and teachings of H. Richard Niebuhr. I have wanted to bring into view the organic unity of his theological-ethical position, and to expose its inner structure and dynamics. Wherever helpful and possible, I have tried to discern and interpret Niebuhr the man and thinker in his wholeness as he comes to expression in the sentences and paragraphs he wrote. Underlying the method followed in this book is my belief that the proper evaluation and appropriation of the contributions of H. Richard Niebuhr cannot be made without a grasp of the pattern and unity of his thought as a whole, and a clear appreciation of the intentions which animated his teaching and writing. Though these things could likely be said of the work of any first-rate thinker, they are especially true of Niebuhr. His was an independent tack in theological-ethical inquiry. The categories of analysis that seem to work in relation to his contemporaries in theology most often fail to really fit the shape and contours of his own work. Therefore my effort has been to bring the organism of his thought into view, to try to clarify the intentions animating it, and, through the study of its development, to locate and clarify the more or less permanent features it exhibits.

The critical reflections on "Faith on Earth" in chapter 5 provide the transition to the tasks of this concluding chapter. Here we will try to step back from our presentation of the dominant features of Niebuhr's thought and their development, and to take stock of the living legacy resulting from his life of work as theologian and ethicist.

1. NIEBUHR'S DEVELOPMENT IN REVIEW

Our glimpses of Niebuhr during the 1920s showed us a young scholar-teacher-administrator responding to pulls in several directions. Dominant among these directions was that one which employed the critical sociological-historical methods of Troeltsch in the analysis of the cultural and societal "compromises" of the church. *Compromise,* for Troeltsch, was not mere accommodation. Rather, it described a process and situation of mutual influence and interpenetration between the Christian message and community and the larger community and culture of which it is a part. As Niebuhr looked at church and society—or as he would later call it, "Christ and Culture"—he saw that the church's dividedness, owing to multiple patterns of compromise, rendered it unable to provide the centering and coherence-giving focus of valuing which could sustain a moral and ethical common life. Nationalism, the economic injustices of capitalism, racial injustice, exploitation, and violence—all these, Niebuhr saw, were sanctioned by idolatrous attachments to false faiths and loyalties. Yet the church was so implicated in fealty to these idolatrous values that it could speak no clear word of prophetic criticism, nor could it point to a central allegiance that really had power to supplant and expose the false loyalties that were being served. What took the form of idolatry in practical terms, was manifest in *relativism* in theoretical terms. Niebuhr's work in these years centered in the exposure of the divided church and its relativistic faith. But he was also working toward a theological position, beyond Troeltsch, that could speak with power of an Absolute beyond the relativities, and which could constitute the basis for a theocentric ethic that would relativize the relativizers.

Our analysis—in agreement with Niebuhr's own interpretation of his career—sees the early 1930s as the period in which there emerged the pattern of faith and thought that was to be characteristic of him throughout the rest of his career. His trip to Germany and Russia in 1930, his encounter with radical Marxism and Communist philosophy of history, the influence upon him of Tillich, and the powerful challenge to his liberal past represented by Karl Barth—all these were elements in the ferment out of which Niebuhr shaped a genuinely new theological approach. Newly seized by what he called the "conviction" of the sovereignty of God, Niebuhr saw that either God is the One who meets us in all the events, conditions, and relations of our lives or there is no God. Either God is the Being on whom we are ultimately dependent, whether we are conscious of or acknowledge our dependence or not, or we have no God. Convicted by the priority in being, value, and power of this God, Niebuhr struggled to find ways to express and symbolize and communicate his conviction and its implications for human faith and life.

Our study identified the emergence of three clusters of imagery by which he sought to depict the relation between humankind and the God who is sovereign Being. The first is an amalgam of Marxian philosophy of history, Whiteheadian process-metaphysics, Tillichian analysis of the Unconditioned manifesting itself in history, and all this deepened and radicalized by a fresh apprehension of the revolutionary apocalyptic thrust in the teachings and faith of Jesus. We identified this first cluster of imagery as the *process-structural* metaphor in Niebuhr's thought. Correlated with it is

251

the image of "man the patient"—human beings acting and reacting in history, impinged on and limited by each other; but, through each other and through nature, also being impinged upon and limited by the One in all the many. It is this first metaphor which seems dominantly to underlie Niebuhr's treatment of "Response to God the Governor" in his lecture course on ethics; and this metaphor is the central one in the lectures that become *The Responsible Self*.

The second principal image Niebuhr came to employ had been present in his thought from the very earliest period. Here he spoke of God as the source of all being and value, and of God's valuing —universal and inclusive in scope—as constituting the standard against which human valuing is to be tested. Correlated with this *value-valuational* metaphor Niebuhr spoke of "man the valuer"— the person as centered in what or whom he loves, and as dependent upon the valuing of others for a sense of worth. Revelation brings the transformation of valuing, relativizing lesser centers of value under an overarching and reorganizing commitment to the Creator, whose loyalty to all being is the ground of its goodness. This metaphor plays its role in Niebuhr's lyrical description and analysis of the impact of revelation in *The Meaning of Revelation*; it is central whenever he discusses faith in terms of the triadic structure of trust and loyalty as in *Radical Monotheism and Western Culture* and "Faith on Earth." It constituted the core of his discussion of "Response to God the Creator" in his ethics lecture course.

Whereas the first two of the three metaphors Niebuhr employed in this formative period of his thought were largely *impersonal* and only partially anthropologically based, the third is clearly personal and moral from the outset. This third image is that of *God the covenanting person*. God the self-binder, God the Father— loyal and intent on bringing to fulfillment all that issues from him. The faithfulness of God breaks through the suspicion and alienation that separate distrustful persons from him in the life, death, and resurrection of the man—and Son of God—Jesus Christ. As in *The Meaning of Revelation* and "Faith on Earth," this metaphor bears the weight of disclosing the faithfulness and steadfast love of a God who, in our natural religion of suspicion and doubt, is known as enemy and destroyer. The correlative image of the person—"man the promise-maker" or "man of faith"—lays bare the betrayals and treasons that fracture the tacit covenant underlying corporate life, as well as the positive potential for membership in a universal community of mutual trust and loyalty. This third cluster of images is central in Niebuhr's discussion of "Response to God the Redeemer" in his ethics lectures.

With the emergence, by 1937, of these three central metaphors, the structural and dynamic features that mark Niebuhr's subsequent work were in place. Coupled with them—or pervading them —was Niebuhr's profound appropriation and reshaping of crisis theology's confession of the absence and harsh judgment of God. In a developmental psychology of faith that grew in importance throughout his career, Niebuhr showed how our "natural religion" is one of enmity and suspicion toward the One who plants us in the thus-ness and so-ness of life. Revelation and the redemptive activity of God come as the conversion of this suspicious natural religion to trust in the One over against us as being both good and powerful, loyal and righteous.

In Niebuhr's work after 1937 I find no significant shift in this fundamental pattern of his thought. Various elements in it will be lifted up for special development and refinement. The perspective will be brought to bear on different kinds of problems, requiring elaboration and clarification as it is so applied. But all in all there is a massive continuity in the basic form and dynamics of Niebuhr's thought after this formative period.

While I think that the judgment expressed in the previous paragraph will bear up under scrutiny, I do want to acknowledge and call attention to a major change of focus that we can see occurring in Niebuhr's thought between 1938 and 1945. Though not a change in the fundamental pattern of his thought, it does represent a consequential alteration in the way he understood God to be related to and active in history by means of that pattern. As such it resulted in revisions in his understanding of his personal vocation as theologian and teacher, and—as is the case when one is an influential teacher and lecturer—undoubtedly contributed in decisive ways to the shaping of church life and ministerial leadership, and to the tone and ethos of theological education in the following period. Let me try to explain.

When we examined Niebuhr's writings of the early thirties we saw, particularly in connection with his development of the *process-structural* metaphor, a man living in the consciousness of a radical break in the continuities that maintain the fabric of human life. Every institution in the society was experiencing threat, and the ideological underpinnings that sustained them were collapsing under the strain. Freshly grasped by an understanding that if there is God, he is the Lord of history, Niebuhr seems to have felt that an authentically Christian interpretation of the agonies of that time would have to be at least as radical in its faith in the historic process as were the Marxists in theirs. Steeped in the prophetic faith of Isaiah and Amos, newly aware of the radical eschatological theme in the faith of Jesus, Niebuhr called for a posture of alert, expectant watchful-waiting. The role of Christians in the crises of the period, Niebuhr thought, was not to rush around making frantic and short-range interventions on the basis of reactive and superficial analysis. Rather, the task was to ask, "What is God doing? What is the meaning of this judgment by which we are being judged?" Only by discerning the intentionality in the judgment might Christians take action that would matter. Niebuhr was convinced that God is present and active as a structure-intending-righteousness in the events and processes of history. In a radical way he expected the transformation of social, economic, political, and religious institutions and relations. And he expected Christians, who had some clue to the meaning of this corporate judgment, to participate in the leadership of the reconstructive efforts, responding to the will and way of God. *The Kingdom of God in America* is, in part, intended as an aid to those leading the reconstruction of corporate, national life.

At some personal cost Niebuhr continued to try to stand in this radical prophetic tradition through the national and world trauma of World War II. We have seen his troubled efforts to interpret God's involvement in the war and its implications for Christian response to the war. Consistent with the eschatological faith that had come to expression ten years earlier in "The Grace of Doing Nothing" and "The Mind of Jesus and the Social Gospel," Niebuhr undertook to reconcile the facts of unprecedented slaughter of noncombatants and the moral ambiguity introduced by the inhumane tactics of all sides, with an understanding of God as sovereign power and love. Reports of friends and students from those years attribute to this struggle with the war the acute depression which all but immobilized Niebuhr and hospitalized him for a time in the early forties.

By the time the war was over a shift, which had begun as early as *The Meaning of Revelation*, seems to have come to completion. In the writings of 1931–35, when Niebuhr spoke of revolution he seems to have meant a major overhaul of the social, political, and economic structures of society, coming by way of war and violence if necessary. By the time of *The Meaning of Revelation*, however, the "continuing revolution" of *metanoia* and change which revelation sets in motion had become principally an event in the mind and heart of individual persons. Though the prophetic expectation of divine reconstruction through historic events painfully maintained itself during the war, in the postwar years it largely gave way to a focus on the evolution and revolution in personal and communal faith, and to the analysis of the phenomenology of the moral life.

As *The Responsible Self* and "The Illusions of Power" [1] show, the prophetic, process-structural analysis of contemporary events did not disappear from Niebuhr's thought. Also he continued each year to address himself to the topic "Response to the Governing Action of God" in his lecture course. But we do have to note a certain slackening of the eschatological tension that had been so characteristic of his work in the thirties. There is a coming to terms with the slowness and mystery of the coming kingdom,

[1] *Christian Century Pulpit*, 33 (1962), pp. 100-103.

manifesting itself in a kind of truce with the existing patterns of social-institutional life. Correspondingly we have to mark an increased investment in the exploration of the dynamics of the life of faith. Though Niebuhr devotes much of his time and energy to writing about the church and its renewal in the postwar years, his ideal of the universal community of faith is neither continuous with nor dependent upon the visible organization called church. The church's importance derives, rather, from being that community where Jesus Christ is remembered and present with power to reverse our distrust of and hostility toward God, thereby beginning the reconstruction of faith.

2. NIEBUHR'S CONTRIBUTIONS

Others have written well about Niebuhr's contributions as churchman, as ecumenist, as teacher and reformer of theological education.[2] Since our focus throughout this study has principally been on the development of Niebuhr's thought and ideas, I want to assess his contributions as *theologian* and as *ethicist* here. And then, having lived in close interaction with Niebuhr through his writings for more than five years, I am unable to resist offering in conclusion a brief expression of my appreciation for Niebuhr as *companion*.

NIEBUHR AS THEOLOGIAN

More clearly than any other American theologian of his generation, Niebuhr sized up the dilemma which theology confronted in the split between the liberals and the Barthians, and created a genuine third way. His was a genuine synthesis, a novelty. His effort to

[2] See L. A. Hoedemaker, *The Theology of H. Richard Niebuhr* (Philadelphia: Pilgrim Press, 1970); John D. Godsey, *The Promise of H. Richard Niebuhr* (Philadelphia: J. B. Lippincott Co., 1970); and the forthcoming doctoral thesis by Jon Diefenthaler of the University of Iowa on Niebuhr's early career, centering on an assessment of Niebuhr's impact, through *Kingdom of God*, on the interpretation of American church history.

ground his theology in the massive objectivity of a sovereign God, while characterizing that sovereignty from the standpoint of the experiencing subject, gave his theology remarkable scope and flexibility. Not only could it incorporate and hold together without paradox most of the affirmations of the two principal contending camps of that day; this approach also enabled Niebuhr to combine the best insights from the social sciences with the findings of biblical scholarship without falling into enslavement to either perspective.

Working always within the framework of the monistic confidence in the oneness, greatness, and goodness of God, Niebuhr could convert the dilemma posed by relativism into theological advantage as theocentric relativism. To be sure, all our concepts and symbols for the sovereign God-in-relation-to-man are time-bound, partial, and distorting. God is transcendent—epistemologically as well as actually. But, Niebuhr claimed, relative perceptions of the Absolute are still perceptions of an Absolute; and inadequate metaphors for the relation of sovereignty between God and man are nonetheless metaphors for the fundamental reality with which we have to do. Following what he saw as the theological strategy of the Bible, Niebuhr employed a multiplicity of metaphors, which in their very multiplicity acknowledged both the absoluteness and the mystery of God.

The other side of the coin from his "conviction of the sovereignty of God" is Niebuhr's freedom, within the comprehensive framework of that sovereignty, to explore and bring under theological control the range of subjective interpretations and responses which persons and communities make in relation to the One on whom we are dependent. In his "confessional phenomenology" Niebuhr makes profound and original contributions to theological anthropology and to the psychology of religion. His understanding of the evolution and revolution in faith's development—epitomized in Whitehead's formula about God as void, enemy, and companion —enables him to show how doubt, anger, fear, and evasion toward God are all to be understood as being moments in faith. His account of revelation as the interruption of our suspicion and of our hostility toward Being, and as the precipitant of a process of continual revolution, intelligibly broadens our understanding of that phenomenon until we can all claim truthfully to be under revelation. Yet, through his analysis of the impact of the risen Jesus Christ on the broken structure of personal and communal faith, Niebuhr is able to proffer powerful christological insights without becoming entangled in traditional arguments about Christ's two natures or the doctrine of the atonement.

For these theological advantages and strengths, however, Niebuhr's approach pays a considerable price, especially in loss of concreteness, determinateness, and religious-ethical sufficiency.

First, consider what happens to the *objective pole* in Niebuhr's theology of the sovereignty of God as he carries out his description and analysis of the subjective responses of persons and communities. There is always the *affirmation* of the trancendence, oneness, and greatness of God, but this affirmation often tends to become merely formal, regulative, and largely devoid of positive content. At least two features of Niebuhr's way of working contribute to this abstract quality of his treatment of the objective pole. The first has to do with Niebuhr's lack of interest in and attention to the metaphysical or ontological questions raised by his tri-metaphor depiction of God-in-relation-to-man. To be sure, there are good reasons, after Kant's critical philosophy, to avoid entangling theological confession with metaphysical speculation; and Niebuhr drew heavily on those post-Kantian theological traditions which sought to work within the Kantian limits by subsuming theology under the category of the historical sciences. (This is the background for the bifurcation of *history* and *nature* and of *personal* and *impersonal* we noted in chapter 5.) But the avoidance of giving account of how faith-knowing is related to and different from other kinds of knowing on which we depend, must inevitably result in making the sphere of faith one which has its own special logic and verification procedures. It thereby becomes inaccessible to critical questions from other realms of discourse, and to that degree also not accountable to general requirements of precision in language and logic. To speak only "from faith to faith" is to run the risk of working within too constricted a circle, so that the vision which faith sees and confesses loses in power and credibility because it makes itself invulnerable to questions and protests from those who do not share its vantage point. This is compounded in a theology of the sovereignty of God because its basic premise and ground conviction claims oneness and all-inclusiveness for the God of its faith, thereby incorporating—or co-opting—the standing place of those who do not share its vision. The affirmation of the all-inclusiveness of God, without serious attention to how that affirmation relates to and congrues with other affirmations we make in expressing our knowledge of reality, inevitably leads to a formalization—an emptying and abstraction—of the idea of God so affirmed.

Similarly, Niebuhr's strategy of using multiple metaphors to express (and acknowledge the mystery of) the God-human relation constitutes problems for his theology. Commendable as an avoidance of the idolatrizing of particular symbols for the object of theology, this method contributes to the evocative power and richness of Niebuhr's theology for those of us who stand within the ambit of the circle of confessing faith. But here again, what is gained in suggestiveness and evocative power represents, in some measure, a loss of ability to communicate about the object of faith with the audience beyond this circle. And while it is true that Niebuhr's "confessional phenomenology" represents an effective invitation and mode of access to the circle of confessing faith, those who enter must agree, upon entering, to accept a bifurcation in their way of knowing the world in exchange for the relational richness and orientation to the Transcendent which Niebuhr's version of Christian faith offers. That is to say, they must relinquish the standpoint of "external history" in order to stand within the stream of "internal history." (We should remind ourselves, however, that this may be as effective a way as any to speak about the disjuncture with previous life and thought involved in one's "taking up the cross and following . . .")

A second, related cluster of problems in Niebuhr's theology stems from what I will call Niebuhr's *idealism*. Niebuhr is an idealist in the sense that, like Plato, he sees beyond but underlying the world of appearances—the world in which evil seems powerful and the good impotent—the outlines of a world more perfect and representing the fulfillment of the truncated promises of being of which we are victim. Niebuhr's idealism, however, is more like that of Jesus than it is like Plato's. It is not the world of eternal forms, intuitively known, to which Niebuhr directs our attention. Rather it is the eschatological reality, the promised, coming, and already operative kingdom of God, witnessed to by the prophets and in the teachings of Jesus, which he wants to bring into view. My objection is not to this idealism of the kingdom, nor is it to Niebuhr's interpretation of Jesus as the great idealist of the eschaton. My objection comes, rather, in relation to two misuses of his idealistic framework to which Niebuhr's various presentations of his position sometimes leave him liable. Both these misuses involve the confusion of the *eschatological* (ideal) and the *actual* (historical). The idea and conviction of the kingdom of God are so powerfully established in Niebuhr's own faith that his employment of them in theological work occasionally involves him in the fallacy of misplaced concreteness. As was the case in "Faith on Earth" he sometimes utilizes the *idea* of the universal community of (restored) faith, with its experience of the power of the risen Jesus Christ, as the substantiation for explaining and claiming authenticity and facticity for the resurrection. Similarly, he sometimes speaks as though the idea of a universal cause implies or denotes the existence or being of a universal cause. These, and other instances like them, illustrate points in Niebuhr's theological enterprise at which the circle of faith grows too small and too inward-looking, with the result that premises which should be established by argumentation or at least by clear statements of intent are simply presumed as being shared by others.

A more serious confusion of the eschatological and the historical seems to emerge at points in Niebuhr's description and analysis of the life of faith. The conviction that God is present and at work in the action of life and history can lead to the alert, responsible readiness to respond in alliance with the work and will of the divine action. But it can also lead, when the eschatological tension is slackened, to a resigned waiting or an introverted concern with the adequacy of one's methods of discernment. In this latter case confidence in the present reality of the eschatological kingdom becomes a ground for complacency in the face of the actual or historical present. God subtly shifts from being the eschatological process straining toward the fulfillment of all being, to becoming the inscrutable and morally ambiguous overlord of a mismanaged and corrupt kingdom to whom, nonetheless, we must become reconciled. Obviously I overstate the case. But when the sovereignty of God is understood primarily in formal and regulative terms, the way is left open to affirm the normative objectivity of such a God without much practical moral involvement or cost, thus opening the way for theological rationalization of injustice and too-easy talk of reconciliation. This point will come up again in our discussion of Niebuhr as ethicist.

Mention has been made of the importance of Niebuhr's contributions to the psychology of belief and faith. This final point is not so much a criticism of Niebuhr as it is a recognition that biography and theology are inseparable, and that in a theologian each affects the other. In his accounts of the movement in faith from God as void, to God as enemy and companion, one can hardly avoid the conclusion that God the enemy loomed in Niebuhr's life with considerable reality and consistency. One notes the vividness and power with which Niebuhr characterizes the broken structure of faith. We remember his acute and agonizing awareness of the suffering of the innocent and his identification with Job. We note his probing awareness of the modes of expressing human enmity to an indifferent or hostile God—defiance, fear, evasion. And we observe Niebuhr's special sympathy for the Promethean rebel who protests the injustice of God on behalf of his mistreated companions. Niebuhr knew God the enemy. This genuine anguish gives his testimony to God the companion far more credibility than if it had come easily or glibly for him. But at the same time it carries over as an alloy of grimness and resignation in his affirmation of confidence in God the companion. Whereas other participants in the companionate relation—say Jonathan Edwards—are able, on some days, to sing full-throatedly and joyfully of the excellence and beauty and awesome love of the Companion, Niebuhr's aesthetic of divinity usually remains more reserved, muted, and ambivalent. Somehow it is as though the sovereignty of God is more a burden to be borne than a liberation to the captive. The disclosure of the kingdom, it seems, is a welcomed nullification of the suspicion of ultimate nothingness and deception, but it comes more as an invitation to unlimited responsibility than as releasing news that human liability is limited because there is One, powerful and good, who is responsible.

NIEBUHR AS ETHICIST

Niebuhr's legacy to the field of Christian ethics is as rich as his contributions to theology, if not richer. For him the two fields are inseparable, though each does have its own proper problematic and sphere of accountability. There are signs that Niebuhr's distinctive mode of doing ethics is becoming more widely emulated and developed today than in his own lifetime. The widespread interest in the phenomenology of moral agency and in the contributions of both Gestalt and developmental psychology to understanding moral interpretation and decision-making can be seen as being in continuity with Niebuhr's approach to ethics. Niebuhr's development of the idea of responsibility; his broad contextualism, established in the framework of the sovereignty of God; his understanding of the development of conscience in social terms; his analysis of the moral agent in terms of loyalties and interpretative schemas, as well as in relation to application of moral principles—

in all these respects Niebuhr made original and powerful contributions to the field of Christian ethics.

As was the case with his theology, however, where there are great assets there are also significant liabilities. Earlier I pointed to the tendency of Niebuhr's characterizations of the God-human relationship to become largely formal and regulative, operating more as constraints and limits than providing positive content. This tendency makes itself apparent in Niebuhr's ethics. Niebuhr makes a clear and forceful argument, for instance, for the contention that faith in God as the source and center of all value requires that we give supreme loyalty and love to no other lesser or finite center of value. As a regulative principle this imperative is helpful. It leads to an examination of the structure of our valuing and the objects or causes of our love, and presses us to relinquish or relativize any that have assumed or usurped a position of ultimate care for us. It is a clear statement and guard against idolatry. This imperative becomes problematic, however, when we address the question of how we should order the subordinate, lesser values which we also love and serve. And it becomes even more problematic when it is our responsibility to adjudicate between the conflicting value claims of other persons or causes than our own.

A similar indeterminateness limits the usefulness of the two other principal imperatives generated in Niebuhr's ethics. With respect to Niebuhr's urging that we respond to the experience of limitation as those who trust that in all that impinges upon us God is acting, we can generate the will to do so. But we cannot be assured in our own minds and hearts, let alone demonstrate to others, that our actions—taken in risk and hope—are in fact responsive to the acting and will of God. Nor can we provide much in the way of reliable guidance for the similar efforts of others. When Niebuhr urges us to respond to fellow beings in loyalty to them and to the God who is loyal to them and us, this can be taken as descriptive of a helpful and normative orientation. We can strive to shape our attitudes and impulses toward others in accordance with it. But it is not the kind of moral guideline in accordance with which we could resolve a dilemma in which loyalty to one companion necessarily required betrayal or neglect of another.

For Niebuhr, I suspect, the reality of the Center of radically monotheistic faith was so real and vivid that the ethics of response to that One's being, valuing, and faithfulness seemed to have sufficient normative determinateness. Such faith can be trusted to know and do the "fitting" thing. Therefore it was not necessary to develop guidelines or "middle-axioms" or other heuristic devices for use as aides (and checks) in the process of ethical discernment. Here a theological ethics, grounded in faith in the objectivity and reality of God, places excessive trust in the human subjective perception of and response to that God. For that reason it fails to adequately address the need for determinate specifications of ethical imperatives for concrete situations.

Related both to the previous point and to our earlier discussion of Niebuhr's idealism, we have to recognize the omission in Niebuhr's ethics of any adequately developed theory of *right* or *justice*. In the previous section we spoke of the subtle tendency in Niebuhr's later thought toward the confusion of the eschatological, ideal kingdom with the present, actual, historical situation. Something like this confusion seems to be involved when Niebuhr insists upon the inseparability of being and value. The statement "Whatever is, is good" is a magnificent recognition of and expression of faith in the eschatological kingdom of God. And to the person whose trust in and loyalty to that eschatological reality is sufficient to sustain him or her in the face of the world's vast and often hostile denial of that vision, it is a valid and determinative ethical principle. As a principle guiding the resolution of conflicts between social groups, however, or between persons who either don't know, or know and distrust, that kingdom, it is not a particularly helpful principle. Students of Niebuhr who want to enter into and extend his work as ethicist would be well advised to build onto Niebuhr's idea of the tacit covenant required for human community and selfhood something like the "ideal-contractualist" theory of justice

264

while is brilliantly developed in philosophical terms by John Rawls.[3]

The confusion of the eschatological and the historical does not always involve assimilation of the kingdom ideal to the historical situation. In fact, the dilemma—and the beauty and power—of Niebuhr's theological ethics are more keenly appreciated if we see that in fact the assimilative movement almost always goes in the other direction. It is not that Niebuhr enwraps the historical present in the wings of the eschatological kingdom, thereby sanctioning the status quo. Rather, so vivid is his taste and feel of the kingdom as *fundamental reality*, that his faith and hope lead him to ground his ethical reasoning in the faith-knowledge of that reality. This involves him in an assimilation of historical actuality to the kingdom, and not vice versa.

Paradoxically, it is this tendency to see things from the perspective of the kingdom that issues in the most serious liability of Niebuhr's position for social ethics. In addition to the lack of a developed theory of justice for the adjudication of conflicts, Niebuhr's ethics of the kingdom calls for a posture of expectant waiting, of alert passivity, and of "aggressive suffering" as its only initiative-taking strategy. It banks on the faithfulness of God, and on the paradoxical power of a God whose suffering and crucified Son was vindicated in resurrection. This ethics of radical faith, extended to human events in the life of the world, can result in a virtual paralysis so far as ethical action is concerned. In a mind as attuned to polarities in existence as Niebuhr's, and as sensitive as he was to nuances of self-centeredness in the most altruistic of motivations, the appropriate response to all but the most heinous of abuses of companions seemed to be expectant waiting, and suffering if necessary. Just as in his theology the word *God* has no unqualified predicate, so in his ethics the *will* or *action of God* can have no unqualified specificity. This is the most serious limitation of an ethics that is deeply and consistently Christlike.

[3] John Rawls, A *Theory of Justice* (Cambridge, Mass.: Harvard University Press, 1971).

But we can't leave it there. I must insist that the proper evaluation of Niebuhr's theological ethics involves us in something more
complex than merely pointing to a seeming confusion, in his
thought, of the eschatological and the actual. It requires something
more serious from us than merely suggesting that he needed to
develop a theory of justice. We should remind ourselves that for
Niebuhr the tasks of theological ethics are fundamentally twofold: (1) the critical clarification and ethical evaluation of the real
loyalties and trusts being served as we make moral decisions and
take moral action; and (2) the presentation of the vision of God-
ruling; the effort to focus the eyes of faith on it and to inform active
interpretation and response in faithfulness to the One the vision
discloses. (We fail to appreciate the stringency of this second
dimension of the task, as Niebuhr understood it, unless we see that
any presentation of the vision of God-ruling must be offered in
such a way that it carries within it its own *negation* and *relativization* as an essential quality of its "truth.")

If we call these two tasks of theological ethics the *critical* and
constructive tasks, respectively, we may say that in Niebuhr's work
they received more careful attention than did a third task, which,
for some ethicists, constitutes the prime responsibility of ethics—
namely, the casuistic resolution of specific moral dilemmas through
the application of moral principle and reasoning.

My contention is that Niebuhr's work is short and unsatisfactory
as regards this third task, not because he was uninterested in it or
felt it to be important, but because his way of engaging the first
and second tasks presented him with a very difficult problem of
what I shall call "standpoint."

Niebuhr believed and argued that every ethical system (and every
culture's operative ethics, distilled in customs, mores, and laws)
has its center or centers of value and loyalty. Ethics, in its critical
function, involves the bringing to clarity and ethical evaluation of
such a center or centers of valuing. This clarifying and evaluative
task, Niebuhr believed, could not be carried out from a value-
neutral position. Rather it has its own value-commitments which

are always susceptible of a similar kind of critical evaluation. Niebuhr's engagement in the constructive task of ethics, therefore, aimed at developing the most adequate presentation he could offer of a universalizing standpoint from which the critical and evaluative task could be carried out.

But Niebuhr was a representative and member of a particular faith community and tradition. His constructive efforts attempted to give expression to the most universalizing version of that particular community's vision of supreme value and transcendent loyalty. He tried to be consistently loyal to its central insight—that the universal, or the Absolute, cannot be apprehended and controlled by ritual, ethical, or conceptual means; and that the effort to discern and respond to it involves the faithful in ongoing revolutions and transformations of their images of the good, the right, and the beautiful. The community of the faithful, then, is always "on the way." Individual members of the community are at different points in the pilgrimage. From egocentric, defensive, and self-referencing faith they develop toward a faith more expressive of trust and loyalty to the One who is universal and whose justice transcends human knowing. Further complexity derives from the fact that others, starting from different faith traditions (and sometimes from no formal traditions) seem to be involved in somewhat similar transformations toward loyalty to the One, and this in ways that are recognizably akin to those of their Christian brothers and sisters.

And so we see Niebuhr's dilemma as regards the casuistic task: he can write and prescribe (as he did in "The Grace of Doing Nothing" and in his wartime articles) from the standpoint of universalizing faith in a God who *is* action in creation, governance, and redemption. But such a vision and its ethical correlates speak only to those whose pilgrimage through revolution and transformation has carried them far enough for them to see it. It provides guidelines for action and reaction only for those whose grasp and feel of the eschatological power of the kingdom is vivid and sure, preparing them for acceptance of the suffering, opprobrium, and death which faithfulness to it may entail. (And it is by no means always only their own suffering and death, they must be prepared to accept, but often those of innocents and the noninvolved—as the careers of leaders like Gandhi and Martin Luther King, Jr., show us.)

Niebuhr, in the mid-thirties, compared the ethical posture incumbent on one who thus sees the kingdom to that of a committed Communist, living and working in a prerevolutionary society. His own constructive ethics is written for persons similarly living "between the times"—those who see and want to anticipate an order more universal, more inclusively just, while living and being involved in a present that seems to block and contradict it.

Seen in this light, the kind of criticisms of Niebuhr's position that I have offered here, while having a certain validity, largely seem to miss the real point of his work. We might better say, in summary and conclusion, that Niebuhr's theological-ethical legacy is *most* helpful at the points of generating and renewing moral vision and perspective; in revealing the distortions and perversions of objectivity that result from self-serving loyalties; and in pointing to the relativity of human notions of justice when seen against the context of the righteousness of a sovereign and finally inscrutable God. Niebuhr's legacy is *least* helpful as regards the development of principles and guidelines for decision and action in contexts where consciousness of God-ruling is fragmentary or unacknowledged, or where the operative time- and value-frameworks are so narrow as to exclude a perspective grounded in radically monotheistic faith.

Niebuhr's theological-ethical vision is not merely an appeal to passivity and to faithful waiting. It also calls for initiatives and pro-active involvement. It envisions demonstrations and dramatizations of radical faith and responsibility. It implies the creative and determined juxtaposition of the demands of divine justice alongside the clamor of our clashes over "our" rights. Niebuhr's position calls for persons and communities to generate prophetic, pioneering incarnations of radical faith, both as modes of responsible existence and as models that can enrich the impoverished moral imaginations of companions in an uneschatological time. When and where these things are occurring, Niebuhr would say, *there* is the true church. And there in the midst of them, Niebuhr believed, will be Jesus Christ, the pioneer and perfector of radical faith in the sovereign God.

Niebuhr's favorite name for Jesus Christ was the "mediator of faith." A mediator, he pointed out, is not one who is hierarchically related to the self—who addresses you from a position of superiority, as adult to child. Rather, a mediator is companion, standing alongside, leading and guiding your explorations, but in such way as to acknowledge your own viability and responsibility.

The mediator is not merely a peer, however; he is not merely companionate. The mediator must also be one who has made the pilgrimage, who knows the city of our destination, and who knows how to direct our eyes so as to enable us to discern its outlines. The mediator must know the rigors of the way and be prepared to lead us in the disciplines that increase and maintain fitness. It is required that he know the beginnings of the journey, the script of its record and memory; and he must know the promised future which illumines the meaning and depth of the present.

Friends who knew H. Richard Niebuhr and were his students speak of him in terms that underscore his mediator role and significance for them. Though I never knew him in life, in a different but equally important way Niebuhr, as my companion in this study, has been and is for me the mediator of faith in the kingdom of God. For this kind of companion one feels deep gratitude and respect. But more than that, one feels a responsibility to enter into his faithfulness and to try, as he did, to be a mediator of faith in the kingdom, loyal both to it and to our companions.

We shall not enter fittingly into Niebuhr's faithfulness and work if we merely emulate the style and content of his theological vision. Rather than of the *products* of his work, our imitation—for our time—must be of the bold analysis he made of his time and its needs, of his consistent attention to the patterns of our life of faith and moral agency, and of his costly investment in being an enlivening mediator between our present, the Christian memory, and the future of faith. Niebuhr once wrote of Kierkegaard, "This is a peculiar phenomenon in human history—a thinker who is always this individual thinking and who can never be reduced to his thought; a thinker who is always at the same time pointing away from himself to us so that when we think with him we think about ourselves." [4] In a fashion much less contrived and self-conscious, this statement also applies to Niebuhr. Only we might add—

A thinker who, in pointing away from himself to us and our companions, also brings into our view the mysterious, powerful, and faithful One in whom we live and move and have our being.

[4] In Carl Michalson, ed. *Christianity and the Existentialists* (New York: Charles Scribner's Sons, 1956), pp. 26-27.

Appendix

OUTLINE AND BIBLIOGRAPHY
FOR NIEBUHR'S LECTURE Course in Christian Ethics
Winter and Spring Terms 1952–53

Part I. The Function and Field of Christian Ethics
   1. The task of Ethics in the Christian Community
   2. The Relation of Christian Ethics to Theology
   3. The Authority of Scriptures for Christian Ethics
   4. The Uses of Philosophy in Christian Ethics
Recommended Readings: Brunner, *The Divine Imperative*, Book I;
   Berdyaev, *Destiny of Man*, Ch. I; Knudsen, *Principles of Christian
   Ethics*, Chs. I & II; Niebuhr, H. R., *Christ and Culture*, Ch. I.
Additional Readings: Vivas, Eliseo, *The Moral Life and the Ethical*

271

Life, Introduction; Wheelwright, *Critical Introduction to Ethics,*
Ch. I; Reid, *Creative Morality,* Chs. XII-XV; Taylor, *Faith of a
Moralist,* Vol. II, Chs. I & II: Paulsen, *System of Ethics,* Ch. VI;
Hartmann, *Ethics,* Vol. III, Ch. 85.

Part II. The Structure and Dynamics of the Moral Life

1. The Nature of Moral Action
   a) Moral Action as Choice of Good
   b) Moral Action as Obedience to Right
   c) Moral Action as Fitting Response to Action Upon Us.

2. Moral Action as Interaction
   a) The Moral Dialogue
   b) The Triadic Pattern of Interaction

3. The Moral Self and the Moral Community
   a) The Nature of Moral Selves
   b) Self, Neighbor and God
   c) "Of Human Bondage"
   d) The Liberty of the Children of God

Recommended Readings: Ramsay, *Basic Christian Ethics,* Ch. VIII;
Knudsen, Chs. III-V; Berdyaev, Pt. I, Chs. II & III; Vivas, Pt. II.

Additional Readings: Buber, *Between Man and Man; The Eclipse of
God; I and Thou;* Jaspers, Karl, "Nature and Ethics" (Ch. III in
Anshen, ed., *The Moral Principles of Action);* Jaspers, *The Way
to Wisdom;* Mead, G. H., "The Genesis of the Self" in his
Philosophy of the Present; Kierkegaard, *Concluding Unscientific
Postscript; The Sickness Unto Death;* Hocking, W. E., *The Self,
Its Body and Its Freedom;* Niebuhr, Reinhold, *The Nature and
Destiny of Man,* Vol. I; Taylor, *Faith of a Moralist,* Vol. I, Chs. V
and VII; Weiss, Paul, *Nature and Man;* Marcel, *The Mystery of
Being,* Vol. I, Chs. VIII-X; *Men Against Humanity.*

Part III. The Principles of Christian Action

I. The Teleological Principle: The Vision of God, The Kingdom
   of God, Eternal Blessedness and Man's Perfection.

   Knudsen, Chs. VI and VIII; Ramsay, Ch. VI; Niebuhr, Ch.
   VII; Berdyaev, Pt. III.

   K. E. Kirk, *The Vision of God* (esp. Chs. I, II, and VIII);
   Thomas Aquinas, *Summa Theologica* II-II, Qz. i-iv; Rauschen-
   busch, *Theology for the Social Gospel,* Chs. XII-XIV; Calvin,
   Institutes, Bk. III, Chs. IX-XVIII; Wesley, *On Christian Per-
   fection* (See Standard Sermons); Flew, R. N., *The Idea of
   Perfection.*

II. Principles of Obligation and Obedience: The Will of God

Ramsay, II and III; Brunner, Book II; Berdyaev, Pt. II, Ch. I; Niebuhr, Ch. IV.

Thomas Aquinas, II-II. Qq. 90-100; Luther, *The Sermon* (or *Treatise*) *on Good Works*; Calvin, Bk. II, Chs. VI-VIII.

III. Principles of Response to Divine Action.
   a) Response to the Creative Action of God.
      Augustine, *Confessions*, Bk. III, Chs. VII & VIII.
   b) Response to the Governing Action of God.
      Calvin, *Institutes*, Bk. III, Chs. VII & VIII.
   c) Response to the Redeeming Action of God.
      Luther, *The Liberty of the Christian Man*; Calvin, Bk. III, Ch. XIX; Berdyaev, Pt. II, Chs. II & III; Niebuhr, Ch. VIII.

Additional Readings on the Principles of Action
   Strong, T. B.—*Christian Ethics*
   Osborne, A. R.—*Christian Ethics*
   Cave, S.—*The Christian Way*
   Kierkegaard—*Training in Christianity; Judge for Yourselves and For Self-Examination; The Works of Love*
   Gilson, E.—*Moral Values and the Moral Life; The System of Thomas Aquinas*
   Edwards, J.—*The Nature of True Virtue; Christian Love*
   Harnack, A.—*The Essence of Christianity* (or, *What is Christianity?*)
   Nygren, A.—*Agape and Eros*
   Royce, J.—*The Philosophy of Loyalty; The Problem of Christianity*
   Hartmann, N.—*Ethics*, Vol. II
   Dewey, J.—*Human Nature and Conduct*
   Bergson, H.—*The Two Sources of Morality and Religion*
   Ross, W. D.—*The Right and the Good*
   Anshen, R. N. (ed.)—*Moral Principles of Action*

Part IV. Christian Responsibility in Common Life

   1. Preliminary Problems: a) Individual and Social Ethics
                             b) Technique and Ethics
                             c) The Problem of Race

   a) Brunner, XXVI-XXX; Knudsen, IX; Ramsay, VII; Niebuhr, VII; F. D. Maurice, *Social Morality*.
   b) Plato, *Lesser Hippias*; Aristotle, *Nicomachean Ethics*, Bk. VI; May, Elston, *Social Problems of Industiral Civilization*, Ch. I; Leys, W. A. R., *Ethics for Policy Decisions*.
   c) Myrdal, G., *An American Dilemma*, Vol. I, Pt. I; Nelson, W. S., *The Christian Way in Race Relations*, Chs. II, XI-XIII; Loescher, F., *The Protestant Churches and the Negro*; Berry, B., *Race Relations*.

2. Responsibility in Sex and Family Life

Berdyaev, 294 ff; Brunner, XXXI-XXXII; Knudsen, X; Cave, VIII.
Groves, E. R.—*Christianity and the Family*
Nash, A. S. (ed.)—*Education for Christian Marriage*
Anshen, R. N. (ed.)—*The Family; Its Function and Destiny*
Easton and Robbins—*The Bond of Honor*
Baber—*Marriage and the Family*
Folsom—*Family and Democratic Society*
Kirk, K. E.—*Marriage and Divorce*

cf. also pamphlets published by the Commission on Marriage and the Home of the National Council of Churches, 297 4th Ave., N.Y.C.

3. Responsibility in the Economic Community

Niebuhr, Chs. V & VI; Brunner, XXXIII-XXXV;
Knudsen, XIII; Berdyaev, 269 ff; Ramsay, V; Cave, IX.
Cameron—*Economic Life: A Christian Responsibility*
Gore, E. (ed.)—*Property, Its Duties and Rights*
Fletcher, J. (ed.)—*Christianity and Property*
Tawney, R.—*The Acquisitive Society*
　　　　　　Religion and the Rise of Capitalism
Mayo, Elton—*Social Problems of Industrial Society*
Miller, A.—*Christianity and My Job*
Calhoun, R.—*God and the Common Life*
Papal Encyclicals: *Rerum Novarum* and *Quadragesimo Anno*
The Churches Survey Their Task (Oxford Conference Reports), 87 ff.

Sherwing, W.—*Rich and Poor*
cf. also pamphlets on Christianity and Work published by the National Council of Churches.

4. Responsibility in Political Communities

Berdyaev, 248 ff; Brunner XXXVI-XXXVII; Knudsen XI;
Niebuhr, V & VI; Ramsay, IX; Cave, X.
Ehrenstroem, N.—*Christian Faith and the Modern State*
Barth, K.—*Church and State*
Niebuhr, R.—*Christianity and Power Politics*
　　　　　　Children of Light and Children of Darkness
Zimmern, Sir Alfred—*Spiritual Values and World Affairs*
Voorhis, Jerry—*The Christian in Politics*
Heimann, E.—*Freedom and Order*
Merriam, C. E.—*Systematic Politics*, esp. ch. II.
Ryan and Boland—*The Catholic Theory of Politics*
Maritain, J.—*Man and the State*
　　　　　　True Humanism; Scholasticism and Politics

APPENDIX

Papal Encyclicals: On Civil Government and the
                    Christian Constitution of States
Bainton, R.—*The Churches and War: Historic Attitudes*

5. Responsibility in Religious Community

Brunner, XLIII-XLV; Cave, XI
Amsterdam Volume: *Man's Disorder and God's Design*, esp. pt.
    II
Oxford Volume: *Church and Community*

Bibliography

I. Published Writings of H. Richard Niebuhr in Chronological Order*

1920　"An Aspect of the Idea of God in Recent Thought." *METK*, 48, pp. 39 ff.

1921　"The Alliance Between Labor and Religion." *METK*, 49, pp. 197 ff.

1922　"Christianity and the Social Problem." *METK*, 50, pp. 278 ff.

1925　"Back to Benedict?" *CC*, 42, pp. 860-61.

1926　"What Holds Churches Together?" *CC*, 43, pp. 346-48.

1927　"Jesus Christ Intercessor." *IJRE*, 3, pp. 6-8.

　　　"Theology and Psychology: A Sterile Union." *CC*, 44, pp. 47-48.

* Excluding book reviews. For a listing of Niebuhr's book reviews see Paul Ramsey, ed., *Faith and Ethics*, pp. 297-301. Torchbooks; New York: Harper & Row (1957), 1965.

277

1929 "Christianity and the Industrial Classes." *TM*, 57, pp. 12 ff.
"Churches That Might Unite." *CC*, 56, pp. 259-61.
The Social Sources of Denominationalism. New York: Henry Holt & Co.
Moral Relativism and the Christian Ethic. Published as a pamphlet by the International Missionary Council as one of the primary papers for a Conference on Theological Education at Drew Theological Seminary, November 30–December 1.

1930 "Can German and American Christians Understand Each Other?" *CC*, 47, pp. 914-16.
"The Irreligion of Communist and Capitalist." *CC*, 47, pp. 1306-7.
"Religion and Ethics." *WT*, 13, pp. 443-46.

1931 Articles in *Encyclopedia of the Social Sciences*, ed. by E. R. A. Seligman. New York: The Macmillan Co.:
"Dogma," vol. 5, pp. 189-91; "Sectarian Education," vol. 5, pp. 421-55; "Fundamentalism," vol. 6, pp. 526-27; "Higher Criticism," vol. 7, pp. 347-48; "Protestantism," vol. 12, pp. 571-75; "Reformation: Non-Lutheran," vol. 13, pp. 190-93; "Religious Institutions, Christian: Protestant," vol. 13, pp. 267-72; "Schaff, Philip," vol. 13, p. 562; "Sects," vol. 13, pp. 624-30.
"Religious Realism in the Twentieth Century," in D.C. Macintosh, ed., *Religious Realism*, pp. 413-28. New York: The Macmillan Co.

1932 "Translator's Preface" to Paul Tillich, *The Religious Situation.* New York: Henry Holt & Co.
"The Grace of Doing Nothing." *CC*, 49, pp. 378-80.
"A Communication: The Only Way into the Kingdom of God." *CC*, 49, p. 447.
"Faith, Works and Social Salvation." *RIL*, I, pp. 426-30.

1933 "Nationalism, Socialism and Christianity." *WT*, 16, 469-70.
1934 "What Then Must We Do?" *CCP*, 5, pp. 145-47.
"The Inconsistency of the Majority." *WT*, 17, pp. 43-44.

1935 *The Church Against the World* (with Wilhelm Pauck and Francis P. Miller). "The Question of the Church," pp. 1-13; "Toward the Independence of the Church," pp. 123-56. Chicago: Willett, Clark & Co.
"Man the Sinner." *JR*, 15, pp. 272 ff.
"Toward the Emancipation of the Church." *CHR*, 1, pp. 133-45.

1936 "The Attack upon the Social Gospel." *RIL*, 5, pp. 176-81.
1937 *The Kingdom of God in America.* Torchbooks; New York: Harper & Brothers, (1937) 1959.

"Value Theory and Theology," in *The Nature of Religious Experience*, essays in honor of D.C. Macintosh, pp. 93-116. New York: Harper & Brothers.

1939 "The Christian Evangel and Social Culture." *RIL*, 8, pp. 44-48.

"Life Is Worth Living." *IFH*, 57, pp. 3-4, 22.

Two Lenten Meditations: "Tired Christians," and "Preparation for Maladjustment," *Yale Divinity News* (March, pp. 3-4.

1941 *The Meaning of Revelation*. New York: The Macmillan Co.

"The Christian Church in the World's Crisis." *CS*, 6, no. 3, pp. 11-17.

1942 "War as the Judgment of God." *CC*, 59, pp. 630-33.

"Is God in the War?" *CC*, 59, pp. 953-55.

1943 "War as Crucifixion." *CC*, 60, pp. 513-15.

"The Nature and Existence of God." *MOT*, 4, no. 3, pp. 13-15, 43-46.

1944 "Towards a New Other-Worldliness." *TT*, 1, pp. 78-87.

1945 "The Ego-Alter Dialectic and the Conscience." *JP*, 42, pp. 352-59.

Articles in the *Encyclopedia of Religion*, ed. V. Ferm (New York: The Philosophical Library, 1945): "Church: Conceptions of the Church in Historic Christianity" (pp. 169-70); "Ethics: Christian Ethics" (pp. 259-60); "Inspiration" (p. 374); "Revelation" (pp. 660-61); "Ernst Troeltsch" (pp. 795-96).

"The Hidden Church and the Churches in Sight." *RIL*, 15, pp. 106-16.

1946 "The Norm of the Church." *JRT*, 4, pp. 5-15.

"The Responsibility of the Church for Society," in K. S. Latourette, ed., *The Gospel, the Church and the World*, pp. 111-33. New York: Harper & Brothers.

"The Doctrine of the Trinity and the Unity of the Church." *TT*, 3, pp. 371-84.

"Utilitarian Christianity." *CCR*, 6, no. 12, pp. 3-5.

1948 "The Gift of Catholic Vision." *TT*, 4, pp. 507-21.

1949 "The Disorder of Man in the Church of God," in *Man's Disorder and God's Design*. The Amsterdam Assembly Series, vol. I, pp. 78-88. New York: Harper & Brothers.

"Review" of Paul Tillich, *The Protestant Era*. *RIL*, 18, pp. 291-92.

1950 "Evangelical and Protestant Ethics," in J. F. Arndt, ed., *The Heritage of the Reformation*, pp. 211-29. New York: Richard R. Smith.

The Gospel for a Time of Fears. Three Lectures: 1. Our

Eschatological Time; 2. The Eternal Now; 3. The Gospel of the Last Time. Washington: Henderson Services, 22 pp.

1951   *Christ and Culture.* New York: Harper & Brothers.
"Review" of Paul Tillich, *Systematic Theology,* vol. 1. *USQ,* 7, pp. 45-49.

1952   "The Center of Value," in R. N. Anshen, ed., *Moral Principles of Action,* pp. 162-75. New York: Harper & Brothers.
The Churches and the Body of Christ. The William Penn Lecture, Philadelphia, pamphlet, 24 pp.

1953   "The Churches and the Body of Christ." *FI,* 110, pp. 621-23.

1954   "Why Restudy Theological Education?" *CC,* 71, pp. 516-17.
"The Triad of Faith." *ANB,* 47, pp. 3-12.
"Issues Between Catholics and Protestants." *RIL,* 23, pp. 199-205.
"The Idea of Covenant and American Democracy." *CH,* 23, pp. 126-35.
"What Are the Main Issues in Theological Education?" *TEA,* no. 2, pp. 1-11.

1955   "The Main Issues in Theological Education." *TT,* 11, pp. 512-27.
"Isolation and Co-operation in Theological Education." *TEA,* no. 3, pp. 1-6.
"Introductions" to Chapters 1, 8, 9, 13 in Waldo Beach and H. Richard Niebuhr, eds., *Christian Ethics: Sources of the Living Tradition.* New York: Ronald Press.
"Theology—Not Queen but Servant." *JR,* 35, pp. 1-5.

1956   *The Purpose of the Church and Its Ministry.* New York: Harper & Brothers.
"Sören Kierkegaard," in Carl Michalson, ed., *Christianity and the Existentialists,* pp. 23-42. New York: Charles Scribner's Sons.
The Ministry in Historical Perspectives (Ed. with D. D. Williams). New York: Harper & Brothers.
"Training a Preacher." *PS,* pp. 24-25.

1957   *The Advancement of Theological Education* (with D. D. Williams and J. M. Gustafson). New York: Harper & Brothers.
"Foreword" to Karl Barth's introductory essay to Ludwig Feuerbach, *The Essence of Christianity.* pp. vii-ix. Torchbooks; New York: Harper & Brothers.
Articles in *Religion in Geschichte und Gegenwart:* "Ralph Waldo Emerson" (vol. 2, pp. 454-55), "Individual- und Sozialethik" (vol. 3, pp. 715-19).

1960   *Radical Monotheism and Western Culture.* New York: Harper & Brothers.
"Reformation, Continuing Imperative." *CC,* 77, March 2.
"The Seminary in the Ecumenical Age." *TT,* 17, pp. 300-310.

BIBLIOGRAPHY

"Introduction" to the Harper Torchbook edition of Troeltsch's *The Social Teaching of the Christian Churches*. New York, pp. 7-12.

"Science and Religion." *Yale Divinity News*, Jan., pp. 3-21.

1961   "The Protestant Movement and Democracy in the United States," in *The Shaping of American Religion*, ed. James Ward Smith and A. Leland Jamison, pp. 20-71. Princeton: Princeton University Press.

"On the Nature of Faith," in Sidney Hook, ed., *Religious Experience and Truth*, pp. 93-102. New York: New York University Press.

"How My Mind Has Changed," in H. E. Fey, ed., *How My Mind Has Changed*, pp. 69-80. Meridian Books; Cleveland: World Publishing Co.

"The Ethical Crisis." Lecture given at Wayne State University in November of 1961 and published in *Universitas*, Vol. II, no. 2, Spring, 1964, pp. 41-50.

1962   "Ex Libris." *CC*, 79, p. 754.

"The Illusions of Power." *CCP*, 33, pp. 100-103.

1963   "An Attempt at a Theological Analysis of Missionary Motivation." Occasional Bulletin from the Missionary Research Library, New York (originally written in 1951).

The Responsible Self. New York: Harper & Row.

II. Selected Unpublished Materials by H. Richard Niebuhr

A. Dated and in Chronological Order

"Ernst Troeltsch's Philosophy of Religion." Unpublished Ph.D. Dissertation, Yale University, 1924.

"Theology in a Time of Disillusionment." Alumni Lecture, Yale, 1931 (handwritten, 22 pp.).

"The Social Gospel and the Mind of Jesus." Read before the American Theological Society, April 21, 1933 (handwritten, 22 pp.).

"The Limitation of Power and Religious Liberty." Address delivered at the Institute of Human Relations at Williamstown, Mass., August 27, 1939 (typescript, 16 pp.).

"Types of Christian Ethics." Mimeographed, dated 1942, 9 pp.

"A Christian Interpretation of War," Mimeographed, 10 pp. Niebuhr's pencilled annotation: Fed. Council Commission, 1943.

"The Ego-Alter Dialogue and Conscience." Typed, longer version of the published article. Read at New York to American Theological Society, April, 1945.

"The Idea of Original Sin in American Culture." Lecture given at Princeton University Program of Studies in American Civilization, February 24, 1949 (handwritten, 28 pp.).

"The Preacher's Poverty and the Unsearchable Riches of Christ."
Unpublished sermon, handwritten, preached at the ordination
of his son Richard R. Niebuhr, November, 1950.

"Who Are the Unbelievers and What Do They Believe?" Paper
written for Commission on Evangelism—World Council of
Churches, Summer, 1953 (typescript, 10 pp.).

"The Lord's Prayer." Typescript based on a tape recording of a
sermon at Union Theological Seminary, 1953.

"The Administration of the Unforeseen." Typescript of Com-
mencement Address given at Catawba College, 1954.

"A Theologian's Approach to History: History's Role in Theology."
Typescript of address given to American Historical Association
in Washington, December 30, 1955.

"The Church Defines Itself in the World." Typed manuscript,
15 pp. L. A. Hoedemaker dates it 1957.

"The Anachronism of Jonathan Edwards." Address (handwritten)
given in Northampton, Mass., on the bicentennial of Edwards'
death, March 9, 1958.

"Reflections on a 'Protestant Theory of Higher Education.'"
Greenwich, Conn., November 12-14, 1959 typescript, 3 pp.

"Martin Luther and the Renewal of Human Confidence." Address
at Valparaiso University, 1959 (typescript, 21 pp.).

Cole Lectures, Vanderbilt University, 1960. Four Lectures transcribed from tape recording: 1. "The Position of Theology
Today" (21 pp.); 2. "Towards New Symbols" (30 pp.); "Toward the Recovery of Feeling" (30 pp.); 4. "Toward the Service
of Christendom" (33 pp.).

"On the Meaning of Responsibility." Lecture given at Cambridge
University, May 25, 1960 (24 pp.).

"Classroom Lectures on Christian Ethics." (Niebuhr's Notes,
1961.)

B. Materials Not Definitely Dated

"Reflections on Hope, Faith and Love." Mimeo text, probably 1953
and delivered before the Theological Discussion Group.

"The Hope of Glory." Handwritten outline of a sermon Niebuhr
preached often in the 1950s.

"The Mediation of Faith." Handwritten manuscript from the
1950s (23 pp.).

"Between Barth and Schleiermacher." Handwritten fragment, written in connection with "Faith on Earth" (3 pp.).

"Participation in the Present Passion." Published sermon for
which I have not established the date.

"Man's Work and God's." Typed sermon manuscript (9 pp.).

"The Logic of the Cross." Typed sermon manuscript (10 pp.).

"The Old-Time Religion Isn't Good Enough." Typed manuscript
done from Niebuhr's handwritten text from the 1950s.

BIBLIOGRAPHY

"The Knowledge of Faith." Book manuscript of four chapters. Niebuhr was at work on these in 1946–47 according to Prof. Richard R. Niebuhr. Chapters are: 1. "Faith Seeks Understanding" (32 pp.); 2. "Towards Understanding Understanding" (24 pp.); 3. "Faith is a Relation Between Selves" (30 pp.); 4. "The Trialectic of Faith" (41 pp.).

"Faith on Earth." Book manuscript of seven chapters on which Niebuhr worked over a period from 1952 to 1958. Chapters are: 1. "Faith in Question" (24 pp.); 2. "The Method of Reflection" (16 pp.); 3. "Believing and Knowing in Community" (15 pp.); 4. "The Structure of Faith" (23 pp.); 5. "Broken Faith" (23 pp.); 6. "The Reconstruction of Faith" (22 pp.); 7. "The Community of Faith" (19 pp.).

C. Lecture Notes from Niebuhr's Course on Christian Ethics Taken by Students, in approximate Chronological Order

"Introductory Lectures in Christian Ethics." 1946–47. Careful typescript, anonymous (46 pp.).

"Christian Ethics, H. R. Niebuhr." Notes taken by James M. Gustafson in either 1952–53 or 1953–54 (typed, 99 pp.).

"Christian Ethics Notes—Prof. H. Richard Niebuhr." Taken in early 1950s by Carl Nelson (typed, 119 pp.).

"Christian Ethics." Notes transcribed in spring 1952 by Robert Yetter, Gene Canestrari, and Ed Elliott. Very complete, verbatim account, most useful of all available accounts. (Typed, mimeographed, 182 pp.).

"Christian Ethics." Notes taken by Harvey Cox in 1952–53 (handwritten).

"Christian Ethics." Notes taken by Mel Keiser, 1961 (handwritten).

III. Secondary Sources on Niebuhr

Ahlstrom, Sydney E. "H. Richard Niebuhr. He Spoke as a Servant." Dialog, 2, 1963, pp. 8-9.
———. "H. Richard Niebuhr's Place in American Thought." Christianity and Crisis, 23, 1963, pp. 213-17.
Ahlstrom, Sydney E., ed. Theology in America. Indianapolis: Bobbs-Merrill, 1967.
Allen, Joseph L. "A Decisive Influence on Protestant Ethics." Christianity and Crisis, 23, 1963, pp. 217-19.
Beach, Waldo. "A Theological Analysis of Race Relations," in P. Ramsey, ed., Faith and Ethics. Torchbooks; New York: Harper & Row (1957), 1965, pp. 205-24.
Frei, Hans. "Niebuhr's Theological Background," and "The Theology of H. Richard Niebuhr," in Faith and Ethics, pp. 9-116.
Godsey, John D. The Promise of H. Richard Niebuhr. Philadelphia: J. B. Lippincott Co., 1970.

Gustafson, James M. "Christian Ethics and Social Policy," in *Faith and Ethics*, pp. 119-39.
_____. "Introduction," *The Responsible Self*. New York: Harper & Row, 1963.
Hoeaemaker, L. A. *The Theology of H. Richard Niebuhr*. Philadelphia: Pilgrim Press, 1970.
Kliever, Lonnie D. "Methodology and Christology in H. Richard Niebuhr." Ph.D. dissertation, Duke University, 1963.
Ramsey, Paul. "The Transformation of Ethics," in *Faith and Ethics*, pp. 140-72.
Schrader, George. "Value and Valuation," in *Faith and Ethics*, pp. 173-204.
Stassen, Glen H. "The Sovereignty of God in the Theology and Ethics of H. Richard Niebuhr." Ph.D. dissertation, Duke University, 1967.

IV. General Bibliography

Augustine. *Confessions*. New York: Collier Macmillan, 1961.
Barth, Karl. *Epistle to the Romans*. Trans. by E. C. Hoskyns from 6th ed. London: Oxford University Press, 1933.
_____. *The Humanity of God*. Richmond: John Knox Press, 1960.
_____. *The Word of God and the Word of Man*. New York: Harper & Brothers, 1928.
Bellah, Robert N. "Civil Religion in America," in Donald R. Cutler, ed., *The Religious Situation, 1968*. Boston: Beacon Press, 1968.
Bonhoeffer, Dietrich. *Ethics*. Trans. by Neville H. Smith. New York: The Macmillan Co., 1955.
Calvin, John. *Institutes of the Christian Religion*. 2 vols. Trans. by F. L. Battles, ed. by John T. McNeill. Philadelphia: The Westminster Press, 1960.
Dyck, Arthur J. "A Gestalt Analysis of the Moral Data and Certain of its Implications for Ethical Theory." Ph.D. dissertation, Harvard University, 1965.
Edwards, Jonathan. *Christian Love as Manifested in Heart and Life*. Vol. 7 in Edwards, *Works*, 6th ed., Philadelphia.
_____. *Concerning the End for Which God Created the World*. Vol. 6, *The Works of President Edwards in Eight Volumes*. Worcester, Mass.: Isaiah Thomas, 1809.
_____. *Freedom of the Will*. Yale edition, ed. by Paul Ramsey. New Haven: Yale University Press, 1957.
Erikson, Erik. *Childhood and Society*. 2d ed. New York: W. W. Norton & Co., 1962.
Frankena, William K. *Ethics*. Englewood Cliffs, N.J.: Prentice-Hall, 1963.

BIBLIOGRAPHY

Harland, Gordon. *The Thought of Reinhold Niebuhr.* New York: Oxford University Press, 1960.

Jonsen, Albert R. *Responsibility in Modern Religious Ethics.* Washington: Corpus Books, 1968.

Kaufman, Gordon. "On the Meaning of 'Act of God.'" *Harvard Theological Review,* 61, no. 2 (April 1968).

———. *God the Problem.* Cambridge, Mass.: Harvard University Press, 1972.

Kerr, Hugh T., ed. *A Compend of Luther's Theology.* Philadelphia: The Westminster Press, 1966.

Löwith, Karl. *Meaning In History.* Chicago: University of Chicago Press, 1949.

Macintosh, D. C. "Troeltsch's Theory of Religious Knowledge." *American Journal of Theology,* 22 (1919), pp. 274 ff.

Meyer, Donald B. *The Protestant Search for Political Realism, 1919–1941.* Berkeley: University of California Press, 1961.

Moltmann, Jürgen. "The Revolution of Freedom: The Christian and Marxist Struggle," in Thomas W. Ogletree, ed., *Openings for Marxist-Christian Dialogue,* pp. 47-71. Nashville: Abingdon Press, 1969.

Mueller, William A. *Church and State in Luther and Calvin.* Garden City, New York: Doubleday & Co., 1965.

Niebuhr, Reinhold. *Moral Man and Immoral Society.* New York: Charles Scribner's Sons, 1932.

———. "Must We Do Nothing?" *Christian Century,* 49, pp. 415-17.

Niebuhr, Richard R. *Schleiermacher on Christ and Religion.* New York: Charles Scribner's Sons, 1964.

Novak, Michael. *The Experience of Nothingness.* New York: Harper & Row, 1970.

Pannenberg, Wolfhart. *Jesus—God and Man.* Philadelphia: The Westminster Press, 1968.

Polanyi, Michael. *Personal Knowledge: Towards a Post-Critical Philosophy.* Chicago: University of Chicago Press, 1958.

Reist, Benjamin. *Toward a Theology of Involvement.* Philadelphia: The Westminster Press, 1966.

Royce, Josiah. *The Philosophy of Loyalty.* New York: The Macmillan Co. 1908.

———. *The Sources of Religious Insight.* New York: Charles Scribner's Sons, 1912.

Tillich, Paul. *The Protestant Era.* Abridged ed., trans. by James Luther Adams. Chicago: University of Chicago Press, 1957.

———. *The Religious Situation.* Trans. by H. Richard Niebuhr. Meridian Books; Cleveland: World Publishing Co., (1932), 1956.

——— *Die Religiöse Verwirklichung.* Berlin, 1930.

Troeltsch, Ernst. *The Social Teaching of the Christian Churches.*

2 vols. Trans. by Olive Wyon. Torchbooks; New York: Harper & Brothers, 1960.

————. "Das Wesen der Religion und der Religions-Wissenschaft." *Gesammelte Schriften*, vol. 2, pp. 452-99.

Underwood, Kenneth. *The Church, the University and Social Policy.* Vol. 1. Middletown, Conn.: Wesleyan University Press, 1969.

Whitehead, A. N. *Religion in the Making.* Meridian Books; Cleveland: World Publishing Co., 1960.

Wilder, Amos N. *Eschatology and Ethics in the Teachings of Jesus.* 2d ed. New York: Harper & Brothers, 1950.

Winter, Gibson. *Elements for a Social Ethic.* New York: The Macmillan Co., 1966.

Index